The Marquess of Bath:
Lord of Love

Also by Nesta Wyn Ellis:

John Major, A Personal Biography
Britain's Top 100 Eligible Bachelors
Dear Elector, The truth about MP's
The Banker's Daughter

The Marquess of Bath

Lord of Love

Nesta Wyn Ellis

Dynasty
Press

Dynasty Press Ltd
36 Ravensdon Street
London SE11 4AR

www.dynastypress.co.uk

First published in this version by Dynasty Press Ltd, 2010.

ISBN: 978-0-9553507-4-0

Cover Artwork by Two Associates

Photography by David Chambers

Typeset by Strange Attractor Press

Printed and Bound in the United Kingdom

Acknowledgements

I am immensely grateful to Lord Bath for the time and the facilities he has made available to me over several years in the research and writing of this unique biography. Not only did he make himself available for some 40 hours of private taped interviews but he also invited me as a guest to Longleat and his two other residences in order to carry them out. This enabled me to observe at first hand his life with his "wifelet" harem, and other guests, whom I also observed at close quarters at his summer residence near St Tropez.

I also wish to thank some of Lord Bath's personal friends from his Eton, Oxford and Army years who were introduced to me by Lord Bath, and who kindly agreed to be interviewed. Sir Tim Sainsbury, Lawrence Kelly, Sir Ian Rankin, Tim Rathbone (the late Tory MP for Lewes) and Sir James Spooner were particularly helpful in their contributions regarding Alexander's years at Eton, Oxford, during his National Service in the Guards and for some years afterwards.

I was also privileged to have a long first hand interview with Alexander's first girl friend and love while a Debutante, Davina Merry, an artist, who became Lady Davina Gibbs, as the wife of Field Marshall Sir Roland Gibbs, GCB, CBE, DSO, MC KStJ (22 June 1921-31 October 2004) eventually Chief of the General Staff, the professional head of the British Army; and with other ex-girl friends or former wifelets. Among the latter, Shirley Conran, Lucianne Camille, Clare Gordon, Helen Anderson shared their memories with me about their relationships with Alexander.

I also met many more of Alexander's friends and former wifelets at Longleat, during weekends while I was a guest there. A number helped me with their insights into Alexander's life over the years. A number of more recent wifelets also allowed me some extraordinary insights into their relationships with Alexander and with other wifelets.

I wish to thank Michael Creighton, the BBC documentary maker, also a friend of Alexander's over many years, for his insights. I also thank Lady Bath for her comments.

I would also like to thank the librarians at Times Newspapers for the open ended access to files on Alexander and some of the more prominent wifelets, which they allowed me during my early researches into my subject.

Nesta Wyn Ellis,
Paris
Spring 2010

Introduction

Alexander George Thynne, Seventh Marquess of Bath, is more than just an aristocrat, which in this day and age is not without importance to the British people. In the time of Alexander's parents, aristocrats considered themselves of sufficient importance that a biography would be written simply on the basis of who they were. Thanks to the continuation of the monarchy, which gives the hierarchy of titles and the panoply of patronage a significance it might otherwise have lost, there would have been no need for any achievement in the world other than to have been born an heir to a title and some stately pile stuffed with artworks and antiquities. Alexander, however, has rather trendily spurned all that in favour of some very revanchist notions. He stood for Parliament in 1974 as a Wessex Regionalist; he embraced socialism; he sent his children to the local comprehensive instead of to elitist fee-paying schools; and he turned his back on conventional marriage in all but the legal niceties that allow the continuity of his heir's rights to Longleat and the titles. Of course, he has done this while hanging onto his inherited wealth, his estate and his mansion along with its contents, his money and his right to primogeniture, his titles and the rights of his heir. Not only this but he has also fought off his brother, who was given much responsibility for managing the estate by their father, although none of this within the entail which puts the whole lot into the hands of the eldest son.

The British may be one of the last nations to go on loving their aristocrats but evidently they still do. Alexander is so much more than an aristocrat. He manages to combine his lineage with an open rebellion against his aristocratic origins. Yet he adores his house, his estate and the traditions that have made it what it is; and much of his public cavorting is, he says, designed to attract more tourists to keep the place in funds. However interesting aristocratic fortunes and inheritances may be, they would not on their own make Alexander worthy of more than the odd mention in the gossip columns. Rather than be defined by his inheritance of one of England's premier aristocratic titles and a very noteworthy late-Renaissance palace, he is an eccentric in the true English tradition of extreme individuality. As an artist, Alexander is eccentric even among others artists in that he does not exhibit his work except as murals which are included in the tour of his private apartments at Longleat House. He is also an author and a songwriter.

It is possible, however, that all these marvels would have taken up but a small amount of the public's attention were it not for the fact that Alexander has been noteworthy for his lifestyle. This, taking place as it does in the midst of a 10,000-acre estate complete with mazes, kiddie rides, plasterboard castles and a safari park stuffed with man-eating beasts of the jungle, cannot avoid appearing glamorous and weird. And it seems especially surrealistic that all of this fantasy is centred on one of England's most splendid historic monuments, Longleat House. The Disneyland-like fantasy of Alexander's home and his lifestyle is accentuated by his *Wizard of Oz* costumes: the multicoloured velvet caftans and tasselled fezzes in which he invariably appears in public. The element of scandal is added by the highly publicized lewd murals which cover the walls of his enormous fairy-tale castle of a house, together with lascivious tabloid tales of luscious mistresses tucked away in cottages all over the estate. Alexander is probably more famous for his sex life than for anything else. He has renounced marriage while marrying a wife for the sake of the legalities involved in handing on the estate and titles to his son. Otherwise, he says, he does not believe in monogamy. Fine, one might hear people say in the local pub, but he can afford it. On the contrary, he doesn't intend to afford it. Alexander thinks his system of communal living should be supported by the state. But if he lived in a suburban semi or a council flat, funding his women on the state, would he seem as glamorous? Probably not. However, Alexander has made his lifestyle more than a personal indulgence. He claims to have fashioned it into a model for a new society based on communes of unmarried mothers – completely funded, of course, by the state. While playing the role of mega-stud for all he is worth, and without parting with more than a few meals and glasses of plonk in return, Alexander is positively swarming with women who are queuing up to share his bed. How he does it, why he does it and with whom he does it are topics of enormous interest to the gossips; and while there are some who will turn up their noses at such frolics, most people love a good gossip. They also love to know about the lifestyles of the rich and famous. Alexander is both. While not in the Getty class, he is certainly rich enough to be of great interest, for instance in *The Sunday Times* Rich List, which features him under the headline 'Loins of Longleat', his wealth is estimated at £157 million, depending on the fluctuation of land and other values: not much in these days of hedge-fund billionaires but a comfortable little fortune nonetheless. This wealth, which involves his stewardship of one of the most striking and well-preserved stately homes of England, would attract attention even if he were not also famous in his own right. Fame is vintage Burgundy to a marquess who serves only boxed plonk to his guests. He is not one of those quiet money folks who like to live discreetly. His undisputed fame is actively courted and a part of the self-inspired act with which he brings the tour groups to his beloved Longleat in cash-paying droves. It has always been lonely at the top, however; and there are few who know that, beneath the velvet-robed exterior and beyond the glossy pictures in the gossip pages of the giveaway magazines and the newspaper diaries of the partying Bath with a babe on each arm, there is a serious, sad, lonely workaholic who is continually trying to explain himself to himself and to the world. Envied by the man in the suburban bedroom for his access to countless fawning women, for parading his fancies despite being married, for having it all and a stately home to boot, he is still wanting something more. That 'more' is the love that has always escaped him but which does not escape many much more ordinary folks who find their key to happiness in more mundane circumstances. Nevertheless, he has glamour, wealth, flocking females and countless invitations to parties. Poor little rich boy? Can it really be so bad?

Chapter One

Preliminary Sketch for the Portrait of an Artist

The Public Bath

A magnificent party is underway at Longleat, the wonderfully-preserved Elizabethan palace which is the ancestral home of the Marquesses of Bath. The great hall is thronged with dancers in various forms of evening dress, and in the minstrel's gallery a group is hard at it pumping out sound. Portraits of the ancestors gaze haughtily over the bobbing heads, their dignity barely shaken by the revels. Towering above the dancers is a tall figure, six foot four in his famously bare feet, with flowing grey curls surmounted by an embroidered velvet cap and a grey beard, wearing a fabulous multicoloured garment of braid-adorned silks and velvets that covers him from neckline to slightly grubby toes. Alexander Thynn, the Seventh Marquess of Bath – he adopted the spelling 'Thynn' in 1976 – is celebrating his seventy-eighth birthday with some four hundred guests: family, old friends, and recent acquaintances trawled from the Green Rooms of TV stations. TV cameras, never far away from Lord Bath, are circling the room. Outside, on this crisp night in early May, Longleat House is floodlit and the 'long leat' – a small lake fed by a stream which lends the estate its name – lies glittering in the light of the newly-risen waning moon. Before its rise, the cold stars were a scattering of small spotlights in a stage sky which shelters a Disneyland-style aggregation of tourist attractions surrounding the magnificent house itself. This, a building of Italianate, late-Renaissance design, forms a large hollow square, standing three storeys high, topped with four domed towers and a stone balustrade which guards a flat roof. Four flags flutter from the flagpoles which adorn each tower. Scattered around the parkland close to the house are a medley of rides, slides, mazes, wizards' castles, even a discotheque, all of which form part of the income-producing extras paid for by the tourists who have already paid their entrance money to come on to the Longleat Estate. Further away, up the hill, lies the famous Safari Park from which one can hear the occasional roar of one of the celebrated lions of Longleat. These lions were the first inmates of what has become a substantial private zoo housing giraffe, elephant, buffalo, tigers, various gazelle and myriad cheeky monkeys who leap onto the tourists' cars. The original lions were brought in by Alexander's father Henry, the 6th Marquess, in 1965 with the help of the circus impresario, Jimmy Chipperfield, causing something of a media stir at the time. Longleat had already become the first English stately home to be opened to the public in 1949. This measure was taken when it was realized that heavy death duties imposed by the 1945 Labour Government were going to endanger the estate's financial life. Although income from the public visitors to Longleat contributes a healthy chunk towards running costs, the huge value of the Longleat Estate is largely based on its stock of art treasures, while a much smaller proportion of its wealth is attributed to its 9,000 acres of land. A sale of four hundred art treasures for some £24 million in 2004 was said by a spokesman at Christie's, the London auction house, to have barely scratched the surface of the estate's collection. This and the land, however, fluctuate in value according to the markets. The sale of treasures was provoked by the foot-and-mouth epidemic, which closed Longleat and its parks to visitors for more than six months in 2001, cutting off the supply of cash needed to pay staff, feed the animals and keep up the buildings and parks. After this sale, Alexander who had been deeply worried about his beloved Longleat, heaved a huge sigh of relief. The art treasures, many of which had been lying unseen and untouched for decades in the Longleat attics, have created a more liquid fund from whose invested capital an additional income may be tapped to keep the estate functioning if future hard times reduce the tourist cash flow.

Alexander's own financial position fails to reflect the assets of his stately home, of which he is in fact only a glorified caretaker under the legal terms of the inheritance; and he is reputed, when in London, to eschew taxis in favour of his bus pass. He has investments of his own, of course, and also his old age pension. However, while he may give the impression of being a bit hard-up, no one really believes it. Indeed, at Longleat tonight there is no sign of any financial limitation: wine is flowing, the guests are drinking and eating. Old Etonians and former Life Guards officers, Oxonians, pals from Alexander's early life are rubbing shoulders with the likes of Cynthia Payne, Countess Bienvenida Sokolow, better known as 'Lady Buck' from her *News of the World* confessions of love with a senior civil servant, Sally Farmiloe and other celebrants of large tabloid exposure. There are also several 'wifelets'. These represent the hard core of Alexander's seventy-five mistresses and girlfriends since he began keeping score soon after the end his first love affair in the early 1950s. The list, running from day one in 1952 and continuing to the present, includes socialites such as Suna Portman, Shirley Conran and some lesser-known showbiz babes, as well as some quieter names and a few who most of the others would rather forget. Here tonight, however, we only have the most current and most trusted popsies. A few of the former wifelets who linger on as residents of the cottages famously let to Alexander's women friends by the Longleat Estate are now categorized as old friends and are also at the party.

Many of these former wifelets are formidable females: would he dare leave them out? Tenanting the cottages with wifelets was part of Alexander's plan to create a sort of commune of happily coexisting mothers and babies, the latter, of course, fathered by Alexander. It has not quite worked out that way: there is little sign of babies or of happy coexistence among Alexander's women. Alexander, however, has not yet resigned his dream that they would all be one big happy family; but the reality is that these ladies who grace his bed or hang on his arm at London parties are far from happy in each other's company. There is furthermore only one mother of a love child in Alexander's list of current and former mistresses. She is notably absent tonight, not because she could not find a babysitter for the eight-year-old daughter she is raising in a Devon cottage but because she has made Alexander promise that there will be no publicity for her or her child whom DNA tests confirm is Alexander's. Perhaps there was no reason for DNA tests. Another wifelet claimed in an interview with the Mail that the child was conceived by in-vitro fertilization for which

Alexander picked up the bill, and expressed the regret that she had not been asked to be the mother under the same circumstances.

No current wifelet is to be seen on Alexander's arm tonight, for Lady Bath is also there. She visits Longleat for about one week per month, usually preferring to live and work in Paris, where she has maintained her own apartment and her own life – formerly as an actress and later as a journalist and author – throughout her forty years of marriage to Alexander. The two Bath children – daughter Lenka, now forty and the mother of Alexander's first grandchild, and her younger brother Ceawlin, the present Viscount Weymouth and heir to Longleat and the title – are also present, circulating with some of their own friends. Of other close family members there is little sign. The most notable absence is that of the Hon Christopher Thynne, Alexander's younger brother, who with his tall skinny frame and long thin nose so closely resembles the portraits of their late father Henry. Christopher and his wife Antonia feel bitterly about their exclusion from the Longleat Estate, a matter which caused scandal soon after Henry's death, and relations between the siblings have long been in the deep freeze. Alexander has invited his brother, as he usually does, but Christopher prefers not to be seen at Alexander's parties. Christopher's son by another woman is there, however. He is also tall and carries the Thynne nose, resembling his father. His long curly hair and fine eyes make him stunningly handsome. In fact, he is not only named Alexander but is also an artist. He gets on extremely well with his uncle, the Seventh Marquess, and has helped to carry out some of Alexander's designs on the ceilings in the latter's private apartments at Longleat House.

Alexander's half sister, Silvy, from his father's second marriage, has also been invited with her husband; but, despite the fact that her relations with Alexander are reasonably cordial, she has failed to appear. Her mother-in-law Susanna McQuorquordale, a glamorous, bubbly blonde and former beauty queen, is there with her daughter. Of his niece, daughter of his adored late sister Caroline, Duchess of Beaufort, and other relations by blood or marriage, there is no sign. Alexander is still peeved that his mother, who wrote a number of successful books under the name Daphne Fielding after her divorce from Henry, bequeathed her own literary titles to this niece, who is herself an author. This undoubtedly hurt Alexander both publicly and privately, where the snub was added to other rejections which he suffered from his parents. Family feuds are not new to the aristocracy, but Alexander has added to these the scandal of living a bohemian life and allowing, even courting, publicity about his mistresses. Many of these have added their own colourful accounts in 'kiss and tell' features in the Sunday tabloids. This too explains largely why there are no other aristocrats nodding coronets to each other among this colourful crowd. Even so, we are celebrating an extraordinary life. Seventy-eight years ago on May 6 1932, Alexander Thynn was born in London at 95 Seymour Street in Marylebone, London W1. He was the third child to whom his mother Daphne had given birth and the second son. His sister Caroline had been the firstborn three years previously. A son, Timothy, had survived only for about a year, due to a collapsed lung. Under the British aristocratic system of primogeniture, in which the firstborn male child takes all, Alexander became the sole heir to the estate of Longleat, which, at the time of his birth was quite self-sufficient and had no need for tourists to provide income. He would also, in due course, become the Seventh Marquess of Bath, later changing the spelling of the family name from Thynne to Thynn largely because he said people were mispronouncing it as 'Thine'.

Ancestral Footnotes

At the time of Alexander's birth, his grandfather, the 5th Marquess was alive and well; and Alexander's father, Henry, was the then Viscount Weymouth, this being the title taken by the eldest son of the living , Marquess of Bath. The history of Longleat and the present house date back to the era of Queen Elizabeth I. The title of Viscount Weymouth was first bestowed on Thomas Thynne in 1682, approximately one hundred years after the first Sir John Thynne, freshly knighted by the Virgin Queen, had finished building Longleat. The Marquessate was not created until three more generations had passed, when yet another Thomas Thynne became the 1st Marquess. Alexander himself inherited the title of Viscount Weymouth, becoming the 11th Lord Weymouth when his grandfather died in 1947, and when Henry became the 6th Marquess. Alexander became the Seventh Marquess at sixty, after Henry's death in 1992 aged ninety. The title of Viscount Weymouth then immediately passed to his son Ceawlin.

The first owner of the estate was also the builder of Longleat House. John Thynne was a merchant who had found favour with Elizabeth I. Alexander describes him as ruthless and ambitious and adds a few rather more insulting adjectives, but there is no doubt that in a period resembling the Thatcherite 1980s this was the way to succeed. John Thynne got his chance as a result of being introduced to the Tudor Court by a relative who had a minor position as an administrator of the royal kitchens. He was then befriended by the Duke of Somerset and somehow managed to survive some periods of disfavour, including one when his protector lost his head. The house was built in a natural hollow on the ruins of an ancient priory said to have been the site of black rites by its occupants, who were cleared out in short order even before the dissolution of the monasteries by Henry VIII. Originally, the ancient priory was rebuilt as a residence by John Thynne, who had acquired the land. Later, after this house was burned down, the new mansion was begun. It took many years to finish, was a sensation in its time and cost a great deal. Queen Elizabeth I kept demanding an invitation, but John Thynne continued to put her off, saying it was not yet fit to live in. He may have been apprehensive that the queen would question the source of riches on the scale needed to build such a palace. Eventually, however, after being fobbed off a few times, Queen Elizabeth I insisted on an invitation. She proclaimed the visit a success.

Queen Elizabeth II visited the estate in during the 1960s, and her visit is thought to have caused some consternation among those members of the Thynne family who wanted to keep Alexander away on this special day. Alexander was already notorious for his unconventional way of living. A media figure, he was even then the subject of newspaper diary items and longer news and feature stories. He was, very largely, treated by his family as a sort of cuckoo in the nest. When all his upbringing seemed to have been that of a traditional British aristocrat – Eton, Life Guards and Oxford – why has he turned out to be such a rebel against his aristocratic origins?

To begin with Alexander was a proper little Lord Fauntleroy, and when he was about eight years old he remembers two of the footmen asking him what he was going to be when he grew up. His reply, he now rather shamefacedly admits, was: 'The Marquess of Bath.' Visibly embarrassed, he elaborates upon this confession of aristocratic 'attitude'. 'The next time I was asked,' he continues, 'I said I was going to be a writer who illustrated his own books, which is rather close to what I have become.' But he adds: 'I still believe that I can be and that I am a good Marquess and that the two careers are not incompatible.'

The two careers are inextricably interlaced since Alexander is absolutely devoted to Longleat and its survival. Were it not for this, he might be much less inclined to seek the limelight, since much of his seemingly extrovert love of tabloid and TV publicity is primarily designed to keep up the stream of paying tourists without whom Longleat could not survive. Even so, Alexander's image as a marquess is not in the mould of conventional landed British aristocracy. In terms of the hierarchy, which descends from the monarch, marquesses rank third in importance, coming immediately after dukes, which are the highest in the land after royal princes. Below them, in order of importance, come earls, viscounts, barons, baronets and knights.

The main difference between Alexander and other landed gentry – many of whom follow the traditional huntin', shootin' and fishin', lifestyle – is that he is an artist; and the uncomfortable truth is that artists don't fit into any class. Whether their origins are peasantry or peerage, or anything between, they tend to fall out of line with the rest of society. In fact, artists – whether of stage, screen, canvas or concert hall – usually form a class of their own. In England this tends to be a misunderstood class sought after only when their fame or their money brings them more conventional status. Wherever they live, however, artists habitually scorn other classes and their preoccupations with status and social acceptance, choosing instead to live in a way which often shocks the latter. In this Alexander is following in the footsteps rather than flying in the face of family tradition. His parents were far from conventional in terms of their marriage and their approach to life. They married against the wishes of both their families. Alexander's mother, Daphne, was from a family which had artistic tendencies. Henry's father, the 5th Marquess, considered that she was too flighty. Daphne's family were also unhappy about Henry's credentials. There was, after all, a recent Bath grandmother, Violet, whose birth had caused a scandal involving the then Prince of Wales (later Edward VII) who may have been her father: in which case, as Alexander gleefully notes, he may be descended from the House of Windsor (or Saxe Coburg Gotha as they were originally). As it is, he claims to be descended from the Plantagenets, from Henry II and his bride Eleanor of Aquitaine via their youngest son, King John of Magna Carta fame. But it was not only the line of descent which may have troubled the families of either partner in this match. It was their behaviour. According to Alexander, they belonged to a wild young set that, following the end of World War One, had become used to letting rip, and this was the case after their marriage as well. However, as Alexander points out, while they were keen to demolish all the stuffy values of Edwardian society, they also held on to their own sense of being part of an aristocratic elite. Alexander himself follows this mould in that he has been doing his best to show that he would like to knock down class barriers by sending his children to the local comprehensive and declaring himself a socialist and by standing for Parliament as a Wessex Independent; but meanwhile he remains almost a secret believer in his heritage, promoting himself, his art and his lifestyle in order to bring tourists into Longleat and thereby continue to finance the upkeep of the house and the domain that he loves. His behaviour has made him an ugly duckling in the eyes of many; and although there is both delight and regret in this status, there is still the nagging feeling that he has failed to turn into the swan he would like to be. He has rejected the easy confidence and status he could have known as the holder of a senior aristocratic title but has failed to gain respect from his peers in his alternative role. He has also failed, due largely to his overwhelming lack of self-confidence, to prove his artistic talent to the world.

The Artist

Yes, he is unique. Yes, he is famous, popular, an object of fascination for the class-conscious British, a celebrity who turns up at art-gallery parties, book launches and other commercial promotions and, until recent reforms, a speechmaking member of the House of Lords. Yes, he is known as an author of three novels, but so far only one of his novels has been published by anyone other than by himself, even though another has been made into a film. Yes, he made a record in the 1960s, upon which he sang his own songs and accompanied himself on the guitar. And yes, he is written about as an artist, and his murals are a feature of fascination to fee-paying tourists who do the guided tour of Longleat. But fascination is not enough. Alexander craves genuine recognition as an artist. He wants his work to be valued. One problem is that he has never exhibited except on the walls of his house and has therefore never allowed the world to judge him formally as an artist. However, Alexander's work makes a claim to uniqueness, not only in that he has chosen to express himself in murals rather than on canvas. His Expressionistic style owes some of its origins to his two periods as an art student in Paris during the 1950s. There is much originality to his style and to his method of applying paint very thickly, often combined with wood shavings and sawdust. His use of colour on the wood surrounds, window frames and radiators of his private quarters also shows a great love of strong and beautiful contrasts, such as deep indigo with azure, bright yellow with magenta, turquoise, rose. How uplifting these colours are to the inhabitants of these rooms during the long grey winter months! Alexander's talent as an artist first emerged at Eton, where he was encouraged by his art teacher. He exhibited there and won prizes; and several of his old friends such as Sir James Spooner, Sir Ian Rankin, Sir Tim Sainsbury and Tim Rathbone comment on how much they preferred Alexander's style in his schooldays when his work was traditionally realist rather than the post-Paris Expressionism with which he has covered the walls of his private part of Longleat House.

The former Conservative MP Tim Rathbone said Alexander was very good at portraits while at Eton. Indeed, he is still very good at portraits and can at times bring to life even a long-dead historical character, working from old pictures or tomb effigies. His portrait of Eleanor of Aquitaine, one of his early ancestors, which hangs in the conference suite, is such a vivid image of a celebrated mediaeval beauty that it might have been painted from life. However, many of his life subjects seem not to be recognisable from their portraits. Apart from the heads of ancestors and wifelets, which decorate the staircases and conference rooms of Longleat House, most of Alexander's work is on a very large scale, stretching over entire walls in big rooms or along the long galleries. Much of it is painted on hardboard panels which have then been stuck onto a painted background and is removable. Alexander has very little which could easily be taken down and shown in an art gallery. He has expressed an overwhelming lack of confidence when asked why he does not exhibit. Once he even confessed in front of a group of his friends to having declined to submit a picture for a charitable competition for fear of it not winning. He also suffers generally from a lack of self-confidence as an individual, the causes of which will emerge as his story unfolds.

The Soldier

At school, Alexander seems to have been popular and self-confident, not in the top rank academically but very talented at art. His school pals confirm this. The crisis of self-confidence came later. After Eton, he was obliged to do his two years National Service and, like most of his school mates, went into the elite Life Guards and began officer training. This was where Alexander's confident and successful self-image began to be dented. To be named Alexander with all that this implies to those who know anything about that dauntless Greek may give one a lot to live up to. Certainly Alexander Thynn, Seventh Marquess of Bath, knew of his illustrious namesake from an early age. The British upper classes are steeped in the classics, and it would be impossible to evade the constant references to historic significance of this name at school and university. Alexander says that he 'was certainly aware of the significance' of his name's history and of the high standards of achievement set by its illustrious owner. People do tend to expect something important of the bearer of such a name. Why was Lord Bath named Alexander? Most firstborn males in the family since the days of the first John Thynne have been named John, Thomas or Henry Frederick. The name Alexander was brought into the Thynne family when the 3rd Marquess married Harriet Baring, one of whose family names it was. Alexander Thynn is no Alexander the Great. His brief military career in the early 1950s has given him and his friends an abundant source of amusing anecdotes which point to the opposite. Although he would clearly have loved to emerge from the army cast in the mould of the sort of military leaders whom his father admired, Alexander was not officer material. Several of his old friends suggest that his failure to demonstrate military talents during his National Service in the Life Guards has left a deep scar on Alexander's psyche. Some have also mentioned the marked stutter, which Alexander developed in his teens, as being a great obstacle to gaining the respect of the ranks when issuing military orders.

Alexander ruefully admits that he did not reach the heights of leadership to which he had originally aspired. 'I had the idea that I'd succeeded so well at my preparatory school, becoming captain of the school,' he says, 'and I'd succeeded at Eton, getting elected to Pop (the Eton Society, the self-electing society at Eton with privileges) and so on, and so I should in the army: but then I was suddenly going into army training and finding the faith in myself was crumbling and I was not being awarded the best honours. I was actually passing out as an officer all right, but it wasn't with a stick at Mons,' he continues, referring to the Officer Cadet School at Aldershot, 'and things like that which would have been in the tradition that I'd imagined.' His old friend Sir Timothy Sainsbury, a member of the famous grocery family and a former Conservative MP and government minister, was with Alexander in the Life Guards. 'I don't know that any of us were great leaders of men,' he recalls, 'but some were keener and more efficient soldiers than others. Alex had a romantic and dashing approach, which didn't always produce the right results. Someone was saying we oughtn't to put Alexander's troop on the flank because he's so liable to get out of touch. But I do remember on one occasion that he achieved a great coup by starting off very early one morning on some exercise. He discovered a whole squadron of the other regiment still having their breakfast, and the umpire said he had won.'

At the time Alexander was serving with the British Army On the Rhine (BAOR). 'It's not true that Alexander was a failure in the Army,' observes his friend Laurence Kelly. 'We were on the border, and the Russian tanks were patrolling on the other side of it. The BAOR could not possibly have dealt with an attack. So it's not true to say that a junior office was not competent. They could not have risked it.' There is no doubt, however, that Alexander was troubled by the fact that he did not reach the heights in the army he was expected to by his family. Michael Croucher, a BBC TV director friend from fairly early days of filming at Longleat, says, that in understanding what went wrong for Alexander: 'You should realize that the army was important.'

Alexander's perception that he had failed during his military training helped influence his decision to drop out. After the army he went up to Oxford; and it was after this, his friends say, that he disappeared. What really went wrong? Laurence Kelly, who became one of Alexander's close friends but who had not been among his Eton buddies, was also in the Brigade of Guards at the same time. 'We were a privileged stratum of young men pitch-forked into an unexpectedly rough situation,' he says. 'The first thing was Caterham, where there was a fearsome thing called the Brigade Squad. We lived in a long hut. There was a Captain Gow there who became a general. There was also an uncle figure called a "Trained Soldier". He was teaching us how to polish boots, fold clothes and not come back drunk. Then there was an experienced sergeant in charge of squad. It took four to six months to break in the young men. If you passed that you then went to Mons Officer Cadet School where you learned about tanks, armoured cars, guns and lived in another long hut. Then we were moved to Germany. Alexander was touchingly naïve and approachable,' he adds. 'But at that time he was a great splutterer and squeaker. By the time he went to Oxford he had developed a few more complexes and a carapace. Henry had ditched Daphne by this time.'

Alexander wrote in *Two Bites of the Apple*, Book Three of his online memoir, that he had a terrible fear in his heart that he would not match up to all the promise he had shown as a schoolboy. He felt that the 'fundamental weakness' in his personality might now come to the surface once he was exposed to the 'rough and tumble' of fending for himself in a world outside the protective and orderly structures of his upbringing. However, when he arrived at Cumbermere Barracks for his induction into two years of National Service in the Brigade of Guards, he found a high percentage of Etonians, including many of his own friends, amid the new arrivals. As a result of this, he found immediate acceptance in the Officers Mess. But this good start did not lead to glory.

Even if he were not to be a military star, Alexander did experience some successes, albeit seemingly accidental ones. When things went wrong for Alexander, they did so with bells on; but at the very end of his army training everything went crazily well out of sheer happenstance. During one brigade exercise, where several different regiments of the Rhine Army were playing the two opposing sides in a war game, he describes his comic bit of luck. 'I'd been really irritating my colonel and my squadron leader and everyone else, but then suddenly...if you've seen *Private Benjamin*...all that sort of thing was happening to me. I was getting lost in the woods, coming out somewhere and saying, "What's that? Oh, it's enemy headquarters."' He laughs uproariously, his face pink, his eyes sparkling. He loves to tell the stories of his successes but does so while laughing hugely and yelling loudly in imitation of his own roared orders, words tumbling out, laughing and gabbling incoherently.

'There was an episode where I'd been drinking far too much,' he continues, 'and my squadron leader, probably to get me shot with a rubber bullet, quickly sent me off in the middle of the night to where the enemy line was, which is a hopeless thing for an armoured car to be doing. Suddenly there were thunder flashes, and in a drunken reaction I began shouting like Rambo "Come on now. Get the bayonets!" And the enemy were hearing this, and suddenly lights came on everywhere and there were tanks everywhere racing away. And this was where we made a breakthrough and captured a bridge over which they were going and suddenly everything was going right.' When Alexander tells other stories of his army days, he tells them self-critically, and yet, is keen to emphasize that in the end he came out with commendations. To add to these final triumphs in the war games, he became British Army Officers Welterweight Boxing Champion. He makes that too sound like a happy accident. 'I went back from the exercises to what I thought was just a boxing course,' he says, 'but I found that they were really getting us to enter the army officers boxing championship, which I happened to win.' Telling the story, he is visibly exhilarated, laughing uproariously at the memory of the wave of success with which he ended his National Service. He is being modest about his boxing. His school friend, Tim Rathbone, remembers that 'he was very good at boxing, very light and quick, and he had been given his first boxing training at the age of three and a half when his father sent him to a London gym.' These final successes saved Alexander from leaving the army with a total sense of having failed to reach the standard his father expected. He would have liked to have left the army knowing he was good officer material and a natural leader of men, but that was certainly not the case: so much so that it undoubtedly served to steer him in a direction opposite to one in which a talent for leadership has any great usefulness. It drove him inwards to his art, and ultimately his ambition to prove himself a leader was transmuted into an intense desire for recognition as an artist.

The Aristocrat

So if Alexander was hardly the model Guards officer, he is also far from a standard British marquess. But is there such a thing? Past aristocrats, especially during periods like the liberal and licentious Eighteenth Century, had a devil-may-care vigour. They lived for the present with lustiness and libido to the fore. The nineteenth century saw in a more prudish fashion, which continued into the twentieth century. The image of the British aristocrat is now somewhat staid. There have been attempts to show that they earn their own living or at the very least that they do not flaunt their wealth, flogging off the odd Goya or Titian to pay for a new roof on the stately home, turning the family palace into a public amusement park. Even the Windsors now open Buckingham Palace to the public and the Queen has started going to Sandringham by public train. Today's aristocrats, following the Royal Family, complain of the cost of keeping up the family home. They lead fairly quiet lives, attending private dinner parties in London or otherwise sticking to their estates where they hunt, shoot and fish while entertaining an exclusive circle of friends. This, however, is the *Country Life* version of the image. The more colourful ones, like Alexander, tend to find themselves in the diary columns of the tabloids. The English like to label them eccentric, but surely if they have enough money in the trust fund they can indulge their individuality? Marquesses, more than most, seem to have cut out a role for themselves. The quieter aristocrats dislike these flamboyant ones, regarding them as letting the side down. The British public also likes the myth of the superior caste, which they can respect. They do not want their aristocrats to be too much like themselves. Many prefer the myth of a higher form of hereditary life. Alexander, even if he has inherited his wealth and titles, is very well known and therefore seems extremely accessible. He regards himself as a meritocrat making his own way as an artist and writer. However, he still feels he must defend himself against the criticisms of those who demand conventional respectability from their aristocrats. In reality, Alexander lives quietly enough and with an effortless dignity. His publicity gives the contrary impression that his life is one long bawdy bacchanalian orgy. It consequently seems as if he were always on the edge of apologizing, of explaining his eccentricities, of wanting to be understood.

Father Son Dynamics

The key to Alexander's life lies in his teens and twenties. His childhood with its fun-loving parents and strict nanny and governesses seems far from disastrous, and his schooldays were happy. But in his home life, his teens were more tormented than most. His relationship with the father he had adored and tried to emulate fell apart.

Alexander had been set on a career as the Marquess of Bath, with hopes about his gift for leadership. As a child, he adored Henry and wanted to create himself in Henry's image. He absorbed much of Henry's admiration of fascism and tried to follow his philosophies. Then came several betrayals, of which the most critical for Alexander was the humiliation of being beaten at the age of fifteen for washing his dog in the kitchen. Alexander relates often that it was not only the fact that he was beaten but that he was beaten at an age when he would not have been beaten at Eton. At fifteen Alexander was already bigger than Henry and, being a great success as a boxer, could have hit him pretty hard. He did not. He submitted instead to his father's will out of respect and was therefore doubly humiliated. Alexander then turned against his father and all the ideals which that father had represented. This was not the only betrayal which marked the key turning point in Alexander's life and aspirations, but to Alexander the incident was crucial. When he describes what happened that day, he still goes red in the face and shouts out in mimicry of his father's despotic manner.

After that event, there were more battles with Henry, and the deterioration of this relationship has had a profound and continuing effect on Alexander's life. When he later passed through an 'Angry Young Man' phase, this humiliation was more a symbol than the sole cause of his enduring rage. Alexander is now the unrepentantly angry young man grown grey but no less angry, still trying to knock down everything which his father held out to be right. He is also, however, a strangely conservative upholder of his first-born place in society, as the inheritor of an important title and a splendid family seat. As many of his friends remark, he is deeply conservative and a traditionalist while giving the impression of a 1960s hippy; but as he points out, his parents were also a combination of rule-breakers and upholders of their elite position. To what extent is he merely following in their footsteps? How much of his polarity is personal and how much a media-enhanced amplification of his parents' stance?

How much is Alexander his own man and how much simply a product of his environment? The answers to these questions will become clear as his story is told. The two opposing pictures of the rebel and the traditionalist will struggle for domination like two snapshots superimposed upon each other. At first sight the hippy dominates. When out in public, Alexander is invariably dressed strikingly in one of his rather spectacular caftan-style robes or in tailored velvet jackets which are far removed from the sober styles of Savile Row. Some of these garments are, when examined in detail, very intricately constructed. Others are African caftans given as gifts. Many of the jackets are made and designed by the same private designer: Helen Anderson, a former girlfriend who first met Alexander in the South of France during the 1970s. Ms Anderson, a school pal of John Lennon's in Liverpool who spent a period in the fashion business, has since returned to her original craft of painting and has recently done a portrait of Alexander, which she says is 'the only full-length portrait of Alexander in existence' and which has been installed in one of the libraries at Longleat. 'He asked me to design and make a jacket especially for him to wear in the portrait,' she says. 'It's a green velvet jacket with embroidered lapels. I must be the only case of a painter having to design and make a jacket for one of their portraits.' Another wifelet, Yelena (number 40) made many of Alexander's other clothes. His wardrobe is packed with this kind of exotica; but at home alone or at weekends with friends, Alexander does not often dress up. He wears velvet trousers in jewel colours, again specially made for him, and old jumpers sometimes with holes in them or looking a bit stained. In this gear he generally looks the part of the artist, the odd blob of paint often adding authenticity to the image. He might dress up in one of the caftans for dinner on Saturday night, but that depends who else is there and whether or not he is trying to impress them.

However, he has also been seen in pinstripes. When he took his seat at the House of Lords after becoming the Seventh Marquess of Bath, he evidently was intimidated enough by tradition to leave his robes at home and adopt the conventional uniform of the three-piece suit. His flowing curls were reined into a pony tail and his normally bare or sandaled feet squashed into black shoes. A wifelet who once accompanied him to the Lords where he was to make a speech complained that she had to wear 'a little navy blue suit' instead of her usual fetching leotards and capes, to go with Alexander in his pinstripes. Sadly the need to dress up every week for sessions of the Upper House has passed. Alexander sat with the Liberal Democrats in his brief six-year period as a hereditary peer. He took his role seriously enough, attending the House each week. He made several speeches of which he was inordinately proud. I was present in March 1999 when he read out to guests at his Sunday lunch party the speech which he was to make the following afternoon on the subject of Lords Reform and Devolution. It was, however, Lords reform which brought to a close this period of exercise of his hereditary right to govern. Despite his keenness to take his place in the Lords as the Second Chamber of Parliament, Alexander was not one of the few hereditary peers who stood for election to stay on under the reforms which excluded the majority of hereditary peers from the automatic right to take a seat in the Lords. The thrill of making speeches in Parliament has been reluctantly resigned. Alexander has had to go back to other methods of making headlines, getting mentions in the press about the wifelet scene or attending London parties.

Philosopher and Politician

Alexander once told me that if he had the choice between being simply very rich or being what he is, he 'would choose to go where the power is'. This seems a surprising statement. One would not suspect Alexander, the artist, the rebel against the status quo and the upholder of his own heritage, to be a seeker after power. The statement explains much about a man who has long sought to overthrow the idea of conventional status while clinging to its reality. By running with the fox while still managing to ride with the hounds, Alexander has played a consummate power game. In a world which, since his childhood, has ceased to tolerate the conventionally aristocratic idea of hereditary rule, Alexander has managed to stay at the top and get the best of his inheritance while playing the populist. It seems, as he is bound to admit, that even in present-day England, where the political power of the hereditary aristocrat has been curtailed by legislation, his position as a marquess and proprietor of a substantial estate is still a higher form of power in British society than that exercised by a self-made multimillionaire. Titles still count. A title can still open doors even in commerce, as Prince Edward's spouse, Sophie Rhys Jones, was once foolish enough to admit to the press. As for Bath, would anyone care about his paintings, his wifelets or his philosophies, if he were just plain Alexander Thynn?

Even in republics like France, titles have a subliminal glamour. In England, the overt importance and influence of the aristocracy is, as a hierarchy, dependent upon the continuation of the monarchy for its survival. The luxury of espousing socialist views while enjoying the privilege of wealth or titles has been largely encouraged by the existence of the House of Lords, which requires peers of differing parties for its legislative function. Alexander, a hereditary member who sat on the Liberal Democrat benches in the House of Lords, is in a strange position as a self-proclaimed rebel against class advantages who continues to enjoy those advantages in abundance. Take, for instance, the question of the monarchy. Alexander prevaricates when asked his views on its continuation. He diplomatically replies that he believes 'political union of the European states will automatically take care of the future of the monarchy'. By this he means that national sovereignty and therefore national heads of state will cease to exist. The ultimate European plan is to subdivide the nations into cantons, which will be directly under the aegis of the European super-state. It will be goodbye to the nation state and to the British form of constitutional monarchy. In translation, Alexander expects, accepts and, dare we say, desires the end of the United Kingdom's constitutional monarchy. He also confesses that he cannot publicly admit this.

Alexander first promoted the notion of the end of British constitutional monarchy in 1974 when he made his first attempt to be elected as independent MP for Wessex to the Westminster Parliament. The British Parliament will also cease to exist under a politically unified EU subdivided into administrative regions rather than nations. Alexander is keen to remind the world that his own region of Wessex, stretching from Lands End to Winchester on the Hampshire–Sussex borders will be a more powerful entity than present-day England in the European super-state. Meanwhile, Alexander's ambitions in the political sphere include becoming the elected representative for Wessex in the House of Lords. That, if it became constitutionally possible before the removal of the British Parliament, would be his way of overcoming the reforms of the Lords, which has denied him his hereditary seat. There are at present no directly elected representatives sitting in the House of Lords: the prime minister's office remains the channel for patronage and the source of new members of the House of Lords. Before the arrival of the EU super-state, Alexander proposed the idea in one of his Lords speeches for a House of Lords in which some representatives would be nominated by their local regions in a sort of 'People's Patronage'. After the British Parliament has ceased to exist, he believes, it would be possible for him to become the representative for Wessex in the politically unified Europe. He has no idea if he will live long enough to participate in such a development, but Alexander has been proved farsighted in making this predication as early as his 1974 Parliamentary campaign. As with all his ideas and philosophies, Alexander has first formulated them and then held to them rigidly. This one, forecasting the division of European nation states into regions or cantons certainly seems likely to be proven right during the present century. However, his friend Tim Rathbone, formerly Conservative MP for Lewes and a famously rebellious 'wet' told me: 'I wouldn't describe Alexander as a sophisticated political animal.'

Alexander's philosophies were founded when he was at Oxford. He studied PPE, (Politics, Philosophy and Economics). Of these the one he liked least was Economics and the one he preferred was Philosophy. He was disappointed to have obtained only a Third Class degree. Perhaps he hoped for a First. He does not say so. A Third, he points out, was not the bottom of the ladder. He could have had a Fourth or even a fail. But he had hoped for better. It was not entirely his fault. 'I remember discussing one examination paper with Alex,' recalls Sir Tim Sainsbury, his Eton and Oxford pal. 'It was a rather strange paper about institutions and not one of the eighteen questions were on the subjects we had been studying. The man who set the papers had departed entirely from what we had been studying. None of the questions we were expecting were there.'

Some problems were related to Alexander's own departures from the strict syllabus. 'He became very interested in cosmology and rather way-out philosophy,' Sainsbury remembers, 'and I think he drifted away from the mainstream and wrote at copious length, and I think it does not help if the examiner can't read or decipher the contents, which I think may have been the case with Alexander.'

So Alexander's main problem was partly a lack of exam technique. With a less abundant imagination he might have been more successful at passing exams. He so desperately needed a good result to prove himself in the eyes of his father and the world, but this disappointing degree meant that his father had been proven right. Henry often stated that the Thynne family were not intellectuals, and it had been important for Alexander to try to prove him wrong. After he came down with the poor degree Alexander remembers that 'Henry was crowing.' By the time he went to Oxford Alexander was completely at loggerheads with his father. Having lost faith in the rigid beliefs of his background and having therefore nothing on which to fall back when his personal confidence seemed to fail him, Alexander decided that he should work out his beliefs in detail and once and for all. The Philosophy course provided the tools with which Alexander could work out where he stood in terms of beliefs about politics, love and marriage, life after death, God and the divine. He learned less about past philosophical ideas than about an academic process of rational argument which he still uses today. It was like learning a martial art. With the help of the mental disciplines he learned at Christ Church College he was able to formulate philosophies of his own. This was important for his own self-belief in that by working out where he stood as an individual he was separating himself from the beliefs his father had instilled into him. He says that he knew that he needed to do this because he also knew that he had to have intellectual weapons with which to fight his father's Blimpish views. Or at least, that is what he believes he was doing. It is possible that even the process of rebellion, of divesting himself of the beliefs held by his class and his education, was a part of the process which had made him. His act of rejection was itself a part of what he wanted to reject. Alexander would argue otherwise; and indeed his Oxford tuition has given him a training in mental argument which he quickly drops into when his ideas are challenged. There are, however, many among Alexander's friends who would say that he is too stuck in his beliefs, that he gets one idea and then insists that he is 'always right'. This tenacity may be the reason why Alexander's philosophies have not changed since he initially formulated them in those Oxford years. He published a book of his philosophies in 2000: it does not show that he has made many observations during the intervening half century that might have modified his beliefs first conceived at the age of twenty-three and later used as the framework for his science-fiction novel *The King is Dead*.

Alexander's beliefs about life after death and deity are explored in this novel as are his views on women and their promiscuity. Alexander's view of the universe is somewhat frightening in that it does not have any sense of good and evil or of the quality of love. To Alexander, the divine is not a singular being but a vast complex which functions on somewhat mechanical lines. He does not believe in an afterlife but in a form of recurrence or repetition of individual life, which he calls 'resurrection' and which differs from established ideas of reincarnation. In the theology of reincarnation, individual souls turn up, life after life, in new bodies and evolve spiritually as a result of their response to the challenging experiences of material existence until they become 'liberated' and do not have to return, life after life, to the struggle of material existence. Alexander's concept of resurrection is one of unchanging repetition in one existence after another without evolution. 'I'll turn up in a sort of android,' he jokes. This would just be Alexander in a new disguise, unmodified by experience. Likewise his view of the universe is not that it is eternal but that it is 'permanent'. Again this implies an unchanging continuity as opposed to one of constant evolution. These concepts fit Alexander's rather rigid personality structure. Change is frightening to him. Rebellion, yes; but change, no. As in his philosophical view of the universe's permanence, his other views are indelible and unchangeable; and his deep conservatism is immutable in the face of a rebellion which is simply a dramatization of his fight with his father.

His Oxford years were also when Alexander started his idea of the collective family. He had by the time he went to Oxford spent nine months in Paris and witnessed the dissolution of his parents' marriage. The period in Paris brought him into contact with ideas such as those espoused by Jean-Paul Sartre, Simone de Beauvoir and the Existentialists, none of whom believed in conventional marriage. It was at this time too that Alexander became disappointed in love and in women. The origin of his philosophy of sexual relationships lies here. The ideas, or rather the impulse which sparked them, came from his anger, his experience of rejection, his assumption that women are always unfaithful and from the bitter pill of his recent past. Although he is married simply for the sake of legitimizing his heir, he has made himself famous as much for his highly publicized extramarital love life as for any of his other activities. This is probably what has brought about Alexander's extraordinary celebrity.

Lifestyle of The Lion of Longleat

Longleat is at the heart of Alexander's beliefs and his life. At Longleat, one can understand his belief in 'permanence'. The massive stone of the four-turreted house, the strength of that square edifice, imply something immovable. One feels that Longleat is indestructible. In the material sense alone the house is permanent and unchanging. Alexander has lived in the house since he was twenty-one, when he was in fact the only member of the family to live there. Whether it was a form of exile or rebellion he does not say. He moved in there when his father parents divorced in 1953 and sold off Sturford Mead, the house on the Longleat Estate which had been the family residence. Alexander has occupied about one half of Longleat House ever since. He clearly loves it and although he has two other abodes, he clearly feels affection for – and a commitment to – Longleat. Indeed he has told me that it is part of his identity. This great square palace, with its uncompromising symmetry, is the foundation of his sense of permanence. It is the rock on which he has founded his life and his beliefs.

Without Longleat, he admits to feeling that he is some lesser being. With Longleat, he is a force. He tries to be his own man within this framework, and this is what gives him his double image as reclusive traditionalist on the one hand and hippy rebel on the other. He has tried to spread his wings. When he came into his trust fund in 1964 he immediately bought himself a duplex in a newly built block of flats near Notting Hill Gate. He says that this was a way of asserting his independence and also of trying to become more sociable after a period of being semi-reclusive at Longleat, and in Paris, where he lived for three to four years after coming down from Oxford. With this flat as his base he was able to begin to circulate more freely on the London party scene. The 1960s were beginning to get into their stride; and Alexander, having already established his personal fashion statement of hippy caftans, bare or sandaled feet and pony tail, became a well-known figure on the edge of the *beau monde*. He says he was never part of the Swinging Sixties, never quite the upper-class swinger like Patrick Lichfield and Tony Armstrong Jones, whose photographic talents and enterprise took them into the heart of the Kings Road scene: home to the models and hairdressers who formed the hard core of the 1960s smart set. His shyness and lack of self-confidence had always been a barrier.

But Longleat was always a magnet for people. Shirley Conran, wifelet nineteen, met Alexander in the later 1960s and briefly became a girlfriend in 1969, the year in which Alexander finally married Anna Gyarmarthy, his Hungarian girlfriend of ten years standing. Now a famous author, Shirley Conran was working as a journalist and already divorced from Terence Conran. She was introduced to Longleat by a friend and for a time, shared the use of a cottage on the estate with another of Alexander's friends: Ben Whittaker, another Old Etonian and a Labour MP for Hampstead, with his wife Janet. The first time she saw Longleat she was being driven there as a surprise by a friend in the midst of a snowstorm. She did not know where they were going. One of the private roads across the estate comes over a hill and then curls down gradually. The house is visible as one drives down the hill, flags often fluttering from each of the four towers. As they crested the hill before driving down to the house, the friend said: 'Look to the right.' Conran looked and the view through the snowstorm has stayed forever fresh in her memory. 'It was one of the most beautiful things I have seen in my life,' she later tells me.

When they went inside the house, she says, 'everything reeked of paint.' Alexander was busy with his murals. 'He has been terribly considerate,' Conran recalls. 'He has painted his murals on boards so that they can later be taken down to reveal the beautiful Eighteenth Century wallpaper underneath.' Alexander was 'tall and slim and very good looking', but she did not, she says, fall in love with him. 'That's one of the reasons I am so fond of him,' she adds. She was often a weekend guest at Longleat House parties. 'It was so beautiful being at Longleat in the Swinging Sixties,' she says. 'I was fashion editor on the *Express* at the time. Everyone seemed so terribly beautiful in see-through clothes and all the women wore lots of makeup. It was so glamorous.'

Not so the Notting Hill apartment, and certainly not today. Alexander still has the same flat in a rather grimy 1960s low rise block where it simply says 'Bath' in a rough scrawl on the doorbell. Many of his visitors have commented on the squalor of this apartment, often likening it to a squat. The living room doubles as a study with a desk at one end and a mattress on the floor – for daytime resting – at the other. Dirty glasses, paper plates with leftovers from days before and pots of mustard, ketchup and foodstuffs litter the coffee table. Alexander cooks there for his friends and wifelets, feeding them on tinned food or ancient deep-frozen stuff from his freezer. In these respects he is very much the unreconstructed bachelor. The flat is the base for his social life. Three or four evenings a week he goes off from here to art gallery viewings and PR parties. It is at these gatherings, seldom in the A-list category, that he meets his new wifelets. He also paints upstairs at the flat and works on his writing, carting his desk top computer back and forth in his car from Longleat. He's a familiar figure at the local pub, The Windsor Castle, where he lunches on such favourites as steak and kidney pie, stew or bangers and mash. Also dating from the 1960s, Alexander has had another residence, near St Tropez, where until recently he stayed each summer for about two months, roughly from mid-July to mid-September. He also bought this place in 1964 when, he says, he was 'trying to woo Anna'.

When he is at Longleat, Alexander lives partly in one wing of Longleat House, the Western half, and partly in a very modern penthouse which he has had created on the top floor under the North Eastern turret. The rest of the top floor of the East Wing is laid out as a magnificent series of beautifully designed very modern conference rooms. The latter he built, together with the penthouse, after his father's death in 1992, at which time it had been discovered that the attic rooms of this wing housed a rather grotesque collection of Hitler memorabilia, together with items commemorating Churchill and Margaret Thatcher. Alexander now sleeps and works upstairs in the penthouse, eats and greets and entertains his visitors downstairs in the apartments which he first called his own home. Guests also sleep downstairs on the West side, in the variously named bedroom suites: the Dowager, the Autobiographical and the Kama Sutra suites.

The penthouse with its hi-tech feel, its 1980s minimalism, its huge open-plan living room which looks out on two sides on Longleat Park, is very much the home of the man who has written and published a science-fiction novel. It is also very much the home of a man who appears to eschew traditionalism. The clean lines, the functional furniture, the beautiful blond-wood floor, the massive floor-to-ceiling console with its giant TV screen, video and CD player, the huge crescent-shaped desk behind which Alexander sits with his computer, like the captain of some space ship, the contemporary moulded foam easy chairs for guests all speak of a need for the occupant to rise above the traditions of the antiquity-packed tourist attractions of his private apartments and the public half of the house. Interestingly, there are no murals here, only smallish ancestor heads which decorate the otherwise modern conference rooms. The more homely touches also suggest an abrupt departure from convention. The king-sized bed is housed in a large alcove off the living room, separated from the rest of the room only by a curtain. Alexander has been known to retreat behind this curtain to watch programmes using an earpiece on the small TV which he keeps by the bedside. Meanwhile his guests may be amusing each other in the main room or watching a different channel on the other TV.

The bathroom is in fact much bigger than most people's living rooms. It houses a giant Jacuzzi bath, complete with toy ducks, which totally fills one wall. This is a party sized tub and one can only guess at the possibilities for social scrubbing which it offers. In addition there is the usual equipment: loo, wash basin, bidet and an enormous corner shower cubicle big enough to accommodate a man of Alexander's size with perhaps a wifelet or two at the same time. The kitchen is the first room one encounters on entering the apartment. It is to the left of the passageway and separated from it by some floor-to-ceiling cabinets. It is one of those ultimate kitchens with a lot of steel and glass. There is a big oven with a gleaming hob, large drawers full of polished stainless-steel cooking pots. A large fridge-freezer with doors opening adjacent to the cooking area forms part of the unit separating the kitchen from the hallway. The hall-facing side of this has shelving packed with glasses and canned food. The latter is an Alexander speciality. One would think he was expecting a siege to see the numbers of tins of tuna, pilchards, beans, sardines and ham packed on shelf upon shelf. A big freezer stocks ancient-looking frozen meat, fish and vegetables. When the couple who look after Alexander are away, weekend guests cook here, using these stores to make up strange mixtures of dishes. Alexander also cooks for friends or family when he is not too busy. He specializes in big meaty stews. Passing through the kitchen, past the canned-food stores, one arrives next in a dining room containing a round teak table and a small modern side table complete with hot plate. The room is subtly plain with a black stone-flagged floor and hessian walls also partly decorated with transparent glittery fabric pulled into pleated arrangements on the walls. There is none of Alexander's vivid use of colour. It's all a little too beige and subtle. Only a rather expensive designer could have put all this together. Yet the effect lacks warmth or intimacy even when there is a group seated at the table. Leading off the dining room to the left is a small sitting room where Alexander keeps his guitar and a chessboard. He is a keen chess player and, according to one friend, is rather good at it. At one time he used to play against a computer but found it too good an opponent. Usually he plays with any guest who can attempt a game, sometimes with a wifelet; and there are chessboards upstairs and downstairs. 'Alexander hates to lose at chess,' his friend Laurence Kelly tells me, 'and displays a lot of petulance if he does.'

This uninspiring rectangular room with white walls leads off to the left to a very small room absolutely crammed with paints and painted boards, with palettes and messy worktables. It leads in the other direction to a corridor which is flanked by windows on the eastern side of the apartment and which gives off to the bathroom on the right but which otherwise leads dead ahead to Alexander's desk and then continues around to the right to the big open plan living room. One also reaches the living room by means of the right-hand exit from the dining room. This is the main route to the living space from the apartment's front door. It passes on the right a spiral staircase, which goes up onto the roof and, after this, a small passageway leading to a narrow room in which there is an even narrower bed. This in turn opens out into another narrow room containing two bunk beds intended for visiting children but sometimes used by adult guests. Back in the main living space, Alexander's bar is on the left as you enter. There is little indication of serious wine other than the occasional bottle brought by a guest as a gift. There are three wooden boxes with taps marked red, pink and white. Carafes are filled from here to be placed on the table where more tooth glasses are available. When staff is resident Alexander and his guests go downstairs for their meals. There is a lift which can be used for this, or one can trail through the conference suites in the North Wing, past rows of ancestral portraits and down the creaky, splintered wooden staircase which houses the remaining gallery of ancestors. Alexander has painted these using prints of old paintings and a good deal of imagination.

It is some distance down these stairs and across two sides of Longleat House to the opposite corner where Alexander's original ground-floor apartments welcome his visitors. Alexander claims that walking up and down these stairs and along the galleries to and from his meals affords him sufficient exercise. He says he does not want to go for walks; and when his faithful old mongrel, Toya, died in March 2001, he said that he would not get another puppy because this would mean going for walks. Toya used to lie all day on her own cushioned bed at the foot of Alexander's bed, a silent companion for Alexander who is otherwise alone in this huge apartment much of the time, sleeping here at night and working by day on his life story and other projects, taking calls directly on his private line. He now has a Golden Labrador, Boudicca, named after the famous Celtic warrior queen, who is his constant companion. He has had a portrait painted by a local artist of himself with the dog, both seated on a staircase.

The huge, curved, ship-like desk carries the desktop computer which is being used to write Alexander's immensely detailed memoirs. Also, on this huge crescent of polished pale wood are phones, directories, executive toys and all manner of other objects. Nearby, toy lions, lion cubs and a chimpanzee lurk and, in an alcove, an ancient upright piano which is virtually unplayable due to missing notes and lack of tuning. Sometimes Alexander's guitar sits on one of the moulded foam easy chairs around the glass coffee table, and he will sit and play a song to anyone who requests it. He sings in a rather reedy tenor the songs he composed in the 1960s, some of which are on his album. From outside, the penthouse is reached by entering the building from the stable yard, turning left and past Lady Bath's Shoppe — a title referring not to the present Lady Bath but to Alexander's grandmother — and passing through a locked door by means of a numerical code and then going up in the silver painted lift to the silver-painted landing and front door flanked by ancestral portraits. One is then confronted by another numerical keypad and, if you don't know or can't remember the code, a normal doorbell. The problem with the latter is that if Alexander is alone, he may not hear it. He wears two hearing aids and is often out of communication even with those if the battery goes flat. Worse, he could be asleep with the hearing aids on the bedside table, in which case, it is as well to have one's mobile phone with one to ring his private line which makes a noise like an old fashioned fire engine. The penthouse is not where visitors are brought at first. As one of Alexander's private guests at Longleat, one comes in to his old apartments downstairs. The entrance used most often by guests being decanted from cars in the yard, where the garages are on the north side, is via the small private garden on the western side of the house. One passes through a gate marked private and is immediately confronted by a large stone upsidedown lion, which blocks both the path and the view. Sliding around this lifesized object, one crosses a few yards of crazy paving, notes, on the right, the dark bronze statue of a Minotaur emerging from the bushes to surprise two stone virgins and descends a couple of steps to a door marked 'Viscount Weymouth'. This is Alexander's private entrance, and the legend under the brass lion-head bell refers to himself rather than to his son Ceawlin. He simply has not had it changed in the years since he became the Marquess of Bath on his father's death. The striking thing about this door is the outsize dog flap. Guests have been known to use this very late at night when all other means of entry are switched off after visiting the Longleat nightclub. Dogs have come and gone with ease but for humans it seems to be a difficult wriggle, but still possible, which seems to make a nonsense of the security.

In the normal upright mode of entry, once through the door, unlocked by another digital code, one crosses a flag-stoned hallway and climbs a spiral staircase carpeted in red. Women's portraits stare from the walls here. It's the start of what Alexander calls his 'Bluebeard's Gallery' of wifelet heads. They are not actually severed heads, but at first sight this is what they seem to be. This is because of Alexander's own special technique of combining oil paint with sawdust and wood shavings, which he then builds up into three-dimensional faces. He agrees there is a caricaturist element to this work, and there are no wifelets who feel that to be recognized by their portrait would be flattering. The wifelet portraits are arranged up the staircase in chronological order. They begin with Davina, a brunette with brilliant eyes, dated 1952, continue through some early debutante girlfriends and then start to develop into a multiracial assortment. The names and dates are pasted on the back of each head. There is one of his wife Anna who was a mistress for ten years before her success at becoming pregnant supplied her with an entrance ticket to the British aristocracy as Alexander's legal bride. She promptly divorced her French film-producer husband, married Alexander, and baby Lenka was born soon after. Her comments on her portrait are, according to Alexander, somewhat acid. But for the moment we are not going to follow the staircase upwards. We arrive in a red-carpeted hallway facing the kitchen whose door is invariably open, showing one of those very ordinary old-fashioned kitchens with a central table and a few old fitted cupboards. There is a good-sized stove in here, for this is the kitchen where all Alexander's meals, for himself or his weekend parties, are cooked by the housekeeper. All Alexander's food is prepared here, unless the housekeeper and butler are away. If he is alone, meals are often eaten off a small table in the drawing room or carried upstairs in the lift to the penthouse. It seems odd that the approaches to Alexander's living quarters involve full exposure to his kitchens. At his St Tropez villa, the front door opens into the kitchen. At Longleat, one might expect something more gracious, as when entering Longleat House through the proper front door. That is not possible with the private entrances, which involve rabbit warrens of passages. Hospitable though this kitchen appears, one does not pass through it to reach the living space. Turning left into hallway one can see three doorways leading to Alexander's drawing room, his dining room and his study library and one at the end which hides the guest lavatory, where Alexander has hung all his old army, Eton and Oxford group photographs. This hallway and its doorways are the social hub of the original apartment into which Alexander moved after coming down from Oxford. Before he built the penthouse, he lived entirely in this wing. It runs the length of the south side and along about half of the west side of the house and going up for three storeys also comprises virtually half of Longleat House. He says he started living here because after his parents' divorce in 1953 his father sold the family home and moved to a smaller place, Job's Mill, with his new wife. There was apparently no room for Alexander there and so he was offered this entire wing of Longleat. As there was great friction between Alexander and his father at this time, it was no doubt a diplomatic manoeuvre to offer him his own quarters. In fact, he loves his home in the great house and one cannot imagine Alexander without it. Yet it is not grand in any way.

'Alexander has always lived in great style but not *in* style,' Shirley Conran observes. 'He's an odd mixture. He has no sense of smell or of taste. I think he has immense focus, but in some ways he's like someone who could be living in Barnes. His living style at Longleat House was nothing like his father's. I thought his father lived a far more luxurious life at Job's Mill with footmen and simply wonderful pictures and furniture.'

Coming out of Alexander's downstairs apartment kitchen and turning right through another doorway, one enters a gloomy hallway with mainly purple walls; turning right again, one is confronted by two striking 1930s pastel portraits of Alexander's parents. Photographic in quality, elegant and slightly reminiscent of fashion sketches in style, these were fashioned in the 1930s by a well-known artist of the day. Gazing down on one with a condescending air from this wall, they seem to reflect the remoteness from real life of the British aristocracy prior to World War Two. The sitters' expressions are bland, their faces unlined by experience, their clothes draped effortlessly on their fashionably tall, thin bodies. Knowing what was to come later, as these escapist people coasted and cavorted towards the war, supporting fascist ideas and living the high life, one thinks of the famous Oscar Wilde novella, *The Picture of Dorian Gray*. In that story the beautiful Dorian maintains his youth and beauty while a portrait in the attic ages and becomes uglier daily, showing the ravages that Dorian's debauched life is wreaking on his soul. Longleat in those days was also the world of Evelyn Waugh's novel, *Brideshead Revisited*. There are echoes of Waugh's fictional aristocratic family in the Baths' gilded youth. It is said by some of Alexander's friends that Waugh based Brideshead on Longleat and the Thynnes. In turn Alexander seems to have echoed *Brideshead Revisited* in his own third novel, *Pillars of the Establishment*, which is described on its book jacket as 'a story of the decline and fall of a noble family'. Alexander says that his parents were 'the leading figures among the bright young things of the 1930s. They were the true *'jeunesse dorée'*. Did the flame of decadent pre-war Society burn brightest before it went out? The 1930s were the final days for this gilded youth. In the 1945 General Election, the Labour landslide and the subsequent huge taxes on inherited wealth took away the glass wall of capital which had sheltered these privileged beings from life's realities within an escapist world of parties and love affairs.

The faces which gaze down from the portraits reflect the tranquillity of their moneyed existence and the apparent vacancy of minds unchallenged by the physical and psychological struggle for survival experienced by the legions of unemployed during the Depression of the 1930s. Even the parents' fashionable embrace of fascist ideas denied the brutal beginnings of Nazi Germany and the undeniable signs of genocide to come. Alexander expresses shame and repugnance for his parents' careless vanities and their callously self-centred lives. Alexander's father, Henry, had not been brought up to inherit the estate. He was the baby of the family who had to shape up to becoming the 6th Marquess after his elder brother John was killed in World War One. Henry never believed that either he or his family had intellect. He considered himself the product of landowning stock of average intelligence. He married a beautiful airhead. Yet, after her divorce and remarriage to a handsome young war hero, she showed herself to be more than a social butterfly and that she was talented as a writer. Henry was a Conservative MP from 1930 to 1935 but that was also what was expected of him, and he was never a creative political mind. To Alexander, as he looks back to his own sheltered childhood of those pre-war days, his parents were merely playing at life. How could they have done otherwise in the playground of a protected existence? They would have to have been unusually compassionate and aware to have wished to step out of their gilded lives into a world of social or political responsibilities. Alexander could have followed in these escapist footsteps if he chose. But he was, somewhere along the way, awakened to something more real and that was also darker in its expression of reality. It seems that Alexander has deliberately placed these cool portraits on a background which suggests a darker element behind their gilded existence. Coming in from the daylight, it is not immediately apparent in the dimly-lit hall that the walls upon which the portraits are hung have been painted with terrifying images. True to the Dorian Gray imagery conveyed by these fashion art portraits, Alexander has cynically and tellingly painted the walls on which these portraits hang and the remaining walls of this hallway in garish swirls of red and purple.

That is still not enough to convey the psychological melodrama of his relationship with his parents. Further down the hall and around the door to the dining room are the convulsed embryonic bodies and terrified expressions of a haunted madness, of figures with wide screaming mouths and goggling eyes, fleeing from the mind's monsters. The cool portraits gaze blankly down the hall towards these monsters, evidently failing to react to the horrors which lurk around them – as indeed Daphne, Henry and so many of their generation failed to respond to the mounting horror of the world's slide towards war and the years of Nazi violence which preceded it. Does Alexander mean to imply also that these charming people were projecting unconscious horrors into the mind of their artistic son? Alexander says that his parents were both extremely charming. Did that charm conceal dark shadows of the mind? It seems so. Alexander has named his mural *Paranoia*; and the paranoia to which he often refers when talking about the first two decades of his adult life is in fact deeply personal. The mural was one of his earliest, but the ideas behind its execution still haunt him. Behind the jovial partygoer stands the secret man whose desire to explain himself to himself and to the world has been driven by inner darkness and solitary despair. There is little doubt from what he says that he blames his parents for the latter.

To the left of the cool parental pastels, a double door the colour of dried blood, which clangs a loud bell when it is opened, leads into Alexander's drawing room. The bell is there to prevent Alexander from being surprised by visitors. He is actually rather deaf and would not hear anyone until they were inside the room. With the bell on the outer door, however, he has a warning that someone is about to arrive or that a tour group is being escorted by a guide through the private apartment where they can enjoy the murals and also receive a talk from Alexander in person.

The murals constitute the earliest part of Alexander's lifework. The drawing room is beautifully proportioned with a high ceiling and a big window overlooking the front gate into the private garden. The mural here is called *The Seven Ages of Man*: it starts with birth and goes on through childhood, adolescence and disillusion, to maturity, decay and death. The ceiling has a centrepiece of a brilliant sun that implies the existence of something beyond all the tribulations of life. In all, the murals fit rather beautifully within the gilded panels fringed by eighteenth-century mouldings. What might have been an uneasy coexistence of 1950s neo-Expressionism with Eighteenth Century gilding works rather well. Otherwise the room is furnished with a mixture of styles from different periods. There is a huge Victorian sideboard loaded with framed photos of his immediate family. A huge roll-top desk is positioned under the window; and an Eighteenth Century commode has had its inside hacked out to accommodate an old 1960s record player on which Alexander can play original Beatles albums. The more modern hi-fi equipment is upstairs in the penthouse.

This room was Alexander's first private pad. There is a divan at right angles to the fireplace where Alexander reclines to read the papers or to entertain his friends. An odd assortment of chairs and sofas clusters around the fireplace. There is a fat sofa, a wooden rocking chair, a chaise longue, a wing chair and some other stools and seats. The day's newspapers sit on the table beside the daybed. It's the English country house home-from-home: a bit uncoordinated, far from posed, far from designer decor, but lived-in, comfy and practical.

The private quarters are part of the public tour of Longleat House because the murals are an important part of what the tourists pay to see, together with Lord Bath himself, who will give a spontaneous lecture on the murals if caught anywhere within the house. The first time I saw Alexander deliver such a speech to a tour group, he and I were having a quiet lunch off a trolley in the drawing room as a break from a long interview session. The outer door had clanged its bell.

'Come in,' Alexander boomed.

A woman's head appeared around the inner door, and she asked if she could bring a tour group in. Alexander leaped enthusiastically to his feet, and some twenty people in anoraks filed in. Alexander welcomed them and began immediately to speak about the murals. The energy and enthusiasm he brought to his descriptions of the work were as fresh as if this was the first time he had told anyone about the work. He has a natural gift of showmanship; and his address, which lasted some five or six minutes with a question-and-answer session afterwards, was that of a practised pubic speaker. A tall figure with an old rust-red jumper stretched over his quite substantial belly, his purple velour bags, and with his hair held back from his forehead by a narrow headband, he looked and sounded every bit the artist. His audience seemed immensely impressed and filed out looking well pleased with the experience of having the celebrated marquess talk to them in so friendly and natural a manner without the slightest pomposity. Later the same afternoon, the housekeeper came in and told Alexander that there was an army colleague asking to see him. Alexander sprang to his feet with the agility of an acrobat from the daybed where he had been lying while I interviewed him. The old soldier came in with his wife and explained that he had been in the ranks while Alexander was doing officer training for his National Service. The couple were not invited to sit down, and Alexander remained standing with them. There was a friendly exchange with the soldier in which some anecdotes of the old days were touched upon, and there was a fair bit of chuckling; but the whole conversation took place in an atmosphere of great deference from the soldier and with Alexander being addressed as 'sir' throughout. In turn, Alexander was very gracious in a completely natural way, but there was in the meeting between these two colleagues of the early 1950s, the unspoken acknowledgement of their generation's experience of the class divide.

On other occasions tour groups have come into the dining room where Alexander has lunch with friends on Saturdays and Sundays. The dining room is entered either through a double doorway from the drawing room or from the hallway. Suddenly the bell goes, announcing someone is coming in through the outer door, and a tour guide pops her head round the door once more to request permission to enter, which is usually enthusiastically given.

The murals in the dining room are of Wessex scenes or of characters like Jeremy Thorpe who, as the MP for North Devon, had his big success as Liberal Party leader in 1974 when Alexander first stood as a Wessex Regionalist candidate in the General Election that year. They are brightly coloured and, like Alexander's ancestor and wifelet heads, usually have a touch of the caricature about them. The style of these is also naive. The figures have blank faces with big eyes. They are childlike and direct. The colours are bright and lovely. Some of the paintwork framing the murals is violet, and the thick curtains on the big windows are bright buttercup yellow. On the ceiling, there are astrological motifs decorated with a star design inset with coloured pieces of mirror glass. This was done by Alexander's nephew and namesake, Alexander Thynne. Some panels, above the sideboard where the ample cheeseboard and fruit basket are always placed, are still waiting to be filled. He will get to them eventually.

At present his great interest is finishing the wifelet and ancestor heads. The latter take over from the former as one ascends the staircase to the penthouse, but the transference to ancestral portraits occurs after walking up a floor and entering by a small doorway into a long gallery, which takes one from the north-western to the south-eastern corner of the house. The gallery features another long mural of vaguely erotic scenes. They fall short of true pornography, perhaps because the figures lack much resemblance to true humanity. They cover a lot of walls and one has to walk some distance.

However, before going into these far reaches one should visit the rooms on the ground and other floors of Alexander's own apartments in the West Wing. Tour groups penetrate here too. The first weekend I spent at Longleat, I experienced the knock on the door which heralded the polite tour guide's request for permission to bring the group into the Autobiographical Suite which I was occupying. I hastened to tidy up the duvet and my things before going to lunch. The Autobiographical Suite is actually an apartment which one enters via an entrance hallway hung with paintings, not by Alexander, and which opens into a large square room, with enormously high ceilings, ugly, sparsely furnished and rather cold, in the North East Wing. It contains two double beds, a *chaise longue* with distinct possibilities and a bedside table; it also has a cosy bathroom, which is the warmest place to sit in the suite if one wants to read a book or do one's yoga. Otherwise the interest lies in the murals, which are among Alexander's attempts to explain himself.

These are very entertaining and made up of panels illustrating cartoon-like scenes from babyhood to manhood, stuck onto an expressionist background of red and yellow swirls. Little brass plates are screwed into the walls with such legends as 'Who am I?' and, 'He isn't one of us,' all of which reflect Alexander's great uncertainty about himself and the pain of his isolation. Apart from those, the entrance hallway to the suite contains some very good portraits of Alexander at various ages. In fact, the long broad galleries leading to the room are hung with a collection of very good paintings by known artists or walled with bookcases containing leather-bound volumes which no one ever seems to read. There are other rooms on the way to the Autobiographical Suite, notably the billiard room which houses a large number of old books and several tables loaded with family photographs. There are billiard tables here and a 'honky-tonk' baby grand. Alexander's murals adorn the walls between the glass-fronted cupboards filled with more beautifully-bound old books. Also on this floor, in the South West Wing, is the Dowager Suite, comprising a large bedroom with a fireplace and an even larger sitting room, both furnished elegantly with Eighteenth Century French and Nineteenth Century English antiques. The walls here are still covered with beautiful *Chinoise* wallpaper, which dates back to the Eighteenth Century. The suite is entirely free of Alexander's murals.

Alexander included me in a tour which he gave to some French Canadian friends of an ex- wifelet who came to Sunday lunch in April of 2001. We went up a floor to visit the infamous Kama Sutra Suite where the murals, to my surprise, turned out to be genuinely erotic. Other murals, as on gallery walls, of naked creatures only vaguely identifiable as human do not seem erotic at all, but the Kama Sutra Suite with its purple walls decorated with copulating couples and trios, with their exaggerated expressions of wild lust and with huge penises penetrating between large buttocks and wide-open legs is pornographically erotic. One wonders at the real-life desires of a man who could spend hours painting these images. Is he a fantasist, or does he really experience the exuberant lust these purple paintings suggest? I have heard him say that in painting this mural he was simply trying to work out his sexual frustrations. That is the great mystery of the present Marquess of Bath. Does the reality live up to the myth? Whatever the answer to that question, the lunch guests seemed embarrassed and fell silent. The ex-wifelet, who had seen it all before, perhaps from the four-poster bed, looked blank. 'Sex with Alexander is normal,' she once told me when she came to my London flat for dinner. The mural is, one gathers, not based on abundant experience.

On this tour, Alexander also took us to the third floor to the Nursery Suite. The impact of this was somewhat sad. His two children are both long past the nursery stage. In fact, they are old enough to have families of their own, and Lenka gave birth to a baby in July 2005. The huge suite of rooms – many furnished as dormitories with several single beds in rows – evidently awaiting their squads of infant occupants from the Big Happy Collective Family seem to reek of absence and neglect. There is even a large room containing a big sauna and a Jacuzzi.

'My children tell me they do use this,' Alexander confides in me without much conviction.

The two huge, empty rooms and their rows of beds speak loudly of Alexander's unfulfilled dreams of life with an extended family. One cannot help glimpsing the deep loneliness of Alexander's life and his absolute lack of the jolly, populated nursery of his dreams. It offers a key to understanding Alexander, Lord of Love. His entire life has been spent trying to recreate the images of family that he obtained from his grandfather and his father. He speaks of the big, jolly family Christmases, the family gatherings that his grandfather and his father too were able to create. But Alexander has never been able to realize this dream. His true family is divided, alienated, while the communal one based on legions of wifelets and brigades of illegitimate children has never materialized. He is married, yes, but he has always lived apart from his wife, except for those first brief months when they lived together in Paris and when they travelled in South America together in his old Jaguar. He has so far failed to find that cosiness for which he yearns. He is a loner, it is true. By choice or destiny, Alexander exists in a solitary state. The Lord Bath of the party spirit, of the tabloid tittle-tattle, of the three-in-a-bed wifelet orgies, fact or fiction, is really a lonely man who once dreamed of achieving that state of bliss that less exacting mortals simply call 'love'. Let us look at the path he has followed in his search for the greatest of all human satisfactions.

Chapter Two

First Love

The Dream of a Soul-Mate

The year is 1951. Picture a fabulously handsome young man. He is tall and built well, with trained muscles of a boxing champion but the large, forward-set eyes and visionary gaze of an artist. The eyes are blue and the hair brown, in a fashionable smooth crop, with no sign of any curls; and his clothes are from the best London tailors. He has recently completed his studies at Eton and is preparing to go into the Life Guards. His friends from those days describe him as a Greek god, and he is also heir to one of England's premier titles and a fabulous Elizabethan mansion. This was Alexander Thynne, Viscount Weymouth as he approached the age of twenty: one of England's most eligible bachelors. 'Indeed, I was a Deb's Delight,' Alexander says of himself in those days, using a term that indicates the kind of rich handsome and eligible husband dreamed of by every young upper-class woman at the time. A Deb was more than just this, however. The word 'debutante' implied being presented at court as the debut of a social career which would lead to a good marriage. Becoming a Deb meant 'coming out' in a far different sense from today's admission of homosexuality. It was the special term for the launch into upper-class Society of a young woman of marriageable age.

Debs would be over sixteen but not much more. Their debut would be heralded by a grand party, usually a white-tie dance given at vast expense by the girl's parents at their own house, if it were large enough, or at a grand London hotel. The dance would usually be preceded by a dinner to which the cream of the debutante's friends and the eligible young men of the season would be invited. For the more beautiful girls, there would be a social whirl of invitations following her dance. There would also be the events of the season: the famous Rose Ball, and Queen Charlotte's Ball, Ascot, Henley, the Society appearances and, of course, invitations to dinners and nightclubs with small select groups. There would also be the country weekends in friends' big houses, where the men would go for the shooting and hunting, the girls for the dances and parties and for the men. The society columns of the newspapers, the photographs in *Country Life* and *The Morning Post* and the unofficial competition to become the Deb of the Year were an important feature in the marriage stakes. The richer girls would be dressed by Paris couturiers such as Dior and Balenciaga and coiffed, corseted and bejewelled by the best. The 'Coming Out' year was the girl's big chance to secure her future through marriage. The main drive of the Season for the Debutante was to make a glittering match. Obviously beauty and charm were the girl's main weapons, and the loveliest young women would be hoping to net a titled husband. A royal prince if there were one available could be the top target of the Season; but failing that, in order of diminishing status, a duke, marquess, earl or even a relatively humble baronet would be acceptable, if they had money, a beautiful house and a good reputation. Mothers would be steering their daughters away from attractions that might lead to trouble in any form while pushing them in the direction of the most eligible men. The latter would also be invited to pre-dance dinners and other select little parties given to throw young people together in this upper-crust mating ritual. Alexander was definitely in line to become a marquess, and nothing short of his own death or a Marxist revolution was likely to prevent that. Invitations to these debutante dances would fall like a blizzard on doormats of titled heirs to large estates. At that time Bath had only the rather junior title of Viscount Weymouth, but as the undisputed heir to a marquessate and a glorious stately home with rolling acres, he was highly eligible. He was also stunningly handsome. Does it not seem a little strange under the circumstances that Alexander Thynne would not have been rather quickly snapped up by some gorgeous girl in pearls? He was, after all, hungry for social life and feminine conquests while somewhat short of money thanks to the family's death duties and to his father's extreme limit on his spending power. The parties provided for all these needs. The eligible men shortlisted as

Debs Delights were themselves usually in search of the right 'gel'. If she herself came from an aristocratic family, this would be an advantage, but for many young heirs to titles and grand estates stripped of their wealth by death duties, a rich bride would take precedence over a titled one. Alexander's priorities do not seem to have been material, however. Young though he was, being only nineteen at his first Season, he was already searching for the woman who would be the love of his life. 'I was hopeful of finding a soul-mate with whom I would have peace of mind and find that my own identity was secure,' he says. He met the woman whom he now calls 'Number 1' during that first year out of Eton when he was waiting to go into the Life Guards for officer training. Alexander would never have revealed Number 1's name to me or to anyone else, but his gallantry was undermined when Laurence Kelly, a charming pal from those National Service days, deliberately revealed it. We were talking about Alexander's army days. He nursed a whisky and water as we sat before a crackling log fire in my London drawing room.

'Have you met Davina?' he suddenly asked me.

'Davina?' 'She's "X",' he said with a cheeky grin. Earlier we had sat together at one of the computers in my study reading Alexander's online account of his army days, some of which referred to Laurence. Among the reminiscences there were copious mentions of a woman referred to as 'X' who was clearly Alexander's first love. Now Laurence volunteered her name and address.

I wrote to Davina Gibbs, formerly Davina Merry, now an artist married to a field marshal and living in the West Country. She invited me for lunch at the Chelsea Arts Club, and we immediately took a liking to each other. She is, as Laurence Kelly told me, very beautiful. Some years younger than Alexander, she is slender, of medium height with her silver hair cut into a fashionable wavy crop and with bone structure to die for. She is vivacious and magnetic and moves with the quick lightness of a dancer. I found her eyes to be as expressive as the ones painted by Alexander in his portrait of 'Number 1', which hangs at the foot of one of the spiral staircases at Longleat.

Oddly enough Davina's portrait, with its intense expression and jaw-length dark hair closely resembles Alexander's portrait of Daphne, his mother. Davina rather vigorously denies any resemblance. While she herself is extremely slim, petite and dainty, 'Daphne was big and tall,' she says. 'Yes, there was a resemblance,' Alexander insists. This extends not only to some of the physical features, for Davina herself is a successful artist while Daphne became an author. There was also a shared vivacity, an ability to be the life and soul of a party. 'Davina was quite similar to Daphne in that sort of way,' Alexander says. 'Her effervescence at parties was something I savoured. I would also try to be at my best. That was a great similarity between us too. When we were being effervescent we tended to be the ones that people were watching and thinking about.' As he speaks these words, one can see the spark this mutual chemistry reproduced in Alexander's eyes, his smile, the inflation of the chest, his confident, extroverted tone of voice. We are thrown back to one of those heady parties of the early 1950s. Fifty years on, Alexander still relishes those moments of being the most talked about, the most attractive, and perhaps most envied couple. He is in that instant expressing the sexual energy that he felt in Davina's presence. Davina saw Daphne at parties. 'I remember going to a party after I had been married for quite a long time,' she says, 'so I was probably in my late thirties or early forties. Daphne was there with a young admirer. She was rather thickened in girth and elderly but so vivacious that she captured the whole room. And Alexander's very like her in that way'. Something else connected Davina and Alexander. At the time that she met him, Davina had already determined to become a painter. Alexander was getting ready to go into the Life Guards. Painting was not yet a career plan, but he had left Eton laden with excellent paintings done during his years there, having won prizes and received many commendations for them. He met Davina through the social circuit of their day. 'Alexander was part of a group which very much made up my whole life,' she tells me. 'One of the main people in it was Serena Rothschild, as she's called now, Serena Dunn as she was when we first met, who really opened up my whole life in as much as I was very much alone and she introduced me to a lot of people. Alexander was in that set, and we all formed a group together of rather wild and crazy and in a way hopeless but I suppose quite amusing young things, slightly bohemian and no doubt totally irresponsible but set on a course of mad enjoyment.' She explains the madness of those post-war years. These were the early 1950s when teenage girls wore Dior's elegant, long-skirted New Look, danced the night away in floor-length full-skirted frocks of layered tulle and expected to become engaged before they went beyond heavy petting. There was a new sense of revelry among the aristocracy. The Labour Government of 1945 had dented their hereditary fortunes, but now Churchill and a Tory Government had been re-elected in 1950. Rationing was ended the following year, and a new generation of gilded youth thronged the stately ballrooms of England. For a brief period it was the return of the grown-up upper-class world which their parents had inhabited before the war: the rebirth of a fabulous fairyland. It was the more so because the war had been a hard time for them as children. Alexander had been at Ludgrove from 1941 when he was nine years old, until he went to Eton at the time the war ended. Davina, who is a few years younger, led a secluded life in her family's house in the West Country and later at boarding school where there was rationing even after the war, and the girls were usually hungry. She seems to speak very personally when she describes those days, 'I think people older than us had a better time because they mixed with their peers and contemporaries socially whereas when the war came younger people like me were completely restricted because of age, money, petrol, everything and so never meeting our contemporaries and worshipping the young people who were fighting because they came into our lives and were billeted on us. They were our heroes, and of course they were old enough to be our uncles, so we were a bit distorted, and when the end of restrictions came it was like a huge cave opening to the sun and we were wild with excitement and totally unprepared and we had been dreaming of the perfect dress, the perfect party, the perfect love...' There were of course the perfect dresses and the perfect parties. Davina describes 'wonderful parties in houses big enough not to need tents, big enough just to have millions of people in lovely big ballrooms and really very romantic situations and you believed in it.' But were there the perfect loves – and was Alexander part of the great romantic experience and the perfect love of which Davina herself had dreamed? Davina was one of the prettiest girls of her age group and there were many possibilities for her. She flirted, for instance, with Alexander's two brothers, Christopher and Valentine; and one of Alexander's school and army pals thinks that Davina was not as keen on Alexander as Alexander was on her. Davina did not pay much attention to Alexander at first. She remembers that he was, 'great fun, charming, enthusiastic, very doggy. But even to me who after all was the younger, he seemed very, very young and puppyish. In fact, my mother called him "Puppy". It was an endearing nickname because he was always bouncing around like a Labrador puppy. I was quite surprised that he could be quite serious really.' He was fresh from Eton at the time and had not yet chosen his career. He felt at a disadvantage. He was keenly aware that he had rivals in whom Davina had shown interest and who might have more to offer, being slightly older and already with a foot on the ladder of their careers. However, this was the period during which Alexander began to think of Davina as his future girlfriend. He went into the first stages of his officer training in England which allowed him some sporadic continuity of his English social life in which he saw Davina, as part of their set, and then, after a few months the regiment was sent to Germany for a tour of duty. 'When I went away to Germany,' Alexander says, 'I was already passionately anticipating but nothing had yet happened. We wrote to each other.' The sense of social unease which has always been a factor in all Alexander's relationships was there, giving him 'a sort of complex', according to Davina. Was this a hint of the 'paranoia' to which Alexander often refers, his constant sense of being out of place with his peers? He remembers himself as gawky and clumsy in company. His descriptions of himself make him seem rather like a P G Wodehouse character who cannot come into a room without knocking over a cake-stand or a table. His greatest strengths were his exceptionally good looks and the fact that he was heir to Longleat and a top title. He was sure that he had been a success during his schooldays: he should have been suave and self-confident, sweeping girls off their feet. But that would have made his life too perfect and too easy. There always has to be something to overcome. For Alexander, it was the fact that his self-confidence was being undermined by the constant criticisms of his father and that he had as yet had no serious sexual experience. So he went off to do his officer training at the cadet school leaving Davina to be courted by older and no doubt more suave and more experienced young men who, even if they lacked titles or glorious country houses, seemed to Alexander to be cast in the Cary Grant mould. Meanwhile, during these first army months he became concerned about his sexuality. He had never had a woman or even a hint of sex with a woman. Could he possibly be gay? The only sexual experiences Alexander had entertained up to that point were some minor homosexual encounters at school. First at Ludgrove, his preparatory school, he had experienced some homosexual foreplay with one boy. He had also brought superior knowledge gained from reading books at home to his schoolmates and had become a sort of erotic gang leader, initiating his schoolmates in the arts of masturbation. This was all boyish stuff and without the deep emotional engagement of more adult relationships. But at Eton, a more serious incident brought home to Alexander the problems of homosexuality in society. It was, according to Alexander, the fashion to go into chapel or whatever group assembly of the school was called and to 'look pretty' in the sense that one was flirting at a distance with older boys and attracting admiration. 'So naturally,' he laughingly tells me, turning his head and flashing his eyes very fetchingly, 'I used to be looking pretty all the time and looking around me like this.' He makes a quick show of turning his head coquettishly and flashing rather feminine smiles from under his eyelashes. It transpired, however, that he attracted the attention of an older boy who, it was later discovered, had been training a telescope at the window of Alexander's study bedroom and watching him undress. This was discovered by the school authorities and became a major scandal. Alexander says he realized after this 'that homosexuality was definitely out.' As Alexander points out, the atmosphere in an institution populated almost entirely by teenage boys was very much one of repressed sexuality where the only outlet was experimentation with other boys. There were maids and the wives of masters, and some boys took advantage of the availability of these women to express their sexual desires. Alexander did not do so, perhaps because he was not inspired by any great attraction to do so. Outside school and after he left Eton, the girls he got to know were well trained in the art of saying 'no'. They were expected to remain virgins until marriage, and Alexander says that for quite some time he expected that he would marry a virgin. The problem was what to do with one's terrible sexual urges. Masturbation was the solution, but this was not enough, and after a disturbing period in which Alexander's sexual doubts were intensified by the case of a misinterpreted encounter which led to homosexual interest from another soldier, he was induced to take a full sexual initiation in an establishment which was frequented by the bloods of the day, including the spy Guy Burgess. This was called The Bag 'O Nails and was essentially a hostess club situated in Mayfair. Alexander was taken there by his army pals. 'I felt it was something I had to do,' he explains, 'a hurdle to overcome before getting on with life. And there wasn't the inhibition of thinking that this was a degenerate thing to do. It was just the usual thing. Looking around the officers' mess, I don't know how many of them but I should think fifty percent of them had gone to such places.' The main problem was whether Alexander would know what to do. 'I had read enough sex books,' he adds. He had not only read them but, according to a couple of his Old Etonian pals, had taken a large sex manual from his father's personal library back to school with him one term and he and the other boys had spent a long time poring over it. 'I remember one incident when it was discovered that he had some book in his bedside table which was supposed to be pornographic,' Tim Rathbone recalls. 'It may have been meticulous directions for making love. Anyway, it was discovered and the House Master, a very pompous man called Leslie James, wrote a very pompous letter to Alexander's father saying he was horrified by this book on Alexander's bedside table and he was sure he would like to know about this since it wasn't appropriate reading for a boy of sixteen. He got a very brusque response from the then Lord Bath saying: "You're completely wrong. I think it's absolutely marvellous that Alexander is reading this and learning about life while he's still at Eton."' Alas, textbook knowledge was no help to poor Alexander when girls remained unavailable. Anyway, the first experience of sex was daunting for other reasons. 'Knowing what to do wasn't the problem,' Alexander says. 'It was more the chatting-up with the intention. I mean, how do you get onto the subject? Do you say, "well, shall we go upstairs?" But of course, it wasn't upstairs. It was going home to bed. To her home that is.' Of course, Alexander also had a lot to drink at the Bag O' Nails. 'I think I drove up from Windsor, and the drinking started when we got there,' he reveals. 'I had to buy a lot of champagne. And that annoyed me slightly, you know. We got through the bottle of champagne, and she was obviously on a percentage thing so we had to have another bottle, and I was irritated because having got another bottle, I had to drink it.' It was the time-honoured hostess club system where the management expects the hostess to oblige the client to buy at least two very expensive bottles of champagne: meanwhile the hostess slyly pours hers onto the carpet. Alexander was drinking his share and became pretty well oiled. Then there was the need to drive back to the prostitute's flat. 'Driving home with her, driving a Rover 2000, a policeman did stop us,' he remembers. 'He sort of popped up out of nowhere when I was trying to stop and came up and talked fiercely at the window, and I was being very submissive. It would have meant not passing the breathalyzer, if he'd got one. Only I hadn't done anything awful, and he just let us by.' At the prostitute's flat, Alexander thinks that 'it was over very quickly. I don't remember much really. What I remember was that there was all the embarrassment about should we be doing this during the King's funeral. It was the period when we were supposed to be in mourning; and I was sort of feeling, how awful of me to be coming here.' He can't remember exactly how much this initiation cost, apart from the champagne. He thinks he paid the prostitute five or ten pounds. It sounds cheap, but the equivalent today would be about £150 with the champagne costing about the same per bottle. He would have spent the equivalent of about £500. It had been an expensive night out and not too much fun, but he had passed his test and felt now that he was really one of the boys. However, there was still no love relationship, other than the fantasy with a remote Davina, and when his regiment moved out to Eastern Germany that prospect became even more remote. All that could happen was that the two wrote each other letters. Was he in love? Attracted, certainly; romantically dreaming, yes. Then as now, Alexander was unable to speak of love. Other definitions prevail. One way of putting it is that he felt emotionally involved with her, but there was still very little he could do when they were separated by distance and his duty. In England, Davina went on flirting with and dating other men. Alexander was in an emotional and sexual limbo. He could only dream. There were no other prospects.

Dating local women was frowned upon as Germany was still technically considered the enemy and, as Laurence Kelly remembers, anything in the way of a relationship with a German woman would have been considered fraternization. Germany, however, had plenty of brothels, and this is where the officers and soldiers went to relieve sexual impulses. 'One would be coming out of the brothel and as you did you would be saluting the senior officers who were coming in,' Laurence Kelly remembers. He thinks, however, that Alexander did not use the German brothels even though Alexander claims that he did so sometimes. Otherwise, he says, he had no more sexual experience until his relationship with Davina began to develop after his return from

Germany. 'I think I did, in London, pick up somebody in the street,' he says, 'but after that, no. Never since, no.' During this period of his life Alexander dreamed constantly of having his own love relationship, and it was Davina who was now the focus of his aspirations. When he returned from Germany he says 'it was with this feeling of, "'Well, so who is my girlfriend? Surely it's her.'"'

Yet, it was not long after his demobilization that he left England and Davina again and went to Paris to study art. This was to be the first of two periods there: this one, from 1952 to 1953, predating his four years at Oxford, lasted nine months and coincided with the period of his parent's divorce. There were interludes when he returned: once, for instance, for the Queen's Coronation where he was among the chosen few who were actually at Westminster Abbey during the ceremony. During these interludes he continued to pursue Davina, and their relationship developed. In Paris, he lived in digs with a French family at the rue Turin near the Gare St Lazare. He took classes at various art schools where he enrolled on a casual basis. His goal at this time was to find himself again after an army life, which, for all its wild eleventh-hour successes, had demoralized him and undermined the self-image gained at school of being successful and a leader of men. In Paris he was able to begin to create for himself a new identity as a painter, but that too was far from confidence inspiring at first. Also his relations with women were not encouraging. He seemed to be the object of sly humour among a group of girl students. They would giggle and snigger when he appeared. He had no physical relationships with women in Paris during the entire nine months. He did not visit brothels either. 'I suppose once I was having sex,' he says, 'although it wasn't fully-fledged sex, with my girlfriend, I couldn't intersperse that with going to a brothel. I'd evolved beyond it.' As to affairs with other women, he adds: 'I was thinking that I had a girlfriend and I would be home in two months or whatever.' The girlfriend was Davina, and it was with her that an intense sexual attraction was developing into an emotional relationship. The relationship was frustrating because in those days girls said 'no' almost all the way to the altar; and as Alexander says: 'I think of what we did as having sex but it fell short: it wasn't complete penetration.' In those days Alexander, in common with other men of his age and class had expected that he would marry a virgin. Now he says, he does not think he has ever 'had a virgin'. In those days when he was dating virgins, he was not experiencing full sexual intercourse while later on he thinks he must have missed the boat. Alexander's experience may have been that of a man patiently courting a young woman with whom he was sufficiently involved to think of as a possible future mate. However, his ideas were changing. During his months in Paris, Alexander had absorbed a number of current philosophies. The 1950s were the days when Sartre and his lover Simone de Beauvoir and the Existentialists dominated bohemian society. Their views that marriage was old hat and that free love was the order of the day had an influence on Alexander's developing philosophy. One of his beliefs based upon personal experience was that it was easier for women to get sexual experience than for men.

Later, when he had had more girlfriends, Alexander says that 'I was always finding myself in the position that the woman had more sexual experience than I did'; and he concluded that 'no woman was ever' capable of being faithful to one man.' Eventually however, he says, this was also the reason why he realized he would never find a woman who was capable of becoming the soul-mate he had long imagined. Therefore, trying to be faithful himself was useless. Davina is angry about this. 'Rubbish,' she bursts out, 'Alexander never had any intention of being faithful to one woman.'

He insists, however, that it was upon his conclusion about women's flightiness that he based his theory of 'polygyny' in which monogamous marriage is replaced by a form of polygamy. It falls short of actual polygamy in that the women are allowed to have other men and there is no actual marriage. This, Alexander feels, would satisfy women's needs to have more than one man while the man would feel less of a booby for his lack of experience compared to the women. But is Davina correct? Alexander seems to imagine that he was capable of being faithful. His failure to find love during his first stay in Paris may have been partly due to his feeling that he had a girlfriend already. His unfulfilled sexual and emotional feelings for Davina made it harder for him to bond with someone else.

He was attracted to Lita, a South American art student, but got nowhere with her. Would he have then had two girlfriends, or was he just looking for a woman who would say 'yes' to a full sexual relationship while continuing his courtship of a girl he thought of as a possible mate? 'There was my time of not bonding,' Alexander says of that period, his expression unhappy, 'but I was not looking for just anybody to fill the gap. I was always trying to see more of somebody who I was seeing already.'

This was also hard because of the geographical separation alone. Although Longleat was not very far from Davina's family home, her availability was limited because she had her own life with friends who were permanently in England; she could not just drop them every time Alexander turned up. There was a happy side to the relationship, however, and Davina remembers Alexander during this period with a lot of affection.

'He was very amusing,' she says. 'He had a great sense of humour, and he was very creative and he was very good looking and attractive and all that and very stimulating. I really thought that in those days he was going to be a very good painter. He used to get annoyed with me because I told him that he put paint on his clothes deliberately to look like one. I imagine that he thought that he did. I remember a duffel coat totally daubed in bright green paint which I'm sure he'd painted on: but it looked terribly attractive. He got frightfully cross about that. Because it was true, but you see that was exciting and different, and he wasn't nearly so intellectual then.

'He was very original,' she continues. 'There were so many young Guardsmen and army and university people who were terribly straight, upright nice young men, but Alexander had a terrific originality. He was totally bohemian in some ways and believed entirely in himself, and was a great…I can never say the word even now, he's tried to teach me all my life…a great Existentialist. He believed in that terrifically. I used to think he was rather a bore about it, but I was also fascinated by Sartre and all those people; and this was absolutely fascinating to me because I hadn't been brought up to understand any of those things.' There were other strains too. It was with visible pain of voice and facial expression that Davina told me that she was also hurt by Alexander. 'He made me cry,' she confides. 'He hurt me very much.' Alexander denies that he made Davina cry more than once. 'I can remember just one occasion,' he says. 'I don't remember what I'd said. I certainly hadn't done anything. It was talk rather than actions, and she was crying in the street. What I remember is being embarrassed by the way she was quietly crying and I was slightly shielding her from the public and members of the public were coming up and saying "what are you doing?" One chap was not actually saying anything but trying to intervene because both of us were ignoring him. Then he just went off. But that's the sort of thing I remember, rather than what the hell it was I'd said. I think it was more toughness of talk than anything I'd said that should make somebody cry particularly.' Alexander returned to England in the summer of 1953, and in the following October he started his first term at Christ Church College Oxford. The relationship with Davina became serious during that first academic year; and then, in August 1954, it broke up. This devastated Alexander. The pain is still evident when he speaks about it today. He falls silent for a moment, and his face clouds. 'I was very sad over the initial breakup of my first affair,' he says. I asked him did he ever feel that passionately about anyone else. 'To feel passionately,' he says after a long silence, 'you need the break, and sometimes there hasn't been the break in my relationships. They do go on. But there was something more recent than that. Yes, it does upset me, the breakup of a very good relationship, but I didn't feel so fragile. I felt more fragile then, over my first affair.

'I could contend, all right, she doesn't want me or she wants somebody else. That's going to be her future, not with me. And, no, I had a much more resigned feeling about it, not expecting different. Life does treat one that way, sort of thing.

'It mended,' he adds, 'and went on but it was not with such a feeling of sadness that happened when it broke the second time.' Someone wrote that it ended because Davina's parents did not approve of Alexander. 'I don't know if that was the case,' he concedes. 'I don't think mine approved of Davina either.' He thinks Davina's parents thought him 'not well enough behaved, for their daughter anyway'. This, however, was not the reason for that first break with Davina or even the second. Before that, the relationship had become serious. In the summer of 1953, after he had completed his first nine months in Paris before going up to Oxford, Alexander went to stay in Scotland where relatives of Davina had a house. 'It was a few months after things had gone serious between us,' he says. 'I came back from Germany in October 1952 then went to Paris, and this was the following summer and things were still taking off, but not with her mother's and father's approval. My father was the one initially against it. He didn't like Davina's mother because of her grandmother. He thought they were flighty or something. And also when he met Davina, she wasn't playing up to him.' He laughs. 'I've had girlfriends who would flirt with the father-in-law, but Davina wasn't trying to and that probably influenced what my father had said too.' On Davina's side the influence of Katie Crighton, Davina's aunt, was powerful. 'I think Davina's family were worried that I was too…um…not the stability thing that they were looking for, for their daughter's future husband,' he says. 'I know that Davina also told me that her aunt, Katie Crighton, had asked her the question which showed the doubts in the family of was I an honourable person. I think they were asking: would I marry her if I got her pregnant? I think that was what Katie Crighton meant by "this honourable thing". In my own opinion, that was what was worrying them. Or one of the things, maybe many things.' Alexander feels that these family opinions undoubtedly influenced Davina against him. 'Certainly it will influence anyone if you know your family doesn't approve,' he says. 'And that was the case. They didn't approve. I suppose they didn't trust me to do these things if the case arose or whatever.' Did Davina's family perhaps wonder if he intended to marry her in any event? 'Yes. I think that would have come into it,' he replies. 'And I probably wasn't showing enough signs that that was my intention. And I think if I'd been asked bluntly and answered with candour, I would have said: "This is not the time for marriage. It's after university. So in three years time I'll give you my answer." That would have been the line I would have taken.' Alexander does not believe in long engagements. 'I think if that's your intention you don't string it out,' he continues. 'You leave the moment of saying you're engaged until just before you marry. Well, that's the way I still think. I wouldn't call it an engagement until such a time. And that might have upset them.' In that instance of parental disapproval from both sides, the romance fitted the pattern of Daphne and Henry's early relationship. Henry's parents were set against him marrying Daphne, the wild daughter of a bohemian family and Daphne's parents were none too keen on Henry. Henry's father, the 5th Marquess of Bath, sent Henry to America for a year in the hope that the separation would cool the affair, but Daphne persuaded Henry to go through a secret marriage before he went. When he came back from America, Henry persuaded his parents to agree to marriage: and they had no option but to admit that the young couple's love was stronger than they had believed.

Daphne and Henry then had to go through a second wedding because they could not tell their families that they had married already.

Davina and Alexander never reached this stage because Alexander's view of marriage had been soured by his parents' more recent divorce disaster: otherwise the course of their lives might have been different. How real was the possibility of marriage between these two? 'There were times when it seemed I did want to marry Davina,' he says, 'and times when not. It's a bit difficult, and I would have to take it step by step and explain.'

Davina is spiritually-minded, a committed Christian who nowadays also meditates (TM) and does yoga. Alexander was already developing his alternative religious ideas about God being the Universe, and then there were Jean Paul Sartre and Simone de Beauvoir, believers in free love. Would Davina have married Alexander? 'We had a terrific love affair for two or three years, really,' she says. 'We broke up because I don't think either of us was willing to commit our lives to each other, and I was feeling trapped and unhappy because I knew that Alexander wanted more than one friend, more than one woman. I'd break invitations to see him. But with my upbringing I couldn't just go off when I wanted, you know, and go away and things, so he obviously had to go off and find other women and he did, which was fine. We just drifted, really.' Even now, some fifty years after those times, there is a sense of desperate, pent-up emotion in Davina, as she goes back over the sad memories of that love. Are her words tinged with regret? It seems so. For Alexander, especially, life might have been very different had he been able to marry Davina, another artist and a woman who was well educated and from an upper-class English background.

Alexander also seems strained when he talks about the relationship. It was not only the tensions of two very young people intensely attracted to each other but not yet in a full sexual relationship. Nor was it not only the inevitable tensions of two emotionally immature people trying to adjust to an adult passion but also the growing knowledge that a fundamental conflict existed in their beliefs and makeup. As Alexander evolved his new philosophies during that first year at Oxford, he expounded them to Davina.

'At the time of the first break she took the line that it's your religion and things like that,' Alexander reveals. 'She said: "I couldn't marry somebody who wasn't a Christian." And I was saying: "Well, I can't be."' Alexander's religious beliefs were partly due to the influence of Alexander's father, who was an atheist. Even so, there was a basic Anglican influence in his childhood. 'The governess used to take us to church every Sunday while she was there because it was a social thing,' Alexander explains rather cynically. 'She wanted to be seen as the person looking after us. In any case I was good at Religious Studies, although when my father came back he said religion was really what women believe, that men know that it's a lot of bunkum. That was his line at the time although, later, he became a Rasnishist, (a follower of the Indian teacher Rasnish). But at the time I suppose he did encourage me to look at atheism. It didn't become atheism as such but it became humanism and more latterly, pantheism, and I was always very glad I had my father's sceptical influence in the formation of my religious views.' This was the only forceful religious influence in Alexander's life. 'Otherwise I wasn't under any strong religious influences,' he goes on. 'My mother was a wishy-washy Christian, but very wishy-washy, so I don't know quite where this formative influence would have happened. So I can look to my father's influence and think of it as formative in that it actually gave me the freedom to work out what God is.'

Davina's views were irremediably Christian, however. Yes,' Alexander recalls 'Well, at least she describes it as that, and she did find it impossible to digest my scepticism, or I suppose my looking in another direction. But that was the first time we broke up and I think she got over that to some extent. There were more and more frequent disagreements where we were upsetting each other,' he adds. 'They weren't fierce quarrels; but we were upsetting each other, and it turned out that what I was upsetting was her confidence in Christianity but not by me attacking Christianity. I was only saying what I believed. I think that it comes up as an explanation in Davina's own thoughts as to what she sees unacceptable in me,' he adds reflectively and rather unhappily, 'but I would certainly not say that it explains why she was finally feeling that I was not the right person for her. I was also in the end feeling that she was not the right person for me so it wasn't entirely one-sided.'

Religion was not the only cause of that first break. Davina was also emotionally linked with other men during the period of her relationship with Alexander. 'Well I had somebody I'd been in love with since I was fourteen, and I'd been terribly in love with him,' she reveals. 'But I had a very odd relationship with this man who was, funnily enough, a relation of Alexander's. It's something, which even now, I don't understand, but I think I was violently physically attracted to him but at the same time I knew it was something that couldn't last, couldn't be a marriage. And yet I was so tied to him as well. But he was somebody much more conventional. I don't know…it was inexplicable. He was sort of at the same time as Alexander but off-and-on so to speak, but I don't think I was really in love with either of them, not properly in love, just terribly attracted to them.'

'Did Alexander think you were his girlfriend?' I ask her.

'I was,' she interjects hotly.

'Did he think there was no one else?' I persist.

'Well I think actually he did and I think it would be truthful to say I was his girlfriend,' she concedes, 'because I very much didn't see this other man because of him.

I ask Alexander about this; and he jumps slightly and begins to try to identify the relative. 'Could it have been one of my brothers?' he asks. He seems as worried as if Davina were still his girlfriend. 'I know she flirted with Christopher, to my annoyance,' he continues, looking quite bothered. 'I just don't know.'

Davina's recollections helped to clear Alexander's mind as to the identity of this mystery relative. 'I remember meeting him on a zebra crossing when I was with Alexander,' she confides, referring to the other man, 'and not knowing which one to go with and obediently going off with Alexander and really wanting to jump into the other one's car. And I remember when he got engaged to this other woman: he went abroad and got engaged and married.' At this point Davina's voice breaks slightly. 'He spent his last night in my house and flew from nearby in the aeroplane,' she continues. 'And suddenly the news came through that he'd got engaged to this girl in Australia. Alexander was with me, and he looked in my eyes and said, "a light's gone out", and it never came back.' It took Davina years to recover from the loss. 'Life's so interesting,' she adds. 'You can be so hurt by someone that you know later on is not worth being hurt by.'

'Oh, I know who that was now,' Alexander beams with relief. 'He's a faint relation, a distant cousin. And it was outside Peter Jones, that zebra crossing.'

Alexander now starts to laugh. 'I'm not going to say anything about him, but I think we've identified who that is. Anyway, better than Christopher: I think he was quite a romantic figure in her eyes.'

The old emotions are still there. Alexander does not conceal the hurt which Davina caused him by her rejection of him that summer's day in 1954 after Alexander's first year at Oxford. 'I remember driving over to Longleat to tell him I couldn't go on and it was awful,' she says. 'I was terribly upset doing it, and I hurt him terribly.'

'Yes, I was very sad,' Alexander says soberly.' His voice drops, his face takes on a hurt look. It is over fifty years since that day, but the pain still lives. 'But in the end I don't think I hurt him that amount, Davina reflects rather crossly. 'I mean, obviously, he recovered very quickly.'

'I was pretty miserable after the first break,' Alexander recalls, 'but when the second breakup came, I was already seeing someone else. They sort of…dare I say it…overlapped.' His expression, his manner and tone of voice give away the pain he still feels over the end of his first love. He can barely hide his chagrin. But then he smiles defiantly. Revenge is sweeter when the next love involvement is the close friend of the first. It has a taste of incest and in some ways one is still making love to the first love through the link. This was Number 2 in the Bath annals, another Deb, a girl he met at one of the Oxford Balls with Davina. The defiance is a mask, however. The smile is thin, the tone of voice one of forced jauntiness. Something had broken in him. Alexander's dream of a soul-mate never recovered from that initial breakup of his first affair. Between the first break and the second, Alexander's whole experience of the world of personal loyalty was undergoing a revolution. Between his first meeting with Davina and the ultimate ending of the relationship, which came with the second break, there was a series of betrayals which completely undermined any chance he had of making a go of his relationship with Davina and which destroyed his trust in love.

A Background of Betrayal

Alexander met Davina during a crucial period of change in his life. Not only was he leaving school to join the army, but his parents had begun divorce proceedings. Alexander's first period in Paris coincided with his parents' actual divorce. His decision to go there to study art was to see if he could make painting his career, but it was also to evade the gruesome publicity associated with the divorce. The pain and the public embarrassment of his parents' divorce was something he had to get away from. It was also something in which he felt he had been involved as a guilty party. The breakdown in his parents' marriage occurred when Alexander was ten. His father was invalided home from the war in 1942 after being injured in the battle of El Alamein. Up to that point, Alexander's mother had been having a riotous time entertaining officers from nearby barracks. The parties she held were extremely saucy, and she herself had been having numerous affairs. War seems to make people more sexually active. The need to live in the present because tomorrow may never arrive turns brief encounters into instant passion; the mass deaths seem to create an unconscious response to procreate or at least to make love as often as possible. Alexander became used to seeing strange men in dressing gowns in his mother's bedroom when he came in for his morning kiss. Alexander smiles slightly as he describes this, but he says he was unsure at the time as to whether this was really all right or not. When his father came home to convalesce from his injuries, Alexander took a bold step and confronted both parents with the issue. Despite his own constantly avowed beliefs that monogamy is a form of hypocrisy, there is something in his voice and his facial expression when he talks of his mother's behaviour that reveals that he still harbours some anger and even disgust at his mother's multiplicity of lovers. Those were the days when Alexander hero-worshipped his soldier father, so to some extent the presence of these other men was seen even by a nine-year-old boy as a betrayal of that father and also – since the father is usually the role model for the boy – a betrayal of himself. Furthermore, Alexander sees himself as complicit in the betrayal of his father by his mother; as the passive observer of her post-frolicking mornings, he had become an accomplice in the cuckolding of Henry.

Whatever his parents may have wondered about each other's sexual exploits during the war, the diplomatic code was silence after Henry's return. One day, however, Alexander announced to his father in the presence of his mother: 'There are a lot of new men you've got to get to know.' He says he did it partly out of a desire to know if the presence of these strangers in his mother's bedroom was acceptable and right. 'I suppose with a part of my mind I knew

I was stirring things up or saying it in my mother's presence to see how she would react,' he says. 'It might have been that, only it wasn't so intentional. It wasn't so planned as that. The feeling in my heart was more or less: "Does it matter for Mummy to have seen a lot of men? Surely it doesn't matter, but if I say it in front of Daddy and he doesn't mind, everything's fine." But I knew from the reactions after I'd said it that um, yes, evidently something's wrong here.' It was not solely individual betrayal that began to be registered in Alexander's young mind, but a betrayal of the idea of physical fidelity, of a social order where one's parents, and everyone else's parents, were married to each other and that their intimacies were exclusively for the marriage partner. It is as if the first bolt in the edifice of sexual morality that the baby Bath had learned at his nanny's and his parents' knees was dismantled here; the first perception that wedlock was not living up to its advertised version, was confirmed in this scene. What had been suspected by Henry was now a fact confirmed spectacularly by his eldest son. How could the charade continue? It was not as though World War Two had not, understandably, produced many a bedroom scene of this sort when servicemen returned to their wives; but few, if any, of the key lines in those scenes could have been spoken by a child. It seems as if Alexander is still haunted by guilt about the breakup of his parents' marriage, which, according to his mother, had been a very good one before the war. 'I did write a poem about it at the time,' he says, 'and it was like a ballad of the woman who had her son thrown into prison after seeing awful things and finally she pounced on the luckless lad and took his eyes and tongue and ate them. And for this thing, the wicked wretch was hung.' Perhaps he regrets his words about the other men the more because they also effected a change in his relationship with his father. 'Because I'd identified with my mother, I'd also been wicked. I was part of the guilty side of the family. These things had gone on, and poor Daddy had come back to them.'

Did Alexander learn then the double lesson that he later rationalized into the basis for his philosophy of polygyny: that women are incapable of being faithful and that for the man who is betrayed the pain is very great? Did he have to learn it again when Davina let it be known that she was attracted to a different man from Alexander? Alexander must have been a witness throughout his teens – those formative years when a boy becomes a man – to his father's pain, for it was another ten years before Daphne and Henry divorced. During the first part of that ten-year period during which Alexander was first at Ludgrove, his father returned to the army in a non-combatant role. In this phase Daphne gave herself over to further wartime fun. Later, while Alexander was at Eton, she took up with Xan Fielding, a war hero ten years her junior whom she later married. During these ten years, Henry, charming and handsome though he evidently was, seems to have been without a love, even if not without sexual partners, until he met Virginia Parsons for whom he ultimately went through the divorce from Daphne and whom he then married. All that time Alexander was without a love of his own. It was as if he was mirroring his father's experience of rejection by women. Certainly during that first nine-month period in Paris after his National Service, it was as if he was unconsciously taking on the experience of his father's rejection as a man. He had also been losing his self-esteem. He was in fact having to adjust his self-image, and not for the last time. His National Service had been a crisis for Alexander in his belief of who he was and what he would become – the leader of men beloved of his father and his schoolmasters. For his first nine months in Paris were those of an art student living in lodgings. He was Alexander Thynne, an Englishman. He did not tell anyone that he was Viscount Weymouth or that he was heir to a marquessate.

Despite his very good looks, he did not attract girls. It was not that he felt unattractive. 'I did feel attractive,' he insists. 'But I couldn't attract. I wasn't attracting, was more the case.' Nor was Alexander an unappealing male. 'I'm not blaming Paris,' he confides. 'I think I found that, although I had instant sex appeal when I went to a Deb party or a dance in that period, divorce me from the London scene and that appeal wasn't there. It wasn't "nudge, nudge, he lives at Longleat". It was "what's Longleat?" It didn't translate to Paris.' There he was in all his Greek-god glory, and no takers. Why? 'Oh, I think I could understand it in these terms,' he says. 'When I'm at Longleat, yes, I'd have all that persona attached to me.' He had often felt something of an idiot in the army. At home, he was the butt of his father's ill humour and now, his only field of operation, painting, was one in which his success was unproven, at least in Paris – and for Paris read the real world. He was now learning the hard way that whatever he felt about himself and his work, Paris was at quite another place from Eton when it came to artistic styles and quite another place from London when it came to assessing a man's attractiveness. 'When I was in Paris,' he says 'there was not a lack of confidence in my painting or anything else I was doing there, but there was a lack of confidence that people would register that I was a fine artist.' Lack of confidence in other people's acceptance of him is a deep fault in the Bath psyche. Even now he will not exhibit his paintings commercially, only as a part of his murals at home and he is disinclined to submit a painting on the basis that it might be considered less good than that of another artist. At the time of his first visit to Paris, he says his sense of personal confidence was being undermined at home by his father's criticisms. One example of his father's mockery is vividly recalled by Davina. 'Alexander painted his self-portrait in National Service uniform,' she says 'and his father said: "Who do you think you are? Rommel?"' In Paris, Alexander suffered and strove for evidence that he had a future as an artist. 'I think that I'd dropped out of society and was the bane of my father's life and found it very difficult to endorse my father's view of life' Alexander says. 'With all of that public attitude against me it doesn't surprise me that I wasn't attracting. I wasn't going to give up because I was meeting a certain mockery.' At the same time as this personal battle was undermining him as a man, the divorce was undermining Alexander's position in high society as an eligible man. Divorce has become a commonplace, and unfaithfulness in marriage is not so frequently referred to in Biblical terms as 'adultery'. Distorted shadows of a Biblical sexual morality may linger on in the prurient columns of the tabloid press, but practical reality has stepped in to the management of serial marriage. In 1942, however, when the Bath marriage first hit the rocks, divorce was still a scandal. Memories of the Abdication remained sharp. A few years earlier, a king had given up his throne because politicians believed that public opinion would not have accepted his marrying a divorced woman. Divorce still had a dirty ring to it when Daphne and Henry finally divorced in 1953. It was a sordid matter where adultery was dragged through the courts and the newspapers illustrated it with terms of horror. What people did in private and what they were publicly found to have done were two separate issues. Alexander speaks angrily about the values of his parents in those days when they openly began to go their separate ways. He passed through his teens with a home background and environment which crackled with male rejection and female guilt. Alexander still seems to believe, however, that it would have been better for the marriage to have continued regardless of the fault line which had opened up when he exposed his mother's infidelity. His parents divorced, he says derisively, only because his father had met someone he 'wanted to get off with'. 'I don't blame Virginia,' he adds, 'but it was only when she came along that my father decided he wanted a divorce. Otherwise he had been accepting Xan as my mother's boyfriend.' Rows between Alexander and his father had been increasing in intensity. 'The divorce when it came was a relief because things had been building up,' he says. The divorce seems to have been like rain after a long hot summer, but it was a rain that brought a new crop of ideas fertilized by the years of tension and betrayal. These ideas became the foundation on which Alexander has built his life's philosophy. At twenty-one, the disillusionment with all the values he had been taught during the nursery years and which had been growing and developing throughout his teens now ripened. 'This idea of working towards family stability, and there you are doing this: both of you going off and marrying different people,' he declares angrily, his voice rising, and his colour heightening. 'And what are we supposed to do? Are we supposed to take that as our ideal and follow you? Are we supposed to forget all that you said and think up something new?' That is precisely what he did do. His philosophy of polygyny, based on his experience that women will never be faithful to one man, was Alexander's attempt to create a model in his own life for society to follow. Even so, he is still angry that his parents were not living by the moral code that they were propounding.

'It was the hypocrisy of the teaching that when the nitty-gritty comes down of how you ought to behave, they just did what they wanted,' he says through clenched teeth. 'It was not that they were over-moralistic in giving me that code, but it was being pumped in everywhere and they were endorsing it. And suddenly one had the feeling that you hadn't been given anything in the right way of teaching. You'd got to sort of work it all out.' Alexander's faith in the values of his upbringing and the values of stable married and family life had been destroyed. What is more, they had been destroyed during the period when his own sexual and emotional feelings were emerging and developing. Can there be any wonder that Alexander's first love affair, his relationship with

Davina, failed to reach the conclusion her family had expected? Here was a young man, passionately attracted to a beautiful young woman, with whom he had much in common, but unable to foresee any future with her in marriage. The war had torn away the outer structure of the society in which Alexander had been taught to believe, both in a collective and in a personal sense, but he had still been passing through a series of Establishment structures, which seemed strong and unchanging. After his parents' divorce, not much of this conceptual architecture was left standing. No wonder he still lacks confidence in the world, clinging only to the permanence of his own ideas and to the rocklike permanence of Longleat. It was not only his view of sexual morality which was fractured. Once that had cracked everything else came tumbling with it, and by the time Alexander had spent his first nine months in Paris, he was ready for the period of analysis and introspection that led to his formulation of his own original viewpoint about marriage and family life during his Oxford years. 'Divorce was a much greater scandal in those days and I think it upset people,' Davina recalls. 'Daphne had quite a reputation, but people were upset by the divorce. Daphne was quite upset. She was quite happy to have Xan as a boyfriend and remain married to Henry. Then when Virginia came along, incredibly beautiful, it was suddenly very difficult for her.'

Virginia is described in her obituary in the *Telegraph* in 2003 as being 'the intoxicatingly beautiful scion of a thespian and literary family' who on gala occasions 'drifted through the staterooms, tall and slender, adorned with a giant tiara and smiling her tree-cat smile.' Virginia was already married to David Tennant, son of Lord Glenconner, when she met Henry who fell overwhelmingly in love with her, and she with him. Tennant had divorced his wife, the actress Hermione Baddeley, to marry Virginia. Alexander, heir to Longleat but also to his family genes, no longer looked quite so eligible after this. His decline as an eligible male in the eyes of Society began at the time of his parents' divorce. Did the number of engraved invitations on his mantelpiece decline as a result?

'I think it would be more correct to say that I dropped out rather than I was told to get out of anything,' he says gruffly and with a touch of shamefacedness. 'I don't think I was ever ostracized from London Society. I wasn't aware of reacting to it passively. I was just aware of feeling that I don't belong here and that I must find my own feet.'

There was the added factor from the point of view of the Thynne family image at this time. 'I think that my younger brothers were thought of as being a bit crazed and unreliable partners,' he chuckles. 'Well, I think we all were. But I think the bad reputation was really taking hold with Valentine,' he goes on referring to the youngest of the three Bath brothers. 'I think there was a time in his young life when Deb mothers were pulling their daughters away from him.' He laughs again. 'They were saying "Just look at his older brothers."'

Under the British system of primogeniture Alexander had the advantage of being the sole heir to Longleat and the title, whereas the two brothers would be known to inherit nothing except courtesy titles. Clearly he was tarred with the same brush of family looseness, however; and, future marquess or not, this would have had considerable impact on Alexander's image in the eyes of Davina's family. By the time the divorce itself had happened, Alexander had become an art student and his own behaviour had also changed. He dressed deliberately badly, had unkempt hair and drank a great deal. The view of Alexander held by Davina's family was coloured by these things. Undoubtedly, Davina's family pressed her very hard to give him up. The fact that Alexander was to some extent now socially unacceptable was demonstrated by another rather sad experience of rejection by his sister, Caroline.

Caroline had always been Alexander's closest companion and greatest friend and confidante in childhood. Three years older than Alexander, Caroline had rather dumped him as she went into her teens. He says that she considered him too boyish, while she was now set on becoming a young lady. But there was a further distancing in Alexander's relationship with Caroline. She had at one time had artistic aspirations of her own, having become a drama student at RADA but had given it up, to Alexander's disappointment. She had been a stunning debutante. 'Caroline was, surprisingly, being talked about as the Deb of the Year for three years running,' Alexander says rather proudly. 'It was her sort of world and she was very much at home there.'

Not surprisingly, as a Society beauty and a social success Caroline married well. Her husband was David Somerset, the heir presumptive to the Duke of Beaufort. 'For a long time he was just David Somerset,' Alexander says, 'and it was only because his cousin or his first cousin once removed – I don't know quite how it works out – died without a son and heir, that he inherited the

71

title. But it had been accepted that this was likely to happen from before the time of his marriage to Caroline so that somehow it was always the expectation that she was going to be a duchess.' He laughs rather proudly at this feather in the family cap. However, the aftermath of Caroline's marriage was a distancing of his relations with the sister he so loved and who had been the inseparable companion and confidante of his early childhood. Alexander does not laugh when he explained the way in which the gulf had arisen. 'Caroline and David married in 1949 or 1950,' he says. 'I was still at Eton and about seventeen or eighteen.' Over the next two or three years, however, Caroline became more distant. 'I think she was faintly embarrassed by me,' he says without rancour, 'by the immature things and immature angles that I was sometimes taking on social life.' Caroline and David had a London house. 'I used to stay with them,' Alexander recalls. 'But I felt that it wasn't something that was particularly liked or encouraged and I was possibly embarrassing Caroline by endeavouring to stay there, so I just sort of dropped it.' The problem was more with David than with Caroline, but her first loyalty would naturally be to her husband. Although David had been to Eton, some years ahead of Alexander, the brothers-in-law were, according to Alexander, 'never particular friends so I was having to adjust myself to a life with somebody I hardly knew and didn't especially get on with.' At first, when Alexander was in the Life Guards and very much on the list of men invited to Deb dinner parties and dances, the problems had been less immediate. Then the gulf widened. Alexander became the paint-bespattered bohemian who rode a motorbike. David did not want his deadbeat brother-in-law staying at his London house.

'David was much more in the London social whirl than I was,' Alexander explains. 'And also during that period I was dropping out and going to live in Paris and trying to discover my identity on a new basis.'

His exclusion from his sister's home was just another symptom of rejection by his family. As his twenties got under way, and his manhood came into its earliest expression with the attraction to Davina, Alexander gradually lost touch with his closest and most trusted female companion, the sister who could perhaps have been his confidante and advisor in the alien field of romantic love. So, partly due to this insidious rejection by his adored sister, he lost some confidence in himself; and when it came to his relationships with his female contemporaries, he felt strangely insecure and lacking in assurance, despite his stunning good looks and pedigree. 'Gauche', 'awkward' and 'shy' are words applied to Alexander during this period; and the stutter he had had since childhood was now, according to his male chums of the period, very evident, especially at moments of stress.

Caroline was not the only woman who had dumped Alexander during his teens or even earlier. Before Alexander went to his preparatory school, Ludgrove, there had been a succession of governesses, one rather too pretty in that she had attracted the eye of the 5th Marquess, Alexander's grandfather, and had been dismissed. In a sense, she was, as was Caroline after her, lost by Alexander to another man. However, much more significantly, the main defection to a rival male was that of Alexander's mother. Daphne had settled into a relationship with Xan Fielding. 'My mother first got together with Xan about two years before the divorce,' Alexander recalls. In 1951 Alexander was nineteen and about to leave Eton. Xan, whose first name, coincidentally, is short for Alexander, was a war hero of Crete's liberation who had become a travel writer. He created the role of photographer for Daphne so that she could accompany him. 'My mother certainly wasn't a good photographer,' Alexander informs me rather scornfully. 'I think he just wanted an excuse: "How do we describe you? I'm travelling abroad with my concubine? No."'
'I think his sense of inferiority was to do with his parents splitting up and his mother never seemed to take him seriously enough,' Davina says, 'and I always remember various very pathetic things. I was very spoiled compared with him. My parents were wonderful to me and I couldn't have loved them more all my life and I miss my father desperately because he died very young, but Alexander almost made me laugh and weep by saying "Wasn't Mummy kind: she gave me an old record called 'Bye Bye Blackbird'", which, I mean, was the least she could have done and it was the most awful old record and yet, even that made tears spring into his eyes. I wondered if he need be so grateful, but how pathetic really.'

Perhaps 'Bye Bye Blackbird' was his mother's way of predicting the gulf which soon arose between them. Alexander's life, in which – according to many of his friends and acquaintances – he boasts too much of his many female conquests, seems to be a symptom of these rejections, which all came in his early twenties.

Permanence is something to which Alexander too often alludes. Permanence is there in the solid stone pile of Longleat, the ancient rooms and galleries, the land and the family lineage. Alexander's rocklike persona, which makes him stubborn and unmoving in his relationships, may in fact be an opposing reaction to his fear of a loss of that permanence: to a sense that however solid the rock of Longleat, the torrents of life rushing through it have made unpredictable erosions and swept away all but the rock itself. Permanence is something which has not existed in human terms for Alexander. Staff, to whom he had become accustomed, came and went during his early childhood. His father had gone to the war and returned to find his marriage wrecked by infidelities. Then his father had abandoned him, betrayed, him in Alexander's terminology, by turning on him in his teens. Alexander's relationships with other males are the most difficult: but, at this time, in Alexander's most sensitive late adolescence, the tendency of women to leave him was exemplified by his mother's new life with a new man who became in many ways Alexander's rival and an archenemy second only to his father.

Davina agrees that Alexander, even today, feels rejected and believes that this may go back to those days of his mother's rejection of him. It was as if Daphne's betrayal and rejection of Alexander was a template for the pattern of behaviour towards him by all women. The rejection was evident to others. 'I went to stay with him in Cornwall, at Cowrie,' Davina remembers, 'which was his mother's house from her family. Xan Fielding, who was later Alexander's stepfather, was there and it was a very uncomfortable visit inasmuch as I felt I was not staying with the parents at all. I didn't feel his mother really accepted and loved him in the way my mother did me, and I was so surprised that her eldest son should be treated like that and made to feel like a second-rate visitor. I don't think she meant that. It's how I felt it.' This visit occurred, according to Alexander, 'immediately I came back from Paris the first time. This was during the summer before I went to Oxford.' Relations with Xan were not that bad then. The deterioration took several years. Davina, however, did not like Xan. 'She offended Xan on one occasion,' Alexander says. 'It's in my mother's autobiography, but my mother doesn't describe it accurately. It's something about a girlfriend of Alexander's came and offended Xan by leaving an apple core on his typewriter.' He laughs. 'And as if this was such untidiness. It wasn't.

It was a deliberate gesture done by Davina to irritate him because he'd irritated her. This was her gesture of "Take that up your nose" sort of thing.' He chuckles delightedly. Of course, Xan wasn't the only man with whom Alexander has had difficulties. From Henry onwards, Alexander has a definite problem with male relationships. The present-day Alexander has few male friends. These are, he says, the men he plays chess with. He is not one for going out with the boys, and he has no close male friends today. Not only this, but he is also likely to fly into a rage if a woman he regards as one of his circle brings another man, especially a young man, to Longleat. A woman who would rather not be identified who has been a friend and briefly a wifelet once brought a young male friend to Longleat.

She describes Alexander's rage. 'My friend had brought his dog and he gave an old meat bone to the dog after lunch. Alexander flew into a furious rage and took the bone away from the dog, saying "That's my dinner you've just given your dog." And he took it out on the dog, but it was really my friend he was getting at.' This is one reason why young men are rarely seen at Longleat weekends, unless they are sons of older guests. If they should arrive they are not encouraged to stay; and one weekend a woman friend, who was not yet a wifelet, brought a boyfriend and two other young men to Sunday lunch. They were treated civilly, but Alexander made sure his end of the table was packed with women and when the woman friend asked if she and her boyfriend could stay the night, Alexander made excuses, one of which was barely credible in a staffed establishment such as Longleat. 'That will mean washing more sheets,' he is reported to have said. The history of male relations at Longleat is stiff with father-son animosity. Alexander's tempestuous quarrels with his father are legendary. Previous father-son conflicts have been scattered throughout history. Alexander's relations with his own son, Ceawlin, are not, he says, in this category. 'I think I've laid that one to rest,' he says thoughtfully.

During Alexander's teens, as he began to develop into a man, his father may have seen Alexander as a challenge to his own virility and a cause of his failed relationship with Daphne. Xan was a serious challenge to Alexander's relationship with his mother, not only because of the subtle sexual connection which always exists between mother and son but also because Xan was everything Alexander could not be. 'Xan was nine years younger than my mother and she was about twenty-seven when she had me,' Alexander says. Xan was therefore some seventeen years senior to Alexander, which at the time Alexander says they first met would have made Xan about thirty-five to Alexander's eighteen.

Alexander was becoming a man. Xan was aware that he was himself approaching the age of forty, always a crisis point. Because of the advantage of being old enough to have fought in the war while still young enough to swagger and to become Daphne's new mate, Xan had one great advantage over Alexander. He had attained the one status which Alexander could not offer to his mother or any other woman of that day: he was a war hero. Alexander makes rather light of Xan's heroism. 'He'd been an agent in Crete,' he says. 'He was in charge of half the island and organized resistance there against the Germans, and then after Crete fell or came back into the fold, Xan was dropped into France and quickly captured and should have been shot, but there's a famous agent, a Polish lady who dressed people up as if for a firing squad, and she took him out and released him.' Alexander laughs a jolly little laugh here as if to imply Xan's incompetence at being dependent for his survival on a woman.

In fact Xan had been a British Special Operations Agent in Crete during World War Two. He won a DSO for his wartime work as Commander of Underground Forces in Western Crete with Patrick Leigh Fermor until the liberation of Crete. He later wrote a number of noteworthy books including his own war memoir *Hide and Seek*. He translated Pierre Boulle's *Bridge Over the River Kwai* which became a film about war in the Far East against the Japanese. He also translated Boulle's *Planet of the Apes*. He was, indeed, captured in France by the Gestapo in 1944 in company with Francis Cammaerts and a French fellow officer, Christian Sorenson; and the three men were saved by the intercession of Krystyna Skarbek, the noted Polish SOE agent. He died in 1991, the same year as Alexander's father.

Although she apparently did not like Xan, Davina is rather more effusive about his legendary war-hero status. 'Xan is in almost every book I've read about that era,' she says, 'and I knew many women who knew and idolized him and even some who called their children after him. He was a young and very glamorous latter wartime figure, and he certainly knew it. He was a hero to a lot of women, not just a war hero but a young war hero, much younger than Daphne, and there was a kind of tussle for affection going on there, definitely. Xan eclipsed Alexander, and Alexander wanted to eclipse him in his mother's affections and I think there was a terrible subterranean battle going on between them. And Daphne very much wanted to have another baby and, of course, didn't and there was great sorrow over that.' However, this would also have added to the strain, for a new baby with Xan would have further displaced Alexander in his mother's affections.

The tumultuous events of his parents' new sexual arrangements, following years of tension in the family, were affecting Alexander at a time in his life when he was trying to establish his own identity both as a man and an individual. Not long after Daphne became established as Xan's paramour, Henry met Virginia and wanted his freedom from Daphne in order to marry her. Alexander is scathing about his father's desire to be remarried. 'Just because he'd met someone he wanted to get off with,' he says dismissively. 'Otherwise he was perfectly happy with things as they were.' Alexander would have preferred it if his parents had remained married to each other. It is ironic then that his parents found new loves at about the time Alexander met Davina. But whereas his parents survived their divorce to found new marriages with young attractive partners, Alexander's relationship with Davina foundered and finally failed. His bad relations with his father and his displacement by Xan in his mother's affections made him highly likely to see Xan as someone with whom he should fight in order to prove himself a man. He was sharpening his male self-image against that of this cuckolding hero. Although he was still very much at war with his father, he saw Xan as a challenge to his father. At the same time, he seems to have seen Xan as another father to challenge, and he may have reacted to him as such, for relations between the teenager and his future stepfather went sour quickly. Alexander blames Xan. 'For quite a long time he was trying to have a good relationship with me, ' he says, 'trying to discuss things with me. I really quite enjoyed the discussions, but it just gradually became evident that he had this prickly, domineering side, this prickly, aggressive side. The bad incidents would be when he shot me down for my "pretentious opinions" or something, but I just thought that he was unnecessarily rude and I had an "I'm just not going to be treated like that" sort of feeling. I just resented his abruptness and peremptory sort of telling one I was wrong when I don't think I was wrong actually.'

This was, of course, how Henry treated Alexander: criticizing him, knocking him every time he expressed an opinion. It was business as usual with his new stepfather. Alexander's relations with Xan continued to deteriorate until, Alexander says, 'he eventually became hostile.' How much of this was Alexander's fault? 'Alexander has tunnel vision,' Davina says. 'He is always right. But when I met him he had a terrific sensitivity about what other people thought of him.' Alexander had tried to be someone Xan would have admired, but all the time he was fighting back a violent emotional tide against Xan, the war hero who had stolen his father's wife and now was monopolizing his mother's attention. Xan must by this time have begun to see Alexander as a threat to his relations with Daphne. In any event, Alexander believes that it was Xan who drove a wedge between mother and son. Alexander describes the way in which Xan's influence brought about a situation in which he did not speak to his mother for nearly two years. This was after Alexander's Oxford years, during his second period in Paris where he went to study art, and after Daphne's divorce from Henry and her marriage to Xan. From a fairly early stage in Daphne's relationship with Xan there had been pressure from Xan on Daphne to give Alexander less admiration for his work. 'Xan genuinely didn't admire my painting or writing,' Alexander explains, 'and he persuaded my mother that she ought not to have been encouraging me. I think he was probably responsible for my mother writing to me putting me in my place telling me not to be so arrogantly conceited about my work. Oh, she meant it. I was under attack from her, but I think it really came from him. After her marriage to him,' he went on, 'I think Xan was suggesting to her: "Look you might be overestimating him. He might not be the person you really can appreciate." And she was reassessing our relationship and also at the same time trying to patch things up with my father so that they were regaining a really good relationship after divorce without challenging Virginia. So it was all part of the scenario that I was falling out of favour with her.'

Henry and Alexander were totally at loggerheads by now, so Daphne's re-entry into Henry's camp was seen by Alexander as another betrayal. Until the divorce he says that he had always been assured of his mother's support but that after her remarriage both Daphne's new husband and her divorced husband were telling her the same thing. 'Her new husband wasn't saying: "Yes your son is a genius",' Alexander observes. 'And her previous husband was saying: "He's become quite impossible." So she was finding her re-entry into my father's fold by more or less doing as he asked her.' His reaction, he says, 'when she sent a cutting remark was that I didn't answer and I didn't see her for two years. I felt betrayed and felt there was no use in the continuation of the relationship that had been, so I waited for that situation to alter and her attitude also moderated because she hadn't intended to be that fierce. But the relationship was never the same thing again.' This is behaviour true to Alexander's character. Perhaps since that crucial betrayal and rejection by his mother, he takes criticism as a betrayal which he cannot forgive. It was the same when years later a girlfriend who was not a wifelet wrote a critical letter to Alexander about his treatment of his brother Christopher as written about in the newspapers. 'I replied,' Alexander says, 'but when she wrote again with further criticisms I never had anything more to do with her.' He rationalizes the break with his mother and the consequent loss of closeness. 'Let's say it might have been good for me since my whole philosophy of life seems to be "On my own two feet" individualism and not to look to somebody to be supporting. So it really just pushed me into that. But,' he adds sadly, 'it's also very sad for me that I lost a close mother.'

All the sadder perhaps because, in retrospect, he seems to feel that she may have been right in her criticisms. 'I was perhaps making comments that were conceited in the light of my non-acceptance by society,' he says, laughing shyly. For a man losing his beloved and sexy mother to a young war hero and who had no role model he could admire in his father, there were many uncertainties and a great need for permanence with one woman. 'He was somebody you wanted to protect,' Davina says, 'rather because I think he did suffer very much from his father being so unsympathetic and his mother being cold, perhaps one thought, towards him.' Sympathy, however, was not enough to help Davina overcome the difficulties which were growing in her own relationship with Alexander, and she forced herself to make the break.

Final Rejection: Epilogue for a Soul-Mate

Altogether, Alexander's affair with Davina ran from about 1951 to 1955:

four years which took Alexander from his first fresh hopes of adult life to a disillusionment with his beliefs in the way society was structured, disillusionment with himself for obtaining a Third Class degree instead of the Upper Second for which he had hoped and disillusionment with love. The affair with Davina came to its first ending in August 1954. Some six months later the two got together again. 'It was never the same after the first ending,' Alexander admits. 'We got back together again but not quite in the same spirit, although it did go on into my last year at Oxford.' There is some difference of opinion between himself and Davina as to the exact circumstances of the final breakup. 'The second time, that was really me,' Alexander says. 'Um…but um…' There is a longish silence here as Alexander tries to overcome some difficulty at explaining. 'It was at her party. I just failed to turn up and regarded it as over.' He sounds sad, uncomfortable, a bit ashamed, as if he feels his behaviour was somehow below standard for a gentleman. Certainly it does not seem very courteous. 'It relates to things that were happening to me,' he goes on. 'And then within a month or so I heard she was engaged.' His voice is sad, his manner dejected; but indeed the full story is that, once again, he was rejected by Davina.

'At the time she had just met the man she married,' he says. 'I would say the second time it was my decision, but she would say she had actually met the man that she was going to marry.' Alexander's voice and manner are full of discomfort. The rejection by Davina was complete at this time. But to not turn up at Davina's party: surely that was a major slap in the face? Was it calculated to wound?

'There had been comments made at the previous place we'd gone to together which I found demeaning and which I was not going to accept,' he says. There were mutual friends of Alexander's and Davina's staying at Longleat especially for the dance which was held at Davina's family home a few miles away. 'They went,' he says dejectedly. 'I wasn't going to disrupt their plans.' But wasn't Davina expecting Alexander to be there as her boyfriend and partner for the evening? 'Oh, no,' Alexander responds in a hurt tone. 'That point had been raised. I was no longer expecting it.'

'It was my twenty-first birthday party,' Davina says. 'I'm not even sure Alexander was invited to that.' There seems to be some confusion about this point. The disagreements between them had by then become too many. There was, however, another factor in the Alexander-Davina connection. Davina hero-worshipped men who had fought in the war. Alexander was of course too young to have been able to fight in the war. 'Well, it's nothing I've ever felt guilty about,' he says. 'There wasn't a war in my time, unless I'd gone out to Korea or something.' Alexander, a few years older than Davina but not as old as those heroes of the previous war, seemed just another 1950s angry young man, rebelling against his privileged background, unmarked by the experience of death.

Notably, Davina's husband was Field Marshal Sir Roland Gibbs GCB CBE, DSO MC KStJ. He became Chief of the General Staff, the professional head of the British Army. Eleven years older than Alexander and old enough to have fought in the war from 1940, he was at the time of Davina's dance, highly placed in the army where he continued to serve in a lifelong distinguished career until 1979. He died in 2004, aged eighty-three. Another hero of World War Two, and from an aristocratic family, he was the man for whom Davina ultimately rejected Alexander for the second and final time. They married in 1955. This was perhaps the ultimate rejection for Alexander. 'I learned later that she'd already been on holiday in Germany to the regiment, invited by somebody else,' he says, seeming sad and slightly bitter at the recollection. Evidently, the rejection is still profoundly hurtful. Not only did Davina reject him and marry a soldier, but his mother had simultaneously rejected him for her war hero Xan. Alexander's knowledge that he had not been a success as a soldier was somehow borne out by the response of the two most important women in his life: and in both cases too, he was rejected as an artist. His mother had ceased to be supportive to him in his work; and Davina, although an artist herself, had turned from him in favour of a distinguished soldier. Perhaps all of this reflects the biggest rejection of all: that of his father. It was Henry who accused Alexander of being effeminate because he was an artist, who mocked him and criticized him. Henry had also been a soldier, a war hero of sorts, whose own heroes were strong leaders. It was not only Alexander, the son and lover, who was being rejected by Daphne and by Henry or by Davina when she got engaged to her soldier: it was Alexander the sensitive, artistic man in the deepest sense. The artist was being trashed in favour of conventional images of macho men of war.

'It was because he thought art was not a proper occupation for a man,' Alexander says of his father's accusation that he was effeminate because he was an artist. 'The only worse thing would have been if I'd have said I was going to become a ballet dancer.' The damage to his self-confidence was colossal. So many rejections all so close together and so deeply significant conspired to make Alexander feel hopelessly vulnerable and inadequate. He was shaken in his confidence as a man, and also in his belief in himself as an artist. It was a personal crisis of enormous proportions.

At the same time, the world in which he had believed, into which he had been trained to fit, was undergoing a sea-change: in the country which found itself somewhat the worse off after paying its debts to America for World War Two, among the aristocracy which had become the victim of plundering Death Duties, in the attitude of society generally, which was rapidly becoming more aware of egalitarian values. This was echoed in his family where the breakdown of the established order, however scantily clad it had been for several years before his parents' divorce, finally tore apart the remaining threads of the status quo. Alexander's legal position as heir to Longleat and the marquessate were unchallenged by the changes in his parents' lives, but there were other threats to his financial security which gathered momentum later as his relations with his father continued to deteriorate. Rather more significantly, these events were destabilizing Alexander emotionally and sexually as he struggled to establish his emerging identity as a man. Emotionally, while the world of values, which he had been taught were rock firm, crashed and fell around him, he was at a considerable disadvantage. He was like a rubber dingy cast loose by a yacht, tossed around on emotional waves and expecting at any moment to be punctured on a sharp rock. His remaining time at university after the Davina debacle was spent in putting together the finishing touches to a whole new philosophy of life which would replace the one which his recent life's experience had destroyed. Then the bitter disappointment over his Third Class degree mean that he was forced for the second time in four years to examine himself in a new light. 'The self-imagery had to be readjusted in such a way that it wasn't such a fine image,' he tells me.

Feeling like an outcast from his family and from society in general, he would return to Paris with his new philosophies as his new rock of permanence. Paramount among these philosophies was his idea of polygyny. He felt that he had learned from his mother and from Davina that women were not to be trusted to be faithful and that family could not be relied upon for loyalty. He could no longer believe in the soul-mate. Safety in numbers is the name of the game he invented and dubbed a philosophy of life for men and women. With bitter experience under his belt and with his loner's philosophy under his pillow, it is no wonder that Alexander will not admit to any further falling in love.

'I never use the concept of falling in love,' he says. 'I'm always uncertain to use that phrase and I always avoid using it. I'm not sure it's even accurate to describe what's happening. Madly sexually attracted is quite enough to go along with. At a point to say I'm in love with someone I would begin to say that this means I've begun to lose control of my reason and I'm thinking that this isn't me. So perhaps I'm averse to saying I'm falling. "Falling" sounds not on your feet anymore. I have that feeling of it being something out of control, and I am in control of myself. If I'm dependent on someone's actions, if I think in terms of if she's going to do that or say that; or if I say that I'm going to walk on and she says she's going to follow me; but I say I won't look back and then, I think well, I ought to look back; then that means I'm beginning to get out of control.' The truth is that Alexander wants love, that he has never really known love or dared to know it because he is afraid of it. 'I think there might have been a certain absence of it in my upbringing,' he says. 'Even if I take my mother who I had a good relationship with in those early years, she was affectionate, but it's only affectionate; I wouldn't say "love".'

The nanny who was a closer and more devoted figure all the years she knew him still was not the one who gave love. 'It was loyalty,' he says, 'total self-sacrifice. "I'm doing all this for this family." But I hesitate to call that love. I have to think that if I am describing love I would not use her as an example.' 'He never said "I love you,"' Davina reveals. 'We were careful not to use those terms. He was more concerned with being amusing than romantic. Yet, there was a romantic aura.' Perhaps Alexander does not know love when it stares him in the face. 'I've sometimes thought "all Alexander wants is a cunt,"' one ex-wifelet who seems to love Alexander remarks bitterly. 'He's not interested in the person.'

So has he missed out on love in his life? 'I think it's an area where I could have been inspired more,' he says sadly. 'So there's not much personal experience coming in when I write or talk about that kind of relationship.'

Chapter Three

Safety in Numbers: Wifelets in Theory

The Wifelet Theory

'How does he do it?' asked Scary Spice, phoning after a brief visit to Longleat. She meant, how does Alexander attract so many women? Indeed the question can only be answered at length, for Alexander – who so significantly failed to attract women during one period of his life when he had everything to offer, including youth and exceptional good looks – has had to work at attracting women rather scientifically and has evolved a technique so that even in his late seventies, he is the centre of female attention. Why does Alexander need or even want to attract so many women? He has created his strategy of 'Safety in Numbers' because this focus of female attention has been the much-needed cascade of *faux* jewellery that has never made up for his lack of real gems. That does not mean that Alexander has been entirely without important emotional attachments. There have been special emotional links with some of the wifelets, but these he refers to not as loves but as 'significant relationships'.

Is this a natural reticence which prevents Alexander from admitting that he has ever cared for a woman beyond his ability to rationalize his sentiments, never been head-over-heels in love, never felt that he could adore anyone irrationally? Significantly for Alexander, it is this terminology which defines the cautious emotional responses of a man who, having been defeated in early encounters with the messy emotions of love, has fallen back on a hygienic explanation to separate the loves from the mere escapades or, if he has ever known it, true passion from mere erotic pleasure. There is more than one reason for his attitude.

Flighty Females

I ask Alexander if he had ever found the soul-mate for whom he says he was always looking. 'At first I was looking for a soul-mate,' he replies rather sorrowfully. 'I never found a soul-mate. I also realized I would never find a woman who could be faithful to me. So I worked out a philosophy of polygyny.' Polygyny is an attempt to evade the test of fidelity which monogamy presents. Alexander explains it as being based on his observations of female sexual behaviour. His idea is that women cannot be faithful to one man, partly because they find it too easy to say yes. Alexander has judged women universally by his personal experience. He says he based his theory of the promiscuity of women on the fact that most of the women with whom he had his early sexual relations had enjoyed more sexual experience than he had. This is what finally led him to the realization that he would never find one woman who would be his one and only soul-mate. His sense of male superiority, of being the one initiating the innocent girl, was completely crushed. Surprisingly for one who had read so much from sexual text books in his schooldays, he says he felt gauche and awkward when confronted either in bedrooms or bypasses with these experienced girls.

'It was the realization that I was never going to get a situation in which the expectation of the male having more sexual experience than his partner would arrive in my life,' he says. 'Therefore I was thinking what might arise and I was thinking that there is the polygynous male who might have a wider experience though actually less experience than the women. That way I would be able to gain perhaps a basis of equality. I didn't have to fret about the fact that they all had more experience than me but instead could think that, even though they'd all had more experience, then simultaneously I had a wider selection.'

There is some illogic in his reasoning; Alexander's theory of polygyny is really fairly close to polygamy, but whereas polygamy is a system based on the marriage of one man with a number of wives, polygyny is really a free-love free-for-all. Its central idea is that of a community of women who have children fathered by one central male who takes charge of the children's upbringing and education. However, Alexander protects himself from being unable to satisfy all these women at one time by allowing that these 'wifelets' can also have any number of 'hublets'. He seems not to have faced the fact that there would then be some confusion as to who had fathered any resulting children. As to the financial obligations of any of these men, including Alexander himself, there are apparently none; the state is supposed to pick up the tab for the upkeep of this hypothetical brood of brats. Polygyny also neatly prevents any emotional or psychological difficulty over unfaithfulness of the female to the male since Alexander's theory does not demand that the wifelets are faithful to the central male. By avoiding any insistence on fidelity, Alexander avoids the difficulties which all sexual partnerships encounter when they go through an awkward patch. It is the expectation of faithfulness which precipitates anguish once there is infidelity. How much easier then to banish the concept of fidelity and exclusive relationship? But does not banishing the expectation of fidelity also lower the status of the relationship from one where there is commitment, responsibility and real caring for the other partner to one where passing flings are as important as a partnership which has required some effort to develop into a rewarding love? The reasoning is contrary to biological expectations of the male and female. The female has biologically been the civilizing force in human history in that she has demanded a faithful male to protect her while gestating and a nest provided with food in which to rear her young. Biologically, it is the male who tries to fertilize as many women as possible while needing to guard his female from being fertilized by another male. Alexander's idea of 'hublets' for his wifelets seems to undermine the idea that there are any biological guarantees as for the 'father' of the offspring. Polygamy suits male ideas of biological diversity of females fertilized and guarantees the line of succession from the one father: to introduce the possibility that the wifelets can have 'hublets' would seem to undermine the whole idea. It implies that Alexander does not feel confident that he can retain a woman's physical loyalty. This might be because he feels his sexual performance is not good enough to prevent a woman from straying in search of a better lover. On the other hand, it might be because he has taken on too many women and as a result cannot keep any of them happy. If women, in Alexander's view, are so easily seduced, surely the answer is to keep them permanently satisfied. A man with so many women to please cannot possibly have the capacity to satisfy them all sufficiently to prevent them from saying 'yes' to other men, especially when they know that the man to whom they are supposed to be available is probably with someone else. Alexander is therefore creating the very situation which he would prefer to avoid: the conditions of his own rejection. In that polygyny permits the wifelets to have other men, Alexander is also introducing a little political incorrectness into his philosophy by saying that he is 'allowing' the women to have as much sexual freedom as the male. Usually, however, most women seem to prefer the idea that they have one faithful man who is the father of their children and their protector and whom they are prepared to love. They are only unfaithful when they are neglected by this one man.

Wifelet reactions to Alexander's theory and to his behaviour with other women seem to bear this out. It seems that many wifelets may have had the idea that their bond with Alexander was special. When I ask him again about the question of the soul-mate he becomes very arch. 'Oh you'll get me scalped if you say I've never had a soul-mate,' he says 'I've got to be careful about saying I've never had a soul-mate. I'd have my hair scalped immediately.' He laughs and at the same time disappears into the hammock in which he is rocking himself as we talk. 'So I'm not saying that,' he goes on. 'I'm just saying that's one of the criteria that has always been difficult to find but there have been savours of it here and there on several occasions. Don't ask me which,' he adds with a nervous giggle. I remind him that he has given me a list of wifelets in which he told me specifically which are and which are not what he calls 'significant relationships'.

'Oh, did I?' he gasps. 'Well, I'm not coming out and saying so-and-so was a soul-mate.' But he told me for instance that, Jo-Jo Laine (Number 54) was one with whom he would have loved to have had babies. He also mentioned Una (Number 41) a successful artist, and Irene (Number 42) who was important for four years. Nova Williamson (Number 34) was, he said, 'important. I would have liked to have developed the relationship and had children.' Of Rosemary (Number 18) he said: 'I would have liked children with her.' There were perhaps ten or twelve in all who met the criteria of being important in the long-lost archives of lovers he may have lost but never admitted to be loves.

There are deeper reasons why he cannot ever really admit to having felt, or has perhaps never really dared to feel, the more profound emotions of personal love. The most important cause of Alexander's strategy of Safety in Numbers is his profound fear of rejection based on his already deeply painful experience of rejection by his mother, father and first girlfriend.

From Soul-mate to Bed-Mate

His friend Michael Croucher, a TV producer who has made three films with Alexander for the BBC, believes Alexander's polygyny concept is part of that elaborate system of defences which Alexander has built up to protect himself from the further pain of rejection. He has possibly never given up the idea that he might find the ideal soul-mate. There was, for instance, Jane whose placement in the gallery of wifelet portraits as Number 2 follows Davina's. 'Alexander was very enthusiastic about Jane Willoughby,' says his old friend Sir Ian Rankin. Jane, however, was the one whose escapade with Alexander's brother Christopher also caused him some grief. This event was a further nail in the coffin of his interest in women from his own social circles or in the idea of meeting a woman who might become the soul-mate. Other Debs still followed Jane. They were not, Alexander says, 'significant', although he says he would hate them to identify themselves in that way. Perhaps they were happy to be no more than casual girlfriends, invited to balls, meeting lots of men, seeking the hoped-for eligible prospect while enhancing their image by partying on the arm of a future marquess. These were usually the kind of girls invited down for Oxford dances.

At that stage Alexander had not undergone his definitive transition from the glamorous white-tie image of his Oxford and London social life to that of the scruffy art student. Nor had his taste in women changed. According to Sir Ian Rankin, this transition occurred after Alexander returned to Paris for his second and longer period there. 'It was soon after he left Oxford that the change started,' Sir Ian says, 'when he became a student on the Left Bank in Paris. Then, as far as I can make out, from being fairly smartly dressed, he became a fairly scruffy Left Bank student covered in paint.' In fact, Alexander says, the change had already begun at Oxford. 'I think Oxford was the fertilization. I was taught to think, to challenge existing ideas. I was in an intellectual atmosphere where ideas were discussed and where the processes of arguing a point were very explicit. This was a huge contrast with my home life where there was an extreme lack of intellectual life. I realized what I'd been missing, how poor the atmosphere at home was.' So there was Alexander, heir to a beautiful stately home hung with art treasures but intellectually impoverished; and if the intellectual riches of Oxford showed up the intellectual and cultural poverty of his home life, they showed him that he had to create a new world for himself.

Indeed, in the mid-1950s he was also sharing something with a much wider community of young men and women all over Great Britain who realized that the social order which had been accepted by their parents was restricting and that something new was needed to put in place of the antiquated system of class limitation. This took time to get off the ground for society as a whole, while for Alexander, individually, the transformation was much swifter. It was also one that inevitably influenced his choice of women and which also destroyed his standing as an eligible bachelor with women of his own class. There were, however, few among his girlfriends whose intellectual training would have equipped them to understand Alexander's private revolution. While at Oxford, Alexander maintained close friendships with his social peers. He was, for instance, a member – and later the president of – the Bullingdon, the elite dining and drinking club, with other ex-Etonians and former Life Guards officers, who dressed in specially made Oxford blue tailcoats with ivory lapels, mustard waistcoats and sky-blue bowties. A group photo of this soigné elite from Alexander's time in the Bullingdon hangs in a small guest loo in Alexander's private downstairs apartment at Longleat. The club dinners have been reported over the 200 or so years of its existence as scenes of drunken destruction where the dining venue would be 'trashed' but after which, the members were usually all sufficiently rich to be able to pay for the damage, usually in cash on the night. Tom Driberg, later a Labour MP, said that after one such post-dinner rampage: 'Such a profusion of glass I never saw until the height of the Blitz. On such nights, any undergraduate who was believed to have "artistic" talents was an automatic target.' The behaviour of Bullingdon Club members on the night of their annual dinners has sometimes been raised in the House of Commons. Indeed, there are eight such mentions in *Hansard* to date. The club has occasionally been suspended for a few years. More recent members said to be embarrassed by some of the Bullingdon's excesses include the Conservative leader David Cameron and the Mayor of London, Boris Johnson.

While he continued to mingle with his socially exclusive peers in the exclusively upper-class Bullingdon, the seeds of subversion were being sown in Alexander's intellect. Thanks to the philosophy part of his degree, Alexander was also learning formal techniques of intellectual argument so that he developed the confidence to formulate new ideas to put in place of the old ones from his upbringing. These new ideas were divided, he says, into moral, political and religious considerations. This working out in the head of solutions to emotional problems is typical of Alexander: and once he has worked out a solution he does not want to know about alternative possibilities. Alexander seems almost fossilized in the 1950s and 1960s, for it seems he has not changed his style of dress either. His penchant for caftans and long hair also go back to this period at Oxford in the mid-1950s, when he began his rebellion against the established order of his class. At first it all seemed like a lot of undergraduate fun, which his contemporaries assumed he would outgrow. It amused everyone enormously. Sir James Spooner, another old friend of Eton and Oxford days, remembers 'going to Longleat to somebody's dance in 1954 or '55. His father was looking after everyone and feeding them at Job's Mill.' Alexander may not wish to admit it, but his friends were enchanted by Henry and loved his piano playing, sense of humour and charming manners. Sir Ian remembers 'once going to a party at Job's Mill, and Henry Bath was playing the piano nonstop all evening, and he suddenly fell asleep or passed out and his head fell down on the keyboard but the piano playing went on. He hadn't played a note. It was a machine going on behind.'

The fact that there was no room for Alexander to live at Job's Mill, and indeed no welcome from his father and his new bride, was of course another rejection but one with compensations. He lived in his own apartment comprising half of Longleat House. 'My wife Alison and I were staying at Longleat House,' Sir James recalls, 'and I remember that there was a certain amount of incongruity with Alex in his amazing clothes and a very conventional butler waiting on everyone.' Perhaps the immature Alexander enjoyed the contrast between his home in the ancient pile of Longleat House, and his 1960s hippie poses. But the outer crust of bohemianism was also a manifestation of a very real inner change. The iron had entered into his soul some years earlier. The rebellion against his class was one thing, but it was also now a rebellion against that expectation of his class to marry a White Anglo Saxon Protestant virgin.

All this deep revolt was indeed forged at Oxford. Here he found himself encouraged in his transformation by some dons whose political radicalism opened his eyes to the changing social order in Britain as a whole. While his own milieu outside the university was far from ready to relinquish its elitist concepts or expectations of virgin brides, Alexander – misunderstood as a man as well as a member of his class – was now absolutely stripped of his belief in the emperor's new clothes. The staid minuet of court circles on whose fringes he had cavorted among the Debs during his early Life Guards days now seemed like a redundant mating dance.

When Alexander took up his second Parisian period, which was to last almost four years, he was already primed for his angry rejection of everything that had made him what he was. The problem was that he went to Paris empty-handed. Apart from his new Oxford made theories, upon which the ink was barely dry, he arrived somewhat naked. He had no practical proof that his theories could replace the system that he wanted to destroy. In Paris he found an intellectual climate that was more frankly anti-establishment. In England he may have been the rebel in ermine – taunted by the press, ridiculed, even avoided by many of his contemporaries, disapproved of by his family and his peers – but in Paris he was simply an art student. As plain Alexander Thynne, he preferred to be incognito, without a pedigree that shouted his privileged origins. If he were known as Viscount Weymouth, the courtesy title meant little in France. He was just another *vicompte* in a country whose intellectuals were still in love with its own revolutionary rejection of an aristocratic elite. Only French aristocrats would have found his junior title of Viscount Weymouth and his future title of Marquess of Bath meaningful. Alexander, however, does not appear to have mingled in aristocratic circles while studying painting in Paris.

His lack of a meaningful title in France meant that he had dropped all credentials to male allure except for his good looks. Perhaps these alone did not add up to sex appeal? He wanted to see who he was, stripped bare of this paraphernalia. Alas, it seemed, he had not very much to offer, for on his own admission, women turned away from him rather than towards him. Nevertheless, he had not entirely abandoned the search for a soul-mate, but the image of the soul-mate had undergone some rather liberal alterations in the directions of a free-love mate. His overt search was now for sexual experience. He did not find the multiplicity of lovers he had hoped for. Polygyny was slow to get off the ground. Still he hoped to find close bonds and indeed to develop close intimate relationships. What he knew for sure was that he did not want to marry, except in a formal sense to whoever would give him an heir. However, the hoped for sexual conquests did not materialize. As for love, he did not expect such an emotion to complicate his programme. Polygyny would be his strategy. It would also be his revenge against those who had hurt him more than he could admit and, simultaneously, his revenge against a God and a Christ who had allowed this pain of rejection. There remains a good deal of rage behind the creation of polygyny: rage against his parents and all those who had taught him the creed of a society based on Christianity and monogamy. This rage forms a deep fault line in Alexander's psyche, one which creates a backlash in many of his relationships. It is a fault line well concealed behind Alexander's philosophies and the cold intellectual fabric of the universe according to Alexander. But Alexander needs these solid structures to stand on since he knows that he cannot trust the volcanic forces which flow under the surface of his rational mind, less predictable than earthquakes.

Eros, Passion and the Divine Emotion: Love By Any Other Name

Alexander was aware of these seismic torrents. Indeed, so deeply was he disturbed and confused and so longing to understand himself that he sought out all the popular texts he could find on psychology. Much of this was while he was on his second sojourn in Paris where his inexplicable failure to wow the girls gave him even more food for self-analysis. Among his psychological readings of popular texts were those of Carl Jung, whose interpretations of the dark elements in the human mind brought to the lexicon terms such as 'the shadow persona' and 'projection'. Among Jung's writings one may find much on the psychic interconnections between two people who become deeply emotionally involved. Jung said that when two people come together in a serious emotional and sexual relationship, there is always a radical transformation of both. This transformation, involving the opening up of the shadow persona in each, brings out much that seems uncontrollable in their behaviour. Many of the traits buried in the deep memory because the individual rejects them as acceptable parts of his or her own behaviour are those labelled by Jung as 'shadow' characteristics. Because sex involves the awakening of unconscious energies, the opening up of strong passions also opens the whole package of buried unconscious responses. These are raised to the surface of the mind and then 'projected' onto the partner who gets the blame for becoming all the things the individual has rejected in himself and still rejects, preferring not to admit them as his own. So a complex psychic interconnection of two individuals which first begins with the projection of the higher qualities and aspirations and is labelled as 'falling in love' becomes a more sinister exchange. In Alexander's case, the volcanic nature of his buried feelings has caused him many difficulties with women. Certainly those difficulties, sometimes involving violent behaviour, have been an obstacle to Alexander in his quest for a soul-mate and his dream of a close, loving relationship. Polygyny, cold and mechanical though it may seem in its lack of the divine emotion, need not exclude physical passion. While having experienced physical passion, Alexander has probably never known the deeper passion, that combination of the compelling physical with the intense emotional experience: that thing called 'love'. Indeed, he denies that any of his encounters have been 'loves'. He refuses to admit that he can be rocked by passion.

He does not accept the possibility of being inspired by love, even that first love of which he told me solemnly: 'we were very careful not to use the word "love" to describe our feelings for each other. We didn't use the words "in love". We tended to soft play, which I think is wise. I mean the meaninglessness of the phrase for one thing. One might as well have soft play and build on the thing later.'

But later never came. He was unable to fully consummate his physical relationship with Davina, and this may have brought too much frustration into the relationship for both parties. The fact that he was already saying at this early stage that his and Davina's feelings for each other were not 'love' may have prevented Alexander from ever allowing deeper emotions to take root. Certainly, he did not admit such deeper feelings to himself. What might have been his love with a soul-mate turned into a sexually frustrating intellectual battle; and it turned into that because he had to have a reason to destroy anything which might resemble the childhood myth of his parents' marriage: a myth which had originally been based on strong sexual and emotional bonds. Was Alexander waiting for something more than complete sexual fulfilment? Waiting for the evidence that there was something durable in his relationship? If so, that would also have been the evidence for which Davina was waiting, the evidence that Alexander would commit himself to her. Of course, he could not do that because he was afraid of rejection. But his hesitation made rejection inevitable. Because he could not express his feelings as love, he could not in the end provoke the response as in the old saying 'love begets love'.

Alexander's problem is that, having never known the experience, he is not sure what love feels like. He cannot put his finger on the definition. Not everyone knows how to describe love. In fact, few people could define it according to rigorous philosophical or scientific terms. Those who try are likely to end up like Alexander, denying its existence. His view is that the force which others call love is merely physical attraction: an illusion arising from sexual desire.

Perhaps Alexander also conveys his belief that the idea of 'love' is a weakness in an individual which makes it necessary for them to believe that the overwhelmingly powerful attachment over and above sexual magnetism is indeed an exalted, semi-divine emotion. For Alexander, this is unreal; it is merely an exaggeration of physical processes, something which suggests that he, Alexander is not in control; something he would rather not admit. Yet reluctantly he does admit it. His very fear is an admission of the existence of something beyond his control, something ultimately too powerful for intellectual exercises to combat. He also reveals with a look, a blush, a thrill to his voice that there have been women in his life who have done more to hold his attention than merely excite his hormones. When he speaks of these his facial expression softens into a look of love. But, as he sadly tells me, love has been a deficiency in his life. Indeed, his caution is so great that perhaps he has never been able to risk receiving or giving that madly wonderful expression of feeling.

Poor Alexander. Poor little rich boy. Even the humblest, plainest, most impecunious, least important individual can experience the most exalted feeling of love. Yet Alexander, one of the highest in the land in terms of social position, birthright and material wealth, cannot reach those heights. Alexander is not only a man who has learned not to trust love. He is also from that English social caste which sends their children away from home as soon as possible to single-gender schools which teach them everything they need, except how to love and be loved. In these schools there is a lack of the normal interrelationship of the sexes. Alexander's background is a constant reference point in his story, but one cannot blame his fear of love or his inability to acknowledge that there even is such a thing, only on his coolly absent mother, on his nanny or the comings and goings of assorted governesses or on Ludgrove and Eton. The existence of these entities has protected Alexander from exposure to this destabilizing emotional force called 'love'. He may even have welcomed this protection.

I ask Alexander if he had noticed whether periods of artistic inspiration coincided with the relationships he prefers to call 'more significant'? 'I don't notice any difference,' he says a little defensively. 'I'm working on my various projects all the time.' Evidently the defences work so well that they block out the heights of feeling as well as the pain. Not for Alexander the incandescent passion involving the high-risk surrender of emotional control to another human being: his emotional risks are all carefully and strategically planned.

Combined with his formidable defences against the pain of love, Alexander has another attribute to his character which may block the free flow of inspiration and indeed of inconvenient 'love'. This is his determination that everything which occurs in his life should fit into his predetermined plans. His daily, weekly, even yearly schedules are rigid. His life is structured for efficiency and very much a railway line of prearranged activities. The idea of inspiration entering into his carefully plotted timetables seems too much of an interruption, an inconvenience, a danger to his orderliness. He has his pattern, and he will not allow anyone to persuade him to adapt it. As with inspiration, the act of falling in love would amount to allowing the train times of his life to get behind schedule. Likewise, it is as if his life and his art go on uninterrupted by changes of female companions who fit into the slot marked 'sex'. This is Alexander's administrative department of planned lust. As the disillusioned ex-wifelet realized, her persona was of little importance. Her main function was to be a female presence to fit, when wanted, into the leisure section of

Alexander's life. Her individuality did not matter. It is not that he cannot tell them apart, for Alexander faithfully paints every wifelet and places her picture in his personal gallery. The head of every woman with whom he has had a sexual relationship in his almost eighty years (some seventy-five wifelets at the time of writing) is immortalized in thick, painted sculpture on the spiral staircase which Alexander laughingly refers to as his 'Bluebeard's Gallery'. Few of them are easily recognisable. It is not because Alexander cannot paint good likenesses. He can. However, he does not see the women clearly because his vision of them is confused, as if by a projection of his own imaginary ideal. Alexander is putting an unconscious part of himself into these portraits as much as he is observing the woman herself. This implies that his women are all the same to him in that they become the willing collaborators in the psychological typecasting. Until they fight their way through it and show who they are, they are inevitably playing roles directed by Alexander. But in the process of that fight to be herself, the wifelet's relationship with Alexander begins to fall apart.

If one takes a trip up the spiral staircase, there they are: a recorded history, in paint, of a love life or, let's say, sex life that began with Davina Merry, long before his marriage to the present Lady Bath, and continued with barely a skipped heartbeat after the wedding. They are paintings of – and for – his life; not really of the women or their lives. These portraits are not of the women as individuals or studies in character so much as paintings of Alexander's conquests. This explains why he has never succeeded in bonding closely enough with any woman to admit that the relationship is a love affair. After a time, any woman tires of being an object rather than a subject. These relationships have been Alexander's substitute for the love of which he used to dream before he was damaged by multiple rejections. A few are remembered with a rosy glow that stirs Alexander to enthusiasm as he talks. But where are they now? Alexander says his relationships never finish. Do they really go on as relationships, or do they become merely old acquaintances with separate lives, which simply brush past each other with a news update at a Longleat Sunday lunch? As for love as art, Alexander admits that he is by nature a plodder at his work. One suspects that Alexander has plodded on, more afraid than aware of that wildly uncontrollable force called inspiration which has its source so often in a completely abandoned, totally courageous love. It may not be just bad luck that love in any of its forms has not come his way. It is that he fears the topsy-turvy upheaval that love brings, the changes it forces on the individual who makes that deep connection with another; he fears the transformation described by Jung. Alexander clings instead to the rock of his personality, afraid of letting go of his carefully formulated beliefs. He resists any possibility of a new idea which might challenge his painstaking philosophical constructions of more than forty years ago. He cannot open himself to the flow of ideas, the torrent of feelings, the windswept heights of new creative notions, of an ever-evolving stream of thought. He sticks to the tried and tested. He has formed his philosophy, and that is it. That is what he must follow and prove right. That is what he believes that he must live out. So what challenge could be more subversive to his edifice of ideas about male-female relationships than to find that, after all, there is such a thing as love? Soft gentle love or the mad passionate love that the French call 'amour fou', a love to rock the lifeboat of fixed ideas: a force to change the otherwise unchanging framework of a predictable life; a force to shatter the rock of Alexander's unchanging 'Permanence'. Alexander with his intellectual precautions against love's unfathomable undercurrents reminds one of the overly fastidious housewife, Mrs Ogmore Pritchard, in Dylan Thomas's *Under Milk Wood* who warns her husband: 'And if you let the sun in, mind it wipes its feet.' Love, of course, never wipes its feet. His determination to construct a world that did not contain the ideal and probably impossible concept of faithful love is evidently a reluctant counterattack. Masquerading as a rational solution to the problem, it has also the hallmarks of a violent emotional overreaction. Not everyone who has been upset by parental divorce and its associated traumas has gone to the lengths of working out a whole new philosophy of male-female relationships. Alexander, more sensitive than most, perhaps angrier than most and also guiltier than most because of the part he played in alerting his father to his mother's waywardness, needed to protect himself from further rejections in the 'all eggs in one basket' Christian love and marriage scenario. Hence his development of the collective family theory in which emotional safety lies in numbers. Having married and provided his heir, he has not tried to live in the close and loyal partnership of a conventional marriage but has, rather like a monarch of the old days, opted for a lifestyle of sexual independence within the framework of an official marriage. He was never faithful to Lady Bath, the woman who bore his heir Caewlin and his daughter Lenka. Nor, it seems, did he demand that she be faithful to him, which may imply some risks to patrimony. Nor was she. She was married to someone else. The Baths are still married, after this fashion; but one does not have to dig very deep to discover that this arrangement is not altogether satisfactory for Alexander in emotional terms. Lady Bath has not wished to comment.

However, Alexander is celebrated in the tabloids for his wifelets, envied perhaps by otherwise happily married men for his access to these women who jostle with each other to be photographed on his arm at parties and to be written about in the gossip columns. Sometimes too he has been the object of rather outrageous portrayals in the confessions of ex-wifelets in the pages of the more sensational Sunday papers. The diary columns of national newspapers also carry items about Alexander and his wifelets, often announcing the arrival of new ones on his arm at London parties. In fact, so well known is Alexander for his succession of mistresses that any woman seen in his company or even around Longleat is assumed to be a wifelet.

Leaving the house via his garden with the gate marked 'Private' for a walk around the grounds among the visitors to Longleat House and park, one is aware of a certain look, mingling curiosity, admiration and envy, which seems to suggest that the public takes one for a wifelet. Once, when I was lunching with Alexander *à deux*, off a trolley in his private sitting room, a tour group came through and, after giving his talk, Alexander offered to answer questions. One woman smiled and nodded her head at me. 'Have you painted a portrait of your wife?' she asked shyly.

Alexander blushed a bit.

'Well, you see, this lady is not my wife,' he said rather ponderously.

The group shuffled with embarrassment and giggled sheepishly. Oh, I see,' they chorused in meaningful tones. 'And you won't find her on the staircase either.' Alexander responded with a laugh. Alexander later merrily retells the anecdote to guests at dinner. 'Nesta was most indignant,' he adds. 'She said: "I would not wish to be on *that* staircase."'Is Alexander just the teeniest bit embarrassed by this group's immediate assumption that any woman not his wife might be a mistress? Not at all. He seems to have hugely enjoyed the mistake since he enjoys any opportunity to be seen as the great stud. This, however, is not his declared motive for brandishing wifelets in public. His excuse for this overt declaration of what other men would try to hide is that he is pioneering a great social experiment which will replace the rather imperfect notion of monogamy. However, the theory on which he would like to base a new society of communal families is derived entirely from his own personal experience and arises out of his own pain. In creating this elaborate edifice of the wifelet theory, he is in reality defending himself from the risks of loving and losing one exclusive partner. He is hedging his bets to make sure that he always has a woman on tap and that he is invulnerable to the pain of rejection by one sole object of his affections, because there will always be another to whom he may turn. The strategy is more than a defence. It is also terrific advertising. His Casanova image helps to pull in women who think there must be something good on offer if so many others keep flocking around. However, as a response to the idea that women are naturally promiscuous, the wifelet theory seems to break down, since so many of Bath's wifelets seem to be manoeuvring for exclusivity and many appear hopeful of installing themselves as the future Lady Bath.

The Mother Model

Until the late 1990s when a birth by a wifelet was announced, not one member of his harem had produced children in the course of almost fifty years. Only one other wifelet conceived; and her pregnancy, according to Alexander, was unfortunately fallopian and therefore could not result in a birth. One speculation about the lack of conceptions is that Bath has a low sperm count. His long-time associate Michael Croucher says he thought this could be the reason for Alexander's highly public presentation of himself as a great stud. 'Alexander protests too much,' Croucher observes. 'You don't need an explanation for chasing pretty women. You just don't need to; and someone in his position will be successful with certain sorts of pretty women. That's not being rude about him or the women. You know it's just the world, and the pleasures of the world, but most people just don't need to justify it or talk about it.'

Alexander, however, says he has had a fertility test and is in fine fettle. If there were no reason for doubt, would a fertility test be necessary? There may be another explanation for the lack of babies. The terms which he lays down for the production of the children – that they should be handed over to be brought up by him at Longleat – do not suit most women. Indeed, the new baby, which Alexander claims is proven as his by DNA tests, is being brought up by its mother well away from Longleat and Alexander's influence. 'The baby's mother is someone I'd like to be closer to,' Alexander rather wistfully admits, but he is pleased about the child and will not yet surrender his dream of siring a brood by diverse women, age being no obstacle in this new century of medical miracles.

Alexander, however, does not choose women who are the maternal type. A number of ex-wifelets have married and have children. The majority remain unmarried and have never had a child. These women – many of them former glamour girls, actresses, singers, aspiring models, professional mistresses – may be considered to be the female type which Carl Jung designated the *Hetaera* or Courtesan; many of them beauties who have looked to artistic rather than biological fulfilment. These women seem to be based on the model of Daphne, who despite her period as an aristocratic brood mare, later showed herself to be the bohemian courtesan whose lovers Alexander often refers to, somewhat scornfully, as 'her clientele'.

The psychological arguments for Alexander's polygyny have a greater force than the purely biological. The sexual frustration of his early adulthood, while contemporary with the highly publicized sexual successes of his parents and his powerful rejections by women during those years, have left him with an angry determination to prove himself desirable. The evidence, however, appears to be pointing in the other direction.

Even in his heyday as a Deb's Delight, his sexual aspirations lacked fulfilment. However, if women began to seem fickle and promiscuous, this was his personal experience. With his sexually capricious mother as the model of woman deep in his unconscious, he had been selecting the same type and seeing this promiscuous model in each woman. Evidently, with this seductive image of his elusive mother before him, he was selecting women who enjoyed sex, had no fear of it even in those pre-pill 1950s and who consequently had plenty of experience but who were also less likely to be faithful. There must have been an abundance of virgins from which to choose a girl for that special relationship which would lead to soul-mate status and marriage, but even then Alexander was marked out as a man who might waste a girl's time, even get her pregnant and not marry her. The more ambitious Debs would have been keeping their knees crossed while waiting for Mr Right. Title or no title, Alexander was already known as a man who was unlikely to be Mr Right for a properly brought up gel and her family. In any case, Alexander was not attracted to these girls. After his failed love experience with Davina, the potential soul-mate, he was going after the Daphne model of woman who wanted sexual fun as much as he did himself. It has to be said that the theory of polygyny does not appear to work in practise. The women are viciously jealous of each other and waste no time in murmuring calumnies about their rivals when they find themselves alone with Alexander. There is also open warfare, developing into full-scale cat-fights at times, with blood being drawn. Alexander is not only the cause of this jealousy. He is also ferociously jealous of any woman who starts a relationship with him. He is hugely jealous of her other relationships. This even applies to ex-wifelets. In theory he accepts that the wifelets may have as many 'hublets' as they wish; but in practice he does not want to know about other men in the lives of the women who become his wifelets, even after the relationship has cooled.

'I don't want to know about other men,' he tells me. 'I don't want to meet those others. I am thinking of particular boyfriends of wifelets.' It is another example of Alexander's sense of inferiority: his insecurity. 'When I was a young man,' he says, 'I used to worry about previous boyfriends a lot.' Why would one care about people who were in the past? 'Yes,' he insists, 'it has disconcerted me, and I mean in the period when I was trying to get a good degree at Oxford that a girlfriend had been with one who got a Double-First. It set standards that I wasn't going to live up to and I just felt uncomfortable.'

Alexander can think of only one husband of a wifelet today whom he is happy to meet. 'He's got a restaurant, and I've been invited,' he states cheerfully.

Alexander's relationships with his two brothers, Christopher and Valentine also involved a sexual rivalry. Based on the model of Daphne, the brothers were often attracted to the same girl, and his brothers chased Alexander's women

'That I regarded as something one didn't do,' he admits, 'trying to court any of my brother's girlfriends, but they didn't always have that line and this often led to some abuse.' There was the question of Davina, who in the 1950s had flirted with Christopher. If Alexander had satisfied himself during our conversation that Davina had not been emotionally or sexually involved with Christopher, there had been a problem with other girls. There was one girlfriend of whom Sir Ian Rankin says 'she may have been the girlfriend of all three of them.' 'There came a problem,' Alexander tells me, 'but not involving Davina. It was immediately after Davina. Yes, there was a problem and it was immediately after Davina, and I used to be highly indignant and they characterized that as pomposity or something. So it was that sort of a situation. There was only one incident,' he adds, 'and others unsuccessful but still irritating enough that it happened.'

So the brothers were all attracted by the same sort of woman, those who might have a multiplicity of lovers, women in the mould of their mother Daphne. So if his brothers had made a play for his girlfriends, I ask Alexander, had he ever had a sexual relationship with a girlfriend of either of his brothers? Despite his earlier affirmation that he did not do that kind of thing, he suddenly becomes coy and giggles quite a lot but does not give anything away. One wifelet from the 1960s tells me that she met Alexander's youngest brother Valentine through a boyfriend she had in Trinidad and that she came to the UK to be with him. Then she met Alexander, who pursued her with phone calls and invitations.

There are mysteries as well. There is, for instance, the matter of Christopher's lovechild by a woman who lived in Tangier. Alexander gets on very well with this half-nephew, who is also an artist and who has helped with the restoration of ceilings at Longleat House. Interestingly, and rather strangely, the mother named the boy Alexander. I ask Alexander about this coincidence. He laughs, denying that he is the real father. 'But I could tell you stranger things than that', he adds cryptically and will not be further drawn. In his third novel, *Pillars of the Establishment*, a semi-autobiographical story about the decline of an aristocratic family, Alexander writes uninhibitedly about the sexual goings-on within this 'fictional' family. Much of this is autobiographical exaggeration and quite a lot complete fiction. However, one part of the plot hinges on the wife of one of the brothers who becomes the mistress of the hero – whose character is based on Alexander – and also the mistress of the father who is based on Henry, Alexander's father. Alexander denies, with much laughter, that any of this is linked to a real woman. 'Anyway,' he adds, naming the chief suspect, 'she would sue me if I said any more about that.' No wonder Alexander is suspicious of the motives of any other man linked to women he considers his. There is also another factor. As a child, Alexander was the focus of rival women in the nursery. The most telling example is the long-running strife between Nanny Marks and a governess called Miss Vigers. Nanny Marks appears to have resented all the governesses because they took the children away from her as they became old enough to receive education. In *Pillars of the Establishment* much is made of this rivalry. There is one scene between the fictional Nanny Marks and a governess, in which the governess demands entry to the nursery and hammers on the door, throwing her weight against it. The nanny at a strategic moment opens the door and the governess falls flat on her face into the nursery. With examples of this kind going on, Alexander would have had an early training in female possessiveness and jealousy. He is certainly surrounded by the evidence of these traits in his present life and, to all appearances, seems to thrive on it. But then jealousy and competitive behaviour among a crowd of women, each of whom is vying with the others to be number one, gives a man a sense of being desirable. On the one hand, it is Alexander's fear of putting 'all his eggs in one basket'. On the other, it is his psychological analysis of the female mind. A man who knows that he has a rival for a woman's love may walk off the scene out of pride. Women seem rather less proud. Offer them a rival, and they try harder for the man's attention. Wifelets are made to feel all the more insecure because Alexander is continually and openly searching for a new woman. Every time a new female guest appears at Longleat, whatever her reason for being there, a tidal wave of gossip surges through the wifelet community on the estate. The current wifelets, usually two or three bitter rivals, close ranks momentarily against the newcomer. Their fear is that she might turn out to be the one who will finally ensnare Alexander permanently. There is, however, little chance of this. Alexander prefers the elusive, rather distant, almost phantom version of femininity represented by his flirty mother. She was not with him so much in his childhood. 'She wasn't with me that much,' Alexander concedes, smiling rather proudly, 'but Mummy was always around.' His constant need for yet more feminine conquests can be interpreted as a compulsion to seduce this wayward and unattainable female. At the same time, he has a determination to have his revenge on her and to punish her for her faithless behaviour with other men: behaviour which also turned Henry against Alexander by making him a confederate in betrayal. It is no wonder the wifelets feel that they are not perceived as individuals. They are very much individuals, however, and their behaviour towards Alexander and their interaction with each other shows their struggle to make him see them and desire them for themselves. Sadly, as soon as they convince him that they are not his phantom projection, he sidelines them and brings on another one to play the role. The woman Alexander wants is the fantasy image of his mother. What he seems to get is the replay of warring nannies and governesses from his nursery days. Let's take a closer look at life among the wifelets.

Chapter Four

Safety in Numbers Part II: Wifelets in Practice

How Alexander Finds His Wifelets

The scene is a London drinks party: one of those commercial events often held in a hotel, restaurant or nightclub. It could be for the launch of a book or a perfume, where champagne flows. Or it may be a more intimate gathering serving modest red and white wines at one of those small Mayfair art galleries, opening an exhibition of paintings. The setting varies. The cast changes little, since the lists of people attending these parties are now circulating freely among the several PR firms that organize these events. The stage is set; drinks and titbits on trays are being passed among the crowd by the catering staff. It is about one hour after the event has begun, and the guests are starting to look around for someone more interesting to talk to: a celeb perhaps, albeit off the B-list. Enter a tall figure wearing multicoloured velvet robes and a small, embroidered velvet pillbox hat. Hanging onto his arm proprietarily, a smiling woman gushes to everyone who approaches – and many approach. A group rapidly forms around the tall bearded figure. He laughs and jokes. They fawn and simper, gazing up at the laughing pink face with its frieze of grey curls, the roguish blue eyes. Most of these sycophantic individuals jostling with each other for a word with Lord Bath are women. All are hanging on his words. The middle-aged wifelet clings possessively to his velvet-clad arm and simpers, the very image of a sweetie pie. She flashes smiles at, and makes flattering remarks to a robust figure who turns out to be a White Russian aristocrat who has joined the fawning circle. Later she is heard telling the Russian prince that she is in fact much more aristocratic herself even than a Maharani. She is, of course, wandering far from the truth.

Pretensions of grandeur of this sort are a not infrequent development among those who share Lord Bath's bed.

Cameras flash. There will be plenty of pictures for the glossy free magazines. There may even, if the party is big enough, be pictures in the tabloid diaries. Pictures of the Marquess of Bath surrounded by popsies, the very image of a laughing seducer. So much for hype and glamour. So much for the egalitarianism of 21st-century England. So much for media promotion: fame, wealth and a title attract in a way that mere worth or talent or soul can never do. There seems to be no shortage of women entertaining the idea that they could be the next wifelet, perhaps even the next Marchioness of Bath. Among this bevy of party pretties, Alexander will possibly discover a new wifelet, but he himself never seems to be the one to make the first move. Parties of this sort are Alexander's main hunting ground; but he says that when he meets a woman who attracts him he waits for the signal that there may be interest there. Otherwise he does not press his case. He is, of course, naturally reticent in his pursuit of women, due to fear of rejection and to his gentlemanly nature and strict upbringing. Apparently he is not the man for the ferocious pounce. Alexander waits to be sure that he is welcome. 'If I meet someone, and she shows some interest,' he says, 'then I might send a nice letter and if there's no response, probably not pursue matters.'

When I tell him that two wifelets from the 1970s and early 1980s told me that he had pursued them constantly with letters and phone calls before they agreed to go out with him, he says he thinks that this is unlikely. Lucianne Camille is a tall, ebony-skinned Seychellois, an actress and singer under the name 'Ashanti,' a former mistress of Jimmy Mancham, the playboy ex-president of the Seychelles who was ousted in the 1970's. She is Number 43 in the wifelet gallery, her portrait dated 1982. 'I met Alexander at a party,' she tells me. 'He looked so untidy with his long hair and his sandals and strange clothes. I thought, "Who is this awful man?" And he kept on ringing me up, so in the end I agreed to go and have lunch with him.'

The lunch was not what Lucienne had expected from a peer of the realm, let alone one who was also a marquess. 'He invited me to his flat in Notting Hill Gate,' she recalls, her voice tinged with remembered horror. 'I was beautifully dressed in a white suit. I thought we were going out to a restaurant, but he was planning to give me lunch at the flat. It was awful, dirty and untidy and he was opening tins to make the lunch. I couldn't stand it and I said I was going, so in the end he took me out.' This opening of tins in a grubby kitchen is standard practice with Alexander when it comes to his women friends, and Lucianne did well to get him out to lunch even if it was only to the Windsor Castle, his neighbouring pub. Alexander rather naughtily enjoys playing the bohemian artist and has sneaking pleasure in making socially ambitious people accept his grungy artist's quarters before he exposes them to the glories of Longleat. For Lucianne, an invitation to Longleat for lunch followed, and it was not long before Alexander offered her the thatched, Beatrix Potter-style dream cottage which became her country residence. Lucianne, however, is used to being treated well and has a determination to make sure that she receives respect from men. Other wifelets may have been less sure of their market value.

Parties have been the best sources of girlfriends for Alexander ever since his early days as a Deb's Delight. In those early days there were plenty of invitations. On his return from his second period in Paris and his other travels, Alexander was about to enter his thirties; and by then, most of his old pals had found wives of their own class status and started families. Their social lives revolved around cocktails and dinner parties with other young couples. Alexander shared the experience of many a thirty-something today whose contemporaries have married of being made to feel something of a reject. The barefoot Bath was odd-man-out in more ways than one. He was single, he was an artist, and his years of rebellion had made him rather less acceptable to his own class. His life in Longleat was that of a recluse, and he no longer had the option of staying with his sister in London while going out in search of fun and frolics. Something had to be done to open up his access to wider social circles. Socializing is something Alexander decided to force himself into in the early 1960s. Buying the Notting Hill duplex was, he says, a step in the direction of balance, since his life was otherwise becoming too isolated. The 1960s seem to have been one long party, so there were plenty of opportunities to begin making new social contacts. Thus he began to be a well-know bohemian figure about town, still very shy but inviting people he met at London parties to join weekend house parties at Longleat. He was not, he says, a central figure in the social scene like Lord Lichfield or Anthony Armstrong Jones, but he was making a mark although still very much the recluse at heart. Longleat remains his haven and he has a community of friends there or – as he likes to call them – his family of wifelets tenanting the estate cottages. Many wifelets only use their cottages at weekends, and so Alexander makes the trip to London for three of four days weekly and packs in some social life, accepting invitations to parties very selectively and trawling them for new recruits. The quality of the parties to which he is invited has changed, however. He is now very rarely invited to parties given by his Eton and Oxford contemporaries. He now attends art-gallery openings, book launches and commercial parties given by PR people and other media-oriented types who attract publicity-hungry guests. The guests are not there for sparkling conversation. Most of these people are cruising the parties looking for business connections. Some, like Alexander, are keeping their eyes peeled for sexual partners.

Because of his own media profile and his current sugar-daddy looks, Alexander is a natural target for women who want to bask in reflected celebrity. He is seen as a door-opener by showbiz or social wannabes; and, of course, he is also the Marquess of Bath, one of those rare aristocrats to appear in public outside their own social circles. Hence the mad throng of groupies who fawn around him at the London parties he attends. London parties are not the only source of new recruits. He is open to approaches from women through other sources. Margarita, the blonde artist who became a wifelet in 2000, met Alexander as a result of her agent getting in touch with him to see if he would like to see her work. Alexander invited Margarita and her agent down to lunch at Longleat, and things moved on from there. If completely unknown women want to get in touch with him, he also recommends that they write a nice letter to him. Some have done so and ultimately have clicked. Some have received the customary invitation to lunch at Longleat or Notting Hill and have failed to interest Alexander or equally have failed to respond to Alexander in person, so he has refrained from further pursuit. Once in the early days, his pal Sir Ian Rankin remembers the time that there was a weekend house party at Longleat to which Alexander had invited a woman whom he had contacted via a computer-dating service. 'She was quite attractive,' Sir Ian recalls, 'but she had the most appalling legs. Alex ignored her completely, and eventually another member of the house party scooped her up and went off with her.' More recently Alexander met a beautiful blonde topless model during a photo shoot for a tabloid newspaper. The photo was of Alexander in his full regalia with a naked beauty on either side of him. He was very attracted to one of the girls. 'I said "Perhaps we'll meet again?"' he tells me, 'and she said, rather raunchily, "Oh I'm sure we will."'

Alexander laughs in a delighted way, his cheeks growing pinker, his blue eyes rolling around. He did not, in fact, pursue this girl and the awaited opportunity to bump into her has not arisen.

Some female guests to Longleat bring a woman friend. This is encouraged. It can be a potential source of additional bed partners or future wifelets. 'I shouldn't be procuring women for him, really,' complains Sadie, one recent wifelet who has brought other women to Longleat. Nevertheless she brought two attractive women down with her, one of whom she had only just picked up at a party the night before: the girl had not even been to bed. In doing this, Sadie was really keeping herself ahead of the game with rival wifelets by attempting to provide her own team. She was very keen to have the two women sleep in the dressing-room extension to Alexander's penthouse living room. The dressing room is not in fact a dressing room at all since there are no cupboards or mirrors; it is a very small rectangular room with a narrow bed, and beyond it is another room, similarly small, with two bunk beds for visiting children. Sadie was very keen that her two female companions should sleep in these rooms, transparently in the light of her later comments about procuring women for Alexander, so that they could be lured into the big bed. Alexander tells me that he is rather fond of having a woman on either side of him in bed. 'I think four is the most one can do justice to at any one time,' he says, giggling and rolling his eyes skywards, which he tends to do when thinking about pleasure: a habit which makes him look like a painting of Zeus on one of his jolly days. Is it that one woman alone is an emotional threat? One woman alone might expect to be treated as *the* one, might behave as if she were, in fact, the one and only, might expect or demand an emotional commitment, a declaration of love. Two women together naturally keep up that sense of competition for Alexander's attention which he finds so essential. The way he organizes his weekends, two partners is often the available number. Sadie evidently preferred that they were her own choice rather than Alexander's selection from among her rival wifelets. 'Alexander says he likes *A*,' she tells me. But *A* has confided in me that she had no interest in sharing Alexander's bed with or without Sadie. *A* had in fact slept in the dressing room, while the other woman opted to sleep downstairs in one of the guest suites, several corridors and staircases away from the penthouse. Of course the whole thing may have been a figment of Sadie's evidently overactive imagination, for Alexander in his gentlemanly way made no serious play for either of the two new women. An insight into Alexander's seduction techniques comes from a woman guest who was introduced by a wifelet for a Longleat weekend. She says that she found herself momentarily alone in the big penthouse living room. Alexander appeared and trotted towards her. 'Mmm,' he said, beaming rather like a cuddly nursery teddy. He pouted his lips and gave her a big smackeroo kiss that was more baby boy than adult male seducer. 'Mmm' he said again. The woman was unsure of his intentions but thought that he was making a play for her. However, Alexander's approach was so huggy and asexual that he might simply have been expressing momentary affection. But then Alexander is completely the upper-class Englishman in his inability to seduce a woman's attention with smooth compliments or significant glances. No wonder he waits for the women to make the move. This may make Alexander seem rather passive. He has always been extremely shy, however. There is the ever-present fear of being rejected, and the fact that the dominant side of his personality is the reclusive introvert. His natural inclination is to stay at home alone and continue with his painting and writing rather than go out and meet people. I have even seen him entertain a group of guests in the penthouse for the weekend, breaking away from his desk only for lunch and dinner and then going back to his computer while some guests sat around watching a pornographic film on TV and others lounged on the bed chatting. Alexander drinks a great deal of wine during these weekends. He tipples his favourite pink plonk, served in a tooth mug-style glass or a beer tankard, virtually all day and through the evening. This means that often by dinner or certainly after dinner he is lurching a bit: a fact which may not bode so well for his lovemaking techniques.

He has, in fact, always had to drink plenty in order to overcome his overwhelming shyness. It was one of the problems when he was briefly a Deb's Delight. 'It was anaesthesia more than anything,' he says. 'I don't think I drank any more than my contemporaries. In fact, there were quite a number of my army colleagues who drank more than I did.' However, a wifelet of the 1970s told me that Alexander's drinking was a problem for her. And several of his friends have remarked that his doctors have suggested that he cut down, for Alexander is now a diabetic and follows a sugar-free diet. This is one reason why sometimes he has to skip the pudding at Sunday lunch, unless it has been made without sugar. Usually, however he turns to the copious cheeseboard and fruit bowl. Meanwhile he is invariably a most genial host who keeps up a continuous flow of conversation with the guests at his end of the table. Without his wine he might be less bubbly, perhaps even reticent. At one time Alexander's shyness was so acute that he spoke with a marked stutter. His friends from Eton and Oxford remember this well. Even now there can be a sudden difficulty in expressing himself where he seems unable to form the words that he wants. People might put this down to the drinking, but it is actually the drinking which helps him to overcome his evident tendency to stutter. This stutter was linked to Alexander's difficulties with his father in his teens, and it is when he speaks of the unjust ways in which his father treated him at various times that the stutter becomes most marked. Then Alexander also loses his self-control, grows red in the face and shouts in imitation of his father and in re-enactment of the rage and frustration he felt at his inability to deal rationally with Henry.

His relations with men generally have suffered from Alexander's bad memories of his relationship with Henry and then his brother Christopher, whom Henry favoured against Alexander's birthright interests. For this reason, and because of Alexander's fear that his women will cheat on him, there are few male guests at Longleat. Paradoxically, Henry's painful experience of discovering that he was being cuckolded by Daphne has stayed with Alexander and marked him. Thus the last thing Alexander wants at Longleat is any other male who would provide a second or third focus and possibly lure wifelets or wifelet prospects away from him; Alexander's house parties are not put together with an eye to providing spare men even as company for women who are not wifelets. Alexander wants the women all to himself, whether his contact with them is sexual or not. The weekend guests are all women. Some may bring a son, with whom Alexander might be glad to play chess; but usually Saturday-night dinner consists of Alexander sitting at the head of his table with perhaps four or five female guests including current and ex-wifelets and female friends. Alexander tells me he cannot tolerate other men in the lives of his women. He does not want to know about them for he has always felt inadequate in competition with other men. The few male guests at Longleat are usually there as part of a couple for Sunday lunch. Sometimes there are husbands of early wifelets but only at Sunday lunch, never for Saturday dinner. Sometimes there are men there for business reasons related to Alexander's various projects for Longleat. There is never a single man, or any man who could be seen as a sexual threat to Alexander's rule over his harem of female admirers. Even when men are present at the meal, Alexander is of course the centre of attention, with a woman seated on either side of his chair at the head of the table. These weekends give the public view of Alexander as a bacchanalian party-giver and bluebeard. But this image is far from the truth of the lonely artist who plays host almost as a duty to himself. Rather like people who routinely take exercise after a bad medical prognosis, Alexander gives himself his weekly dose of house-party fun. Like everything else in Alexander's life, these have been organized like a military exercise. These weekend house parties are in fact strictly curtailed into just over twenty-four hours from Saturday lunch to Sunday after lunch. It is very unusual for anyone to stay on for Sunday night or to arrive on Friday. Alexander wants it that way; he likes his solitude. Even the wifelets are only invited for the Saturday night, although they might occasionally remain until Monday. There are a number of them in the cottages, but many of these also return to London after the weekend. A few have made their lives on the Longleat Estate, but they are seldom seen at Longleat House since they have moved into the outermost orbit of the extended family, a few having married.

It's a clockwork routine, but Alexander knows what is good for him. His London social life generates publicity for Longleat by keeping him in the social columns. He meets diarists and also gets his photograph taken with attractive women.

This has the added advantage of making him seem always in demand with the girls. It makes him appear very attractive. If all these women are throwing themselves at him, others may assume there must be something worth running after. On the principle that one attracts more of what one is seen to have, this strategy keeps up the flow of wifelet candidates. Weekends at Longleat are the carrot which then attracts people to him and keeps them around. Longleat is the major bait which he uses to hook his women. The weekends – with the possibilities of meeting other, well-connected, people – are the introduction. Cottages are the next phase. This is how Alexander has built up a legend. It is rumoured, for instance, that he is a wonderful lover and irresistible to women. This may indeed explain the jealousy and infighting which goes on between the wifelets. But then what kind of women are these wifelets?

Is There a Wifelet Type?

During the latter part of his second period in Paris there was a change in the women whom Alexander bedded. There were few, only one in four years, except for a couple in England, until he met Anna Gayermarthy, who would eventually become his wife. Soon after their meeting, he was living with her in his studio near the Luxembourg Gardens. A Hungarian with divorced parents and a big element of mystery which Alexander says he has not sorted out even yet, Anna was a girl with masses of chutzpah and bags of ambition. She was also, like Alexander, a rebel of sorts. She was certainly not a debutante. It was not until the 1960s, however, that the real change in Alexander's women manifested. He was back in England and now installed in his new apartment at Notting Hill Gate. He was once again a frequent subject of gossip in the newspaper diaries. There was much speculation as to whom he might marry. While he was still only a humble viscount, everyone knew that he would be the next Marquess of Bath and that he would in time need to produce an heir of his own. The portraits in the wifelet gallery start to reflect this qualitative change in 1966 when a girl from Ceylon (as it was then known) named Tanya Brassey (formerly Duckworth) appears. This wifelet has earned a slightly more prominent place in history due to the fact that Alexander proclaimed her his 'anti-wife'.

This was in 1966, and the pair went through a so called 'deistic-humanistic anti-wedding' and then lived together for a spell in Alexander's maisonette in Notting Hill and his wing of Longleat. How the anti-marriage differed from any other slightly weird 1960s fake marriage one cannot tell. It was of course simpler to get out of than a legally binding marriage, but it is doubtful if under the present state of the law, Alexander would be willing to risk any claims that could be brought to court by a common-law wife. A female friend of Alexander's recently overheard a wifelet making threats to Alexander to bring a legal action against him on just that basis. That may be a very good reason for remaining officially married. Tanya's relationship with Alexander was stormy. 'She used to throw herself at me, scratching and biting,' he recalls Eventually, according to Sir James Spooner, one of Alexander's Oxford pals, when the relationship broke up Tanya determined to become a celebrity in her own right. She headed for Rome to take a film test, and full of confidence that the producers would foot the bill, she booked herself into one of Rome's top hotels. Alas, the screen test was a flop, no one was willing to pick up the hotel bill, and Tanya, with no money and no job and no place to go, in desperation threw herself out of her bedroom window. The story ends happily for she broke her fall on some bushes and when Alexander heard about the tragic turn of events he very kindly offered her a cottage on the estate. She still lives there. From this period Alexander was being seen around town with a variety of women. Some were artists, actresses, or others on the fringes of the showbiz world, seldom actually really in it. There was, however, no obvious physical type either then or later.

Davina's resemblance to Daphne was more in facial structure than in build, but they were not as similar as Alexander has depicted them. The likeness was truer in other qualities, of personality and psychology, and of artistic talents which both have displayed. Both these women were brunettes, but Alexander has told me his ideal physical type is the archetypal full-breasted, longhaired blonde. From time to time he returns to this Eve image. Otherwise he is happy with any reasonably attractive woman who is prepared to fit into the wifelet picture and to accept being one of a number.

The physical types represented in the gallery of wifelet portraits runs the full range of colouring and racial origins. There are some nationalities that Alexander has not sampled as lovers but he has managed to include a wide enough selection to show that physical type is not the main criterion for wifelet status; nor does Alexander, as do many men of some vintage, run after younger and younger women. His wifelets, who have usually been a few years younger than himself, now range in age from thirties to fifties, and some are even older. Of course this means that many are not in the full flower of fertility since the peak for women is thought to be around the age of twenty-seven; but if there were to be any prospect of him siring his brood of infants, one would think that Alexander would want prime fertility as a qualification to become a wifelet. However, this does not seem to be a factor in his selection of bedmates. Although the wifelets have varied so much in physical appearance, they do have in common the fact that most are of Jung's *Hetaera* or Courtesan type rather than Earth Mothers, which would be best suited to polygyny's aim of producing a collective family. Could it be that Alexander's polygyny theory is just a front for philandering and nothing at all to do with producing babies? His friend Michael Croucher is sure that the hype which Alexander has given to his avowed refusal to live in a normal monogamous marriage is in fact a huge disinformation exercise to lead observers away from the truth. Part of that truth, already discussed here, is that Alexander is lonely but unable to trust himself in a monogamous partnership. Or that Alexander is himself of low fertility and that his trumpeting of seventy-plus female conquests in fifty years could, in terms of a normal sexual youth, all have been accomplished during some ten years before marriage. Alexander was a late developer sexually and the advantage of this is that, like late developers in other fields, he seems to have more staying power than those of his contemporaries, who gave their all in their youth. The seventy-plus wifelets are also well spaced, coming at the rate of one or two a year since 1952. It is not that Alexander has been in a fifty-year series of medium-term relationships since the age of twenty; many of the women he lists as wifelets and whose portraits hang in the gallery are no more than one night stands.

Many of his exes have not found husbands. It is also rare that Alexander has teamed up with a woman who has been married before her relationship with Alexander. When Alexander was in his twenties or thirties this might not have been remarkable, but now in his eighth decade, with new women coming into his life in their forties and fifties, it is notable that a number have been single all their lives. Alexander has been attracting women who prefer the idea of being a mistress to that of being a wife. Even then he has had to exercise powers of persuasion with many of those who wanted to have a continuing relationship with him. The idea of becoming one of a crowd does not at first seem attractive to any woman, especially to such a highly publicized crowd. Naturally, since he is married already and has no intention of divorcing, Alexander has not been looking for the marrying kind of woman. However, it is the marrying kind who usually wants children. Thus Alexander seems to have been shooting himself in the foot all these years: the theory of polygyny is a nonstarter as far as breeding a family is concerned because the type of woman who will accept being one of several women in his life is not usually the type who wants to have a baby. There may have been an exception to this. A wifelet in her thirties expressed a willingness to have a baby with Alexander. This woman said that she had already had babies with two different men, both of whom had in the past provided her with money. Her main hope, she told me, was that Alexander, once the father of her child would also give her financial support. However, she was unable to get the financial agreement she sought; and, coincidentally or not, no pregnancy came about. In 2007, however, that wifelet, now of several years standing was reported to have announced that she was pregnant by Alexander. Alexander declined to comment, and no further newspaper reports on this subject have appeared.

Madonnas and Whores

Two women in his circle are thought to have been earning money as prostitutes. Would Alexander care if he knew? The truth may be that, despite his very good manners and upbringing, Alexander unconsciously sees all the women he beds as whores. Not that the majority of women he beds are whores. The cause of the divide exists in the mind of a man who wants a loving bond with a woman whom he respects but with whom he has either token sex or no sex and who will not respect the women with whom he frolics. This is the Madonna-Whore complex demonstrated in the behaviour of many men. This Madonna-Whore division is expressed by the wife-mistress situation. Many men see their ideal woman in terms of their mother, who is not generally seen as a sex object. They put the mother onto a pedestal and usually marry a girl in the mould of the mother: soon they put their wife onto a pedestal too. However, the man soon starts to need someone with whom he can play out his sexual fantasies. This is the mistress. With her, the man can perform all kinds of sexual gymnastics and act out all manner of psychological twists, or perversions. Meanwhile, once the children have been born he may have no sexual desire for the wife, or perhaps she turns away from sex and becomes a second mother figure, the 'Madonna'. The problem is that many of these men feel that their sexual feelings are ugly and shameful, and they feel that they cannot associate the expression of these shameful desires with a woman whom they respect. The mistress is often treated disrespectfully. Some of these men actually visit prostitutes in order to avoid being disrespectful to their Madonna-wife. They hide their lusts from their wives as they would from their mother. Others simply have girlfriends who are made to feel rather rejected when the married man expresses all his feelings of sexual guilt and dark desires with them and then goes back to his nice home to pat his children on the head and dine with his mother-figure wife.

A man does not have to be married to exhibit Madonna-Whore responses. Single men with a strong Madonna-Whore division in the way they see women often idolize their mothers but treat their girlfriends disrespectfully. Sometimes there is an element of punishment in the way such a man treats his sex partners. It is as if he is acting out his anger against women for cooperating with a side of himself that he rejects or of which he is ashamed. This may be the case if the man's real mother has disappointed or rejected him in some way. Such men invariably have several women in their lives and are sometimes almost deliberately cruel in the way that they play one off against the other. Most will not admit to being consciously cruel in any way, although others will express sadistic or sadomasochistic tendencies during sex. Some are in awe to the point of being afraid of the 'mother-wife' but aggressive and macho towards the girlfriends with whom they have complete freedom of sexual expression. This is the type of man who becomes difficult once he 'gets what he wants' because he no longer respects the woman who allows him to do something of which he is in fact ashamed. On the surface Alexander treats women courteously, but a lack of respect for the ones who share his bed is shown in other ways. The very public existence of several simultaneous mistresses is one way in which Alexander shows disrespect for his lovers. Alexander did not mean any harm by inventing the word 'wifelet', but there is something demeaning about it. 'If I started talking about concubines or mistresses, it might have been regarded by some as disparagement,' he says; but however cute the word 'wifelet' may seem, the disparagement is still built into the expression.

There is on the one hand a wife who has an official status and some privileges, and on the other the wifelets who are in fact mistresses and none of whom have status unless it is the glory of being known to go to bed with a marquess.

If one were to be designated 'the official mistress' as in former centuries in the royal courts of France, then there would be status, power and respect attached to the position. It is, however, humiliating to be treated as one of a crowd of also-rans. This could be one reason why Alexander's lovers and ex-lovers are so often at each other's throats. A mistress who is being discussed publicly as one of several may have good reason to feel upset and jealous when other women are constantly muscling in. The true intimacy of any man-woman bond depends either on complete privacy or on exclusivity. Whereas a mistress can accept a wife and vice-versa, it is very hard for a mistress – who is already seen as a lesser person in the man's life than a wife to whom he shows all the conventional public respects – to accept other mistresses, especially when the whole world seems to know about them. This is one reason why some wifelets have been quoted in newspaper articles over the years claiming that Alexander has told them that she is the special one whom he prefers to all the others.

One way of translating one's status from Whore to Madonna is to bear a child. Alexander's official wife of three decades was not, originally, a Madonna figure, although she may have developed into one since. She was a girlfriend for ten years of his life and for part of that time married to another man. She was in a way playing Alexander at his own game. During that time and after the marriage she is described in newspaper reports and features of the day as acting in soft-core porn films, which tends to make her seem more the sexual plaything than a wife on a pedestal. Once Alexander had invented his theory of polygyny, he decided that he had never wanted a Madonna-like wife. In any case, he shows his lack of respect for his legal wife by publicly parading his mistresses and by his constant assertion that he only married in order to legitimize the heir to the estate. However, Alexander has confessed to having once wanted the archetypal monogamous wife. 'When I was a boy,' he wrote in 2000, 'I certainly imagined that one day I would make a faithful husband and that I would find myself an adoring wife to love and to cherish for the rest of my days.' That dream, however, came packaged with some other notions, notably the idea of the virgin bride. 'I suppose one thought one was taking second-hand goods if one married someone who wasn't a virgin,' Alexander tells me, 'and that led to a sort of macho idea that it would make one a second-class male.' He says that he gradually changed his expectations of marrying a virgin. It seems that this early teaching – which, like so many of Alexander's beliefs, is like an iceberg, mostly hidden below the water – has not been melted down by the heat of his anger. Deep down Alexander is still disappointed that he never found the woman he could cherish for the rest of his life; and his treatment of women also contains the seeds of his early belief that sexually-experienced women are second-class partners. In order to find the wife whom he could cherish and adore for life, Alexander would have needed to have known a model of this kind of woman during his upbringing. At first glance, Alexander seems not to have had a childhood Madonna-figure on whom to pin his highest aspirations of the female sex. His mother does not fit the criteria. Indeed, in his novel *Pillars of the Establishment* he cast the fictional mother as the whore and brothel-keeper.

It is the Whore-image which he applies to the woman he beds. Many of the wifelets start to behave as if they are acting out the role cast for them by Alexander, as if they have ceased to be in control of themselves and have become puppets which can be psychologically manipulated. The reason for this lies deep in Alexander's mind, in a place so secret that even he can deny its existence. I ask Alexander whether he thought he might perceive women according to Madonna-Whore imagery. 'The wifelets are whores,' he says and chuckles, then, thinking better of this remark, goes on: 'No. I've not got that divide.' Since his mother does not represent a Madonna-figure, however, and since he has described her as having a number of lovers, perhaps the only figure who could represent this idealized image is his idolized Nanny Marks.

'No,' says Alexander again. 'Nanny I've never thought of at all sexually.' Alexander may not have realized that it this is very much a part of the Madonna-Whore divide that the Madonna-figure is nonsexual and remains untouchable in that sense even while she is idolized, or rather *because* she is idolized. Alexander has shown that he idolized his Nanny Marks. He even wrote a song to her whose lyrics show how much he has valued her presence in his life. When I asked him to sing one of his songs to me, he sang this song to Nanny Marks, accompanying himself on the guitar. He did so with evident emotion, tears in his eyes.

He also gave her a prominent role in *Pillars of the Establishment*, where he created a device – the Nanny Marks tapes – to tell some of the story of the disintegration of an aristocratic family, a story with many characters based not a million miles away from members of his own family. There are two sons: Bruce, the religious prude who thinks of going into a monastery, and Sebastian, the licentious free-lover. Alexander says that each represents different sides of his own personality in exaggerated form. Other characters are drawn partly from life and partly from the fusion of the characters of more than one real person. Nanny Marks is there under her own name as a commentator on the family's affairs. At the end of this book, Sebastian – the wayward son based on Alexander's libidinous self-image and who has several mistresses and a brood of children living with him in a collective family such as Alexander would like in his own life – writes a passionate letter to Nanny Marks. In it Sebastian apologizes for his neglect of her after all her devotion to him and his brother.

'Dear old Nan,' the letter begins. 'If there is any justice in this world, the time will come when they will raise a statue to you. Not to yourself, because you wouldn't really like that. You would only ever accept other people's admiration if it was in some way linked to all of us. But they could erect a statue to all that you stood for, portraying you as the symbol of a life's self-sacrifice to children you didn't even bear.' This is quite the portrait of a Madonna-figure, pedestal and all. 'With all the love which you so much deserve,' the letter ends, 'and which I am not worthy of offering.' Sebastian's self-abasement in this letter offers an insight into a man's conviction of his own unworthiness to offer love to the Madonna-figure: this is in direct contrast to his libidinous lifestyle with his group of mistresses, none of whom he honours or respects with the special attention or love which would be normal to the husband of a monogamous wife. The sentiment is certainly in keeping with the idea of the untouchable Madonna, far above the unworthy carnality of his life with his 'second-hand' sexual partners who are collaborators with him in the playing out of his 'shameful' desires.

I ask Alexander about this letter. 'Yes', he says intensely. 'I was pouring out my heart. The rest of the book was fiction but that letter was absolutely genuinely felt and expressed.'

So are there any Madonna-figures in Alexander's life today? Alexander has a number of female friends who are not wifelets and who remain outside the circle of his sexual play. They join the weekend house parties but never go to Alexander's bed, nor would they dream of doing so. Many of these are quite high-powered women whom he loves to introduce to each other as one powerful woman to another. Are these then the Madonna-figures in his life? Alexander seems momentarily confused. 'I'm actually thinking that though you're saying the whores, meaning sexy ladies, the sexy lady might be one of my Madonnas,' he says. 'I think there can be the lovely, not necessarily approachable, more platonic friend, who fits this idea.' This, of course, is the whole principle of the Madonna-Whore separation in the mind of a man who has an irreproachable nonsexual female model from his youth. Usually this model is the mother. However, Alexander's mother was the courtesan in his eyes, the flighty and desirable mother who had strange men in her bedroom; hence his sardonic use of the term 'her American clientele' to describe the US military officers from the Yoeville base who were among her wartime lovers. This does not mean that Alexander's mother was a whore, such as someone who was paid for her favours. Nor does it mean that the wifelets are whores since they evidently get very little apart from weekends at Longleat in return for their association with Alexander. The Whore-figure is simply in Alexander's mind: and in his eyes, the description therefore applies to any woman who goes to bed with him. It is the model of his sexy, sexually-active mother which awakens his sexual appetites and which sends him searching for the opportunity to seduce that elusive, long lost, almost mythological female phantom. Yet this elusive female phantom does not command his respect. When Alexander speaks of his mother's sexual exploits it is with a derogatory note. Anger underlies his words and tone of voice. Anger at the way she embraced so many lovers and yet rejected Alexander and his father. Anger at her for the pain she caused them both and is still causing Alexander for turning away from him, for making him feel that his love for her was somehow a poor second-rate thing, unworthy to be offered, because it was so lightly and repeatedly discarded. Anger which drives Alexander to go on searching for conquests, looking always to seduce and gain submission of that elusive phantom, who will ultimately admit that she loves him, and then rejecting her as he unmasks her and finds out that she is not really the 'one' after all. At the same time, he is very subtly punishing the women who accept the role of wifelet by forcing them to compete with other women for his love, just as Daphne made Alexander compete with her lovers for just a little piece of her rather lightly-given love. Revenge would be sweet, but it is always just out of reach. Alexander seems doomed to keep on searching for his phantom, like a character from a Wagnerian opera. Meanwhile the Madonna remains inviolable in his heart, the only possible recipient for his unworthy love.

Wifelets and the Bath Wallet: Cry, Baby, Cry

In contrast with the career women who form his Madonna-cohort, quite a number of the women whom Alexander attracts as sexual partners are desperately in search of a male sponsor. Many appear to have no job or any form of livelihood which gives them financial security. They are, it seems, looking to Alexander to provide for them. One way or another, these women seem to be hoping that becoming a wifelet of the Marquess of Bath will help them financially. There are wifelets who hope to become the next Lady Bath. Little do they know what they are up against. Alexander has no intention of jumping from the frying pan into the fire. Besides, Lady Bath is something of a dragon at the gate to prevent wifelets from making excessive demands, either financially or emotionally. Alexander does not give money to his women. He is kindly and sometimes helps when he is asked. But that depends on what he is asked. One thing is certain. Alexander does not pay rent for wifelet apartments in London – rather the reverse, since wifelets who have cottages actually pay rent to the Longleat Estate: there are no grace-and-favour freebies. He does not give his credit card for shopping sprees, nor does he back business ventures with cash unless they are copper-bottomed. Linda is one who, having little means of support at the time of her ascendancy with Alexander, was hoping that he would fund her in a venture. She also seemed to believe that if she were to have a baby with Alexander, her ship would come in. The first step, however, was to get Alexander to pay her train ticket from London and her taxi fare from Warminster. The drive from Warminster to Longleat is a fair step along winding roads and costs about £15. Alexander is no easy touch. The train fare to Longleat is around £30 return depending on the days of travel. He may pay it on occasion but not as a rule. He is, after all, providing his house for a fascinating weekend with full board and unlimited wine! Guests have to pay for their own transport. Trains are usually met by the butler and guests driven to Longleat, but there may be need of a taxi if the train is too late for the staff driver to meet it.

Linda, whose arrival times were notoriously unreliable, had arrived late one evening when there were other guests in the drawing room and asked Alexander to pay her taxi fare from Warminster. Like many of the wifelets, Linda had no job and was often short of money. She had, in fact, expressed a hope that Alexander might donate funds to back her in a business venture. Alexander says he does help wifelets under certain circumstances, but he does not want to reveal what those are in case he is rushed with demands for money. He was not, for instance, intending to provide financial backing for Linda's project but told me that he had said that she could use Longleat for her event, provided she did all the work of organizing it, and also found her own financial backers. However, as far as taxi money went that night, she was unsuccessful. According to another guest that weekend, Linda arrived very late and demanded that Alexander give her cash to pay the taxi driver. Evidently, he refused and Linda then began to shout. 'You bastard!' she apparently screamed among other things. 'I'm supposed to be having your child!' Alexander was unable to calm her, and eventually sent for the Longleat House security guards, who marched her out. As to the probability of Linda having Alexander's child, the chances seem slim as she had told me and also another woman friend of Alexander's that she might, for medical reasons, have difficulty conceiving. Other wifelets – Sadie, for one – have told me that they have been hopeful of having the rent on their London flats paid by Alexander, but then Alexander has never even paid for the flat his wife occupies in Paris. It is probable that he cannot afford to pay a woman's rent. On the other hand he has had some disappointing experiences.

'I have been disappointed,' he says, 'having given money in the hope that a relationship might go in a particular direction and it hasn't.'

Naturally he would be cautious since he would be wide open to the guiles of females on the make. He would, of course, pay the expenses of any children that were born. But he would also wish to take the children and their education under his control.

Linda was interested by the notion of producing a baby for Alexander to nurture. But she was concerned that, while he might be prepared to pay expenses for the children, he would still not be willing to support the mother. Alexander says he expects the state to support his offspring's mothers. It's all part of the polygyny idea. Quite a number of the wifelets have been or are receiving state benefits already, so not much would change, since Alexander's idea is that he would take charge of the child and pay for its upkeep. Hence, quite a lot of the attraction of becoming a Bath broodmare in order to provide a meal ticket for life is diminished. Many wifelets might prefer not to have children under these circumstances. Alexander thinks their reluctance is because they would only agree to have children if they were to be married to him. He thinks the existence of Lady Bath and his two legitimate children might be off-putting. So persuading women to accept polygyny has not been as easy as it seemed at the dawn of this brave new idea. There is more than enough evidence to suggest that wifelets pay lip service to their acceptance of being one of a number who shares Alexander's affections only while biding their time for better things. They might be one of a number to begin with, but some have hoped – and have even voiced that hope to me – that after some work with their womanly wiles they might even become the soul-mate to end all soul-mates.

Conspiratorial Cottagers: Tales from Bluebeard's Domain

None of Alexander's wifelets actually live with him at Longleat House. The current ones stay over Saturday night in his vast penthouse suite, sleeping with him in the double bed in the curtained alcove off the open-plan living room. There are other wifelets – generally not sexually active with Alexander any longer and a few who have married – who continue to have cottages on the estate. These cottages vary from thatched white-walled nests set amongst trees to rather more modern boxes. The cottages are well spaced out, but these former wifelets, many who have occupied their cottages for twenty to thirty years, know each other well enough. Some are on friendly terms, while others detest each other and are not on speaking terms. Whether talking or not, they are not quite the extended family that Alexander originally planned. Mostly no longer fertile and certainly no longer bed -mates, the longstanding ones are simply taking up space that could be allocated to child-bearers if some should come along.

There is also a snag for the wifelets occupying the cottages as, in addition to paying rent to the estate, they also have to bear the expense of any repairs and decorations that become necessary. Some of the cottages are in poor condition and require serious expenditure before they can be lived in. Besides, the best ones have been allocated years ago. There is also a certain amount of rivalry over the cottages. Lucienne Camille spoke of being afraid that another wifelet might demand her lovely thatched cottage and that she would lose it even after spending money on it. It seems that generally Alexander does not demand the return of cottage keys and has only done so once when Sylvana Henriques, a longstanding friend and former wifelet from the 1960s was asked, pleasantly enough, if she really wanted the cottage since she and her husband rarely seemed to use it. The idea of having his wifelets close by for sexual convenience or friendship does not work out quite as Alexander once imagined. It seems that the cottages, far from being cosy nests where Alexander can do the rounds on a randy night out, turn out to be consolation packages for wifelets who are being sidelined. Besides, Alexander is often in London from Monday to Friday and only at Longleat during weekends for which he imports new wifelets or likely candidates to share his Saturday-night bed. When he begins to weary of longstanding wifelets and wants to devote his personal bed space to newer arrivals, a cottage may be offered to the outgoing woman. This means that a wifelet who has been around for a year or so but who now lives in a cottage either at weekends or for longer periods can still be available for occasional sex if no one else is around or be invited to join a threesome or even a foursome or a fivesome. As time goes on and she passes from the bedroom altogether, she can still come to Sunday lunch, and one of the sights of Alexander's Sunday morning pre-lunch drinks sessions are the ancient ex-wifelets who drop in just to see who else is there, to inspect new wifelets or to stay for lunch around the big table in the colourful dining room. This is the 'Nest of Vipelets' scenario. Jealousy is rampant. Often a nasty atmosphere springs up as an ex-wifelet encounters a newer model. On one occasion Sylvana, a big buxom Caribbean woman with a huge belly, dropped in and gave Alexander a raunchy hug and a cackle as he lay on his daybed among the Sunday newspapers, surrounded by a mainly standing group of guests and wifelets. She would not be staying for lunch she told me in a strong Caribbean undertone from under the bill of her green baseball cap, 'because of that thing there.' She nodded her head towards Mariella and sent a poisonous glance towards the newer wifelet. That was in 1999. By 2000, although still living in her cottage on the estate, Mariella was sidelined. 'Mariella is no longer a wifelet,' Alexander tells me firmly. He also makes it clear that Mariella was never one of those 'significant' relationships, although, he adds that 'I like Mariella very much but I don't want to start making categories.' Mariella was, however, working with Alexander on his online memoir, being the one whose job it was to edit the final version and put it up on the Net. This activity has ceased in recent years due to pressure on Alexander from Lady Bath who objected to his *Strictly Private* memoirs being so publicly available. Several volumes were published also in book form but anyone hoping to see recollections of Alexander's more recent times will be disappointed.

Mariella has a cottage on the estate and is a frequent guest at Longleat dinners and lunches, the more so recently as, in spring 2000, claiming that she had been dumped by her local boyfriend, she was now turning up regularly on Saturday nights and Sunday lunchtimes to occupy pride of place at the wife's end of the table opposite Alexander and roll big eyes at him while her irrepressible black Labrador, Lola, cruised under the table goosing the guests. But she can be unpredictable. Once, after Sunday lunch, I was told by a guest who was there, that Mariella disappeared for three hours with the husband of an old female friend of Alexander's, causing consternation to the woman concerned. The disappearance was later found out to be something to do with a bicycle which needed repairing.

'I'm worried that she's up in the penthouse nosing through things she shouldn't be looking at,' Alexander confides in me when Mariella is very late for Saturday-night dinner.

'What things?' I ask.

'My journals,' he says with a very worried frown. Apparently, no one is allowed to see the handwritten journals which contain the real unexpurgated Bath recollections. Alexander's method is to type up a sanitized version of these old journals himself. Mariella then gets the typed version to work on. Meanwhile, he tells me, she is always trying to sneak a look at the handwritten pages that contain the awful truth. 'She's terribly jealous,' he explains. Of course, the stacks of journals include hot, up-to-the-minute entries about what Alexander was doing last weekend and with whom. 'This,' he says, his manner agitated, 'would lead to all kinds of trouble. I do not want her nosing around up there by herself.'

Usually, one must know the codes to the digital locks on the stairway and the front door to get into Alexander's penthouse. Certain wifelets have those codes. Mariella naturally has them. She also sat through an interview which I did in the penthouse with Alexander on a Sunday evening in January 2000. Partly because she wanted to know what Alexander would say and partly because she suspected me of being some sort of threat to her position with Alexander, she was pretending to be watching TV while we talked over by the desk.

Alexander was clearly rattled and kept trying to get her to leave. She had already said she didn't want to give me an interview herself and didn't want to go on record but then demonstrated that she was listening to us by calling out an answer to one of my questions. 'I thought you didn't want to be interviewed, Miss,' I snapped.

Alexander chuckled. Mariella pouted at the TV screen. Soon after this, the TV programme that was her cover ended and Mariella left. Alexander heaved a sigh of relief. But before he could relax properly he wanted to wait to make sure Mariella did not make a pretext to return. 'Wait,' he said, suspiciously. 'She might be coming back.' It was surprising how tense and anxious he seemed. Only when he was quite sure that she had finally gone did he feel free to talk openly about things that he would prefer Mariella not to know about.

Alexander is a very secretive man, and his technique is to give parts of the story while keeping the other parts under wraps. It would never do for someone else, let alone someone with an emotional card to play, to have access to the full picture.

Mariella clearly feels very attached to Alexander. The previous summer, she tells me, at Alexander's villa in St Tropez, she had been sleeping in one of the

Alexander's father, Henry, 6th Marquess of Bath with Virginia, his second wife

Henry, 6th Marquess of Bath, outside Longleat

Henry, 6th Marquess of Bath with Marquis the Lion (E.S Henderson Collection)

Henry, 6th Marquess of Bath riding a Hippo

Alexander serenades his future wife Anna in his private drawing room at Longleat. One of his early murals is in the background.

Alexander with Anna in London in the 1970's

Alexander discusses his murals for Upper Cut, a new leisure centre in Forest Gate. 8th November 1966

Alexander in 1966, with Tania Duckworth, his anti-wife

Lord Bath at a party with Zandra Rhodes and Margarita, a fellow artist

Lord Bath addresses a guest at a London gallery party, a wifelet looks on centre

Alexander at Longleat House, shortly after becoming the 7th Marquess of Bath

guest rooms while Sadie slept with Alexander in his own bedroom. One night, overcome with loneliness, Mariella asked if she could sleep with Alexander, just alone with him. Over Sadie's objections, Alexander said she could. The rivalry between these two women goes back a little time. Catherine, a friend of Alexander's who had been persuaded by him to allow the relationship to become mildly sexual but is reluctant to become a fully fledged wifelet, tells a story of how Alexander, 'dumped Mariella brutally for Sadie'. 'Mariella was plump and happy and very much in love with Alexander,' Catherine says. 'She had gone with Alexander to a pagan wedding celebration nearby on the Longleat Estate.'

Sadie, a fairly new wifelet dating from April 1998, 'had been told about the party by Lucienne, and she turned up there. Shortly afterwards, Sadie persuaded Alexander to go back to the penthouse with her to bed. Mariella was devastated.'

This was a thoughtlessly cruel rejection and not typical of Alexander's methods. Alexander tells me that the usual way in which he sidelines a wifelet is to 'distance myself and become unavailable'. On this occasion he chose to act rather less tactfully and with no concern about hurting a woman who evidently loves him. Sadie was to have her comeuppance, however, for by the summer of 2000 she was also gradually being moved sideways in favour of two new wifelets. Ten years later, however, she remains on the wifelet list. Favourites come and go at Longleat as in a royal court. In the spring of 1999, Sadie was claiming that she and Alexander were in love and were planning a form of marriage ceremony. Having been involved with Alexander since the previous April, she felt totally threatened by other wifelets and friends of Alexander, especially Mariella and Catherine. She claimed Alexander "slept with his cleaners" at the Notting Hill maisonette. She also accused Mariella of stealing clothes that she had left at the maisonette. After a weekend at Longleat she claimed that a beautiful wrap had gone missing and accused Catherine, of whom she was irrationally jealous, of the theft. She was obsessed with getting publicity for herself and constantly rang newspaper columnists trying to get stories written about herself as the 'glamorous model' whom Alexander was now seeing. She was not, of course, a model. She was at first rather successful in getting a mention, but after a time the journalists began to think that she was not reliable and avoided dealing with her. Her period of being Alexander's preferred companion was eventually undermined when Linda came on the scene later in 1999. For a time, Linda and Sadie would keep Alexander company together.

One firsthand account of a three-in-a-bed scene from spring 2000 comes from Linda. She had up to that time, she said, refused to go the full distance in bed with Alexander on the grounds that he refuses to use a condom. Linda says that she was lying on one side of him at the Notting Hill flat while Sadie lay on the other. However, Sadie has told me that she does not like sex. Although she was at that time well into her forties, she also told me that she had never been in love. Evidently nothing much was happening with these two sexually reticent females other than hostility. Within a few weeks Sadie and Linda were no longer on speaking terms. Sadie is psychopathically jealous of any woman who meets Alexander and has been identified as dangerous and a liar by others of Alexander's circle who have seen her in action. She phoned Longleat one Saturday afternoon and upon being told by Alexander that I was sitting beside him interviewing him, she asked to speak to me and asked for my phone number at home. I reluctantly gave her the number. On the Monday morning, I groaned when she telephoned to relate me a stream of unpleasant tittle-tattle, to most of which I felt it would be unwise to rely. Naturally, she wanted to give me her views on the other wifelets. 'Catherine' she said nastily, 'is now a wifelet' and went on to say other less factually accurate things about Catherine and several others.

She had long ago declared Catherine to be her overriding pet hate, but then Sadie is someone who finds every other woman a threat and usually tries to limit their attraction by telling stories about them: hence the accusations to Alexander that these other women were stealing her things. Other guests at Longleat also came in for accusations of theft. Alexander began to show discomfort when one inquired about Sadie's well being. Naturally, she has told Alexander her stories about the others. Indeed when people started comparing notes of what she had said to them about each other, it seems that she had told many poisonous lies. Alexander tends not to want to be involved in difficulties between wifelets. 'I don't tend to find out what they are saying to each other or about each other,' he tells me. He may have the occasional glimpse when wifelet glares at wifelet across the table or makes a catty remark, but he prefers to ignore it if he can. As for the gossiping that goes on in the cottages, he is largely oblivious.

Both Linda and Sadie were offered and accepted cottages in 1999. Meanwhile, although Alexander was still continuing to share his bed with both of them, and both were serial guests at his St Tropez villa in July and August 2000, two fresh wifelets, Judy and Margarita, had begun to take their places in the big bed at Longleat.

More Tales From Bluebeard's Den

One Saturday night in June 2000, Margarita, a tall blonde artist originally from Denmark, accompanied Alexander to a charity dinner and ball in a tent on the lawn at Longleat. Meanwhile, that same evening, in Alexander's brightly-painted dining room, four women sat around the polished mahogany dining table in Alexander's absence, eating a dinner prepared and left on the sideboard by the new housekeeper. One of the women was that wistful ex-wifelet, Mariella, who recounted over and over again the tale we had heard before of how her boyfriend dumped her. One of the other women present was Catherine. She had brought a girlfriend with her, and they were sharing the rather lovely twin-bedded Dowager Suite on the ground floor.

It was a clear but dry weekend in early June. It had been a day of lemon-sharp sunlight and cold, dry winds. We and other guests had bravely eaten lunch at trestle tables in Alexander's private garden. Outside now, the night was bright with stars, but the air was as tart as frost. In Alexander's ground floor West Wing at Longleat House, the brightly muralled dining room was icy cold. We turned on the electric fire and tucked into a bottle of red wine we had found in place of the *vin de pays*. Our dinner was waiting on the hotplate, and we were alone. It was a Cinderella scene. Mariella sat in the place usually occupied by Alexander, and it was clearly painful for her to be sitting in the dining room in her jeans while Alexander had a ball-gowned Margarita on his arm at the charity ball. She hogged the conversation by talking endlessly about her ex-boyfriend, chewing over all angles of the story she had told before of the way in which he had broken up with her.

Sadie was also one of the topics at the Saturday all-girls dinner in Bluebeard's dining room that June. Alexander had told us that Sadie was joining us; but as she did not, the women speculated on the reasons for her non-appearance. Advance notice of Catherine's presence may have been one of them. But then Sadie was now aware that she was being sidelined and she also knew that Alexander intended to go to the ball with his new fancy, Margarita. Put more than one wifelet together and the topic of conversation is almost certain to focus on other wifelets. Catherine, having been around for several years as a friend before becoming (albeit briefly) a wifelet, had much to impart. She told us that one of the wifelets dating from the early 1980s was a dominatrix who whipped men as a profitable sideline. Does this mean Alexander favours the whiplash? No one admitted to knowing the answer. The women discussed this ex-wifelet for a few minutes. Then they moved on to another wifelet who claims to have been a model but who, Catherine said, was probably making a bit on the side selling sexual favours. She had seen this woman in the Hilton lobby having an argument with an Arab man about money. The bottle of respectable red wine ran out, and the wifelets surveyed the alternative with dismay. Alexander usually drinks rosé. However, when I had arrived before lunch that morning he was drinking white wine and what he offered me from the carafe on the sideboard was also white. Of pink and red there was no sign. For many years Alexander had been in the habit of bringing cheap and very young boxed wine back from Provence each September. It was now June.

'I've run out,' he had explained, somewhat embarrassed. 'The white is all that's left.' I had sipped politely then stopped. The wine was really terrible. Mercifully, when Catherine and her woman friend arrived they produced a respectable bottle of white wine, and Catherine insisted that we should open it at once. Naturally it did not last and indeed there were several more guests for lunch who drank the house plonk with no evident lack of interest. At dinner, however, the spring sun having failed to penetrate Longleat's thick stone walls – the house is always cold even at the height of summer – we were in need of some warming wine. Catherine complained that the house white was 'like horse urine', and certainly it seemed not to have kept well. Eventually, another bottle of red was found and it helped wash down the dinner and the conversation. Catherine informed us that she had noticed that bottles of wine brought by guests invariably disappeared before they could be opened and that she had seen a cupboard in the kitchen, which was 'absolutely full of bottles of assorted wine,' evidently brought by guests. She continued to complain that Alexander is mean and that he should at least serve his guests with the wine they had brought with them. She was no doubt overlooking the wholesome meals and the general open-house hospitality which Alexander offers his weekend guests. Besides, Alexander, while ostensibly the owner of Longleat, does not necessarily have oodles of cash to spend on entertaining others – or even himself, for that matter. He runs the flat in London and the villa in St Tropez without staff and has only a couple to look after him at Longleat. At London he attends parties to which he has abundant free invitations and to which he usually travels by bus. As he is over sixty-five, he holds a bus pass for travel in off-peak hours. Hence, Catherine – who had invited Alexander to go with her to an art gallery party – was horrified to discover that he would wait half an hour in the November rain for a bus rather than take a taxi home. She offered to pay for a taxi, but Alexander insisted on waiting in the rain in his long robes and open-toed sandals. 'Well, you see, love,' he had said in his gentle, slightly troubled way, 'I've got my bus pass.'

Sex, Lies and Voodoo

A surprising number of Alexander's former wifelets seem to have remained single and childless. Many of these women may have been picking men who, like Alexander, are not the marrying kind. Hence his women are mirror images of himself. However, just as Alexander has his lingering longing that a soul-mate might still gladden his life, some of the wifelets and ex-wifelets are evidently hoping to marry. Once they realize that Alexander has no intention of making himself available, they entertain hopes that their status as a Bath wifelet will bring them an eligible bachelor. There is some currency in being the mistress of an aristocrat. One glamorous wifelet of the 1980s, who sold her story about her wifelet lifestyle to the newspapers, is often seen to be desperately advertising her ambition to be married in the newspapers and on successive TV shows. This wifelet had lived in a cottage on the estate and has had much to say about Alexander's dislike of using condoms and about his preference for 'three-in-a-bed' sex. She also told of voodoo rites being conducted by other wifelets who lived in cottages on the estate. The object of the voodoo was to remove rivals for Alexander's attentions.

One of Sadie's constant refrains is that 'the black girls,' former wifelets living on the estate in cottages, were practising voodoo on her. Others have said that Sadie herself goes in for voodoo. There seems to be something about Longleat which attracts black magic, and dark rites of various sorts have been a part of the house's prehistory. Before the present palace was built, an ancient priory existed on the site; but this is said to have been destroyed by church orders even before Henry VIII began his dissolution of the monasteries. The reason was that the nuns were said to be going in for satanic orgies. More recently, Alexander included a black magic element in the plot of his first published novel, *The Carry Cot*. This is a semi-autobiographical tale about baby battering based on some events at Longleat when his daughter was very young. Alexander says that in reality the culprit of the baby bashing was not joining in Satanic rites but that, according to his butler at the time, he became aware that 'something of that sort was going on in the woods near the house.' Another wifelet who went to the newspapers is Jo-Jo Laine, a former wife of rock guitarist Denny Laine and a former model and singer. She claimed that some of the cottage-dwelling wifelets on the estate had used voodoo to bring about a miscarriage of the child she had conceived with Alexander. Alexander says, rather sadly, that the pregnancy was fallopian and had to be terminated because of the danger that it would kill the mother. Alas, Jo-Jo died at a London hospital in October 2006 at the age of fifty-three, following a fall at her former home, the 'House On Pooh Corner' where AA Milne was said to have written *Winnie the Pooh*.

Jo-Jo was one of Alexander's 'significant relationships'. His eyes still light up when he mentions her. Part of the attraction was Jo-Jo's own polyandrous nature. But then, the 'like attracts like' recipe for a tortured relationship may have been a catalyst for the passion that evidently developed between these two. Jo-Jo was different from the average run of wifelets. She already had two children from her previous marriage. Evidence of the closeness between these two in the 1980s exists in some of the photographs which were published in a tabloid newspaper of the two together at Longleat. In some of these, Jo-Jo was topless while Alexander was posed with his arm around her and a love-struck expression on his face. The pictures were taken by the newspaper and a three-page article went with them. In this, Jo-Jo claimed that she and Alexander were 'trying for another baby' but without results. Jo-Jo was clearly fertile, and no doubt a truly passionate physical relationship also caused hormone levels to rise, thus making conception more likely. Alexander says he 'would love to have had children with Jo-Jo, but she was impossible.' Jo-Jo eventually drifted away and returned to the US to have a baby with someone else. Alexander announced proudly to a Sunday lunch party that Jo-Jo was coming to visit. 'And,' he added jocularly, chuckling with a rosy glow of pleasure, 'she is now involved with someone from the Mafia. So she is a Mafia Moll, and I now have Mafia connections.'

Mariella is one wifelet who desperately longed to have a child: yet she did not conceive with Alexander. Linda said Alexander had told her of Mariella's desperation to have a child. Linda, however, said that she was not keen on the idea of having a child which might be handed over to Mariella. This does not seem to be likely since Alexander has always intended to keep charge of his infants himself with the aid of nannies. Jealous fears of this kind may be another reason why, over the years, many wifelets who could have given birth have not been producing babies. If Alexander passed his fertility test with flying colours, have any of the wifelets been tested? It seems not. This means that women can hold out the possibility of conceiving a child as bait to Alexander in order to obtain favours. Two recent wifelets, neither of whom seems capable of conceiving, have talked promisingly of becoming mothers. Both these women have also admitted to me that they have material needs which they hope Alexander will satisfy. In this respect, they may be no different from a suburban housewife. The offer of a cottage at low rent is some sort of security. Alexander, however, is running out of cottages. Alexander is no fool. He is perfectly aware that some women will try to use him. He is of course using them. As he has realized since the day he decided women were incapable of being faithful, he has followed the path of attracting them for pleasure rather than for love. Although Alexander knows and admits that he would have preferred a deep relationship, he has been unable to stand the heat of emotional strain or the exercise of give-and-take that such a relationship would demand. He has opted instead for the occasional spurt of flame from a 'more significant' relationship. For the rest, it is a case of sexual arousal, erotic gratification without emotional fulfilment or sentiment. There have been other women who might have offered a more serious relationship but who have been put off by Alexander's multiplicity of mistresses. Claire Gordon, who had been out with Alexander a few times in London, told me that she had assumed 'Alexander was my fella' and when she was invited to St Tropez during one summer she flew down. Alexander was supposed to be driving down to meet her, but when he arrived there were two other women with him and it was obvious, Claire Gordon said, 'they had been sleeping together on the way down.' From this point on she backed off. 'Claire Gordon was important,' Alexander confides in me. He lost an important relationship for the sake of playing his 'safety in numbers' game. Polygyny may be fine for some, but Alexander may be missing out on singularly real relationships for the sake of playmates he feels he can manipulate. The games he has been playing with women are not unlike chess, and Alexander is a longstanding chess player who loves to win. With women he may not be as successful as he is with chess, but he manages quite well to keep a few circling around him. The one thing he will not permit is the checkmate of his white queen, Lady Bath. If she went, so would the whole game because Alexander depends on the existence of a wife, remote but powerful, on the Longleat chessboard to keep the other pieces in their roles. He uses the wifelets against each other to keep the game in progress, playing on both sides of the board, it seems. 'It's all diplomacy,' he tells me.

Even the political side of the wifelet system is there for a calculated reason: to subvert the system of monogamous marriage that brought him his great disillusionment in youth and to provide a grand statement that he is pioneering a new social order. He is, after all, dedicated to his grand theory of polygyny which, if translated into a political statute, would cost the taxpayer dear. Mothers and babies on the state on a grand scale! Alexander does like the idea of translating polygyny into a way for society to follow. He has created a big lie of jolly lechery to hide the fact of his own deep isolation, loneliness and lack of that personal love. But he has other ways of ensuring that he feels desired and wanted by women. He has devised intriguing ways of distracting his attention from that deep-seated lack of self-confidence and its resultant feeling that he is unattractive to women and that he will be rejected for more successful men.

Longleat is that world apart, that 'Gormenghast' in which Alexander lived during the first decade of his life surrounded in his nursery by devoted women who fought with each other for the privilege of being the focus of his attention. It was an *Upstairs and Downstairs* existence reversed. Upstairs was the nursery and Alexander's baby world, presided over by Nanny Marks. Downstairs was the grownup universe where his parents passed their daytime hours and entertained. During this period his parents were remote, and Alexander and his two younger brothers would be washed and dressed to go downstairs to visit them once a day before bedtime. 'I was perfectly happy with nursery life,' he remembers. 'I did not particularly want to go downstairs.' He laughs. 'I remember once I didn't want to go, and Nanny was trying to get me to go down, and I remember my father standing at the bottom of the stairs shouting "*Come down here at once!*"'

The habit of being the centre of female attention was formed during his first decade, especially in the first five or six years. There is no doubt that Alexander still adores being the centre of a woman's attention and the more women the better. But it seems that most women, singly, do not have the talents or the skills to give him the sense of importance that this attention should give. He does not seem to demand that his wifelets have intellectual skills. Like many people who do not hear too well, Alexander tends to do the talking. The wifelets' role is physical. They do not, evidently, need to be ornamental, since many of the wifelets are not especially so; but they should be present, they should be sexual playthings, they should be focused on Alexander in company, and they should flatter him by showing jealousy (often to the point of being psychopathic) of other women who may be considered rivals for his attention. The jealousy factor is of paramount importance, and it seems at times that Alexander actively encourages the internecine strife which goes on between the wifelets. Such is his insecurity and his need for evidence that he is wanted by women that he turns an apparent blind eye to wifelet infighting meanwhile enjoying these battles for priority which go on whenever wifelets meets wifelet. It is time to take a closer look at some of the wifelets and the way they interact with each other and their ringmaster, the Seventh Marquess of Bath.

Chapter Five
A Nest of Vipelets

Serpents in Eden

As I step off the Air France *navette* from Nice onto the dock at St Tropez I hear a voice calling my name. Alexander towers over the other people on the sun-baked dock. His grey curls are held back from his sun-scorched forehead with a blue and yellow plaited headband. His crumpled turquoise and yellow plaid shirt hangs unevenly over baggy chinos. He stoops to give me a peck on the cheek, and I notice that he seems ill at ease. As I wait by the car for him to pay the parking fee, I wonder if it was simply an Englishman's reticence at giving a woman a kiss, however demure, even in France where people are always kissing each other in public. I have seen him go into a full screen clinch with a wifelet at Warminster station; but what is the etiquette of kissing, however formally, one's biographer? I do not have to puzzle for long. We begin the drive to Ramatuelle, where Alexander has his villa. 'So how are things?' I ask by way of small talk. 'Things have reached crisis point,' he replies gruffly.' His cheeks are pink, and his profile reveals strain. 'Oh?' I say, 'in what way?' There is a slight pause while Alexander seems to gulp a bit. 'Linda and Catherine have been at each other's throats,' he says. 'They are no longer speaking to each other.' 'Goodness,' I exclaim. 'What caused that?' 'It blew up while we were waiting for you yesterday evening,' he says, his voice gritty with tension. After my taxi had taken me to the wrong port in Nice, I had missed the previous night's last boat and by the time I had reached Alexander on his mobile he was already in St Tropez. Linda and Catherine, it seemed, had gone along for the ride.

'But what was the fight about?' I ask.

Alexander begins a fairly long explanation by his standards. There had been some insults exchanged, for no apparent reason, but also Catherine had brought her twelve-year-old nephew with her, and it appears that Linda had caused a division between Catherine and the boy and had seemed to be trying to wean him away from her. 'Well one thing is that Linda seems to be trying to turn Joe against Catherine. Catherine not surprisingly resents it.' Alexander says. He does not add something which I am told later, which is that the previous day there had been friends from London to lunch at the villa and that Linda caused a scene in front of them, attacking Catherine and also complaining that Joe – who for family reasons was living with Catherine in London – ought to have a computer. It seems that Catherine has been receiving some financial help for giving Joe a home, and Linda was publicly accusing her of using the money for herself. This I hear from Catherine later: and the story is backed up by others who were there.

Alexander, his voice tense, describes the verbal vitriol that was being hurled by the two women at each other. 'They've been absolutely awful,' he says miserably. 'They've been screaming abuse at each other.' 'Goodness!' I say, alarmed. 'Couldn't you tell them to stop it?' 'I have,' he responds with a good deal of brio. 'I exploded. I shouted at them that if they didn't stop, they could both leave immediately.' 'So did that help?' 'Well, they've quietened down,' he says. 'But I don't know when they might start again. And the thing is we've got an invitation for tomorrow evening, for all of us to go to a friend's villa for dinner. If they're going to start fighting, I can't take them.' I look at Alexander's profile as he guides the car up the winding mountain roads. His face is screwed up with misery. I have never seen him so disturbed, other than when telling me about past upsets in the family. But this is here and now. I begin to realize that the next few days might prove unpleasant.

'Perhaps I can help to smooth things over, Alexander,' I offer. 'Perhaps,' he replies forlornly. But I did not then know what further tensions were brewing or what paranoid behaviour had been exhibited by Linda when she heard that I was coming to stay for a long weekend. I had, in fact, no idea that I was the object of so much jealousy. This I learned later from Catherine and also from Margarita who had been there until the previous day. But at the time I was quite unsuspecting. I did not see myself as anything other than an observer when Alexander entertained his friends and as far as the wifelets went I thought it should have been abundantly clear that on weekends to Longleat and on this visit to St Tropez, I was working on my book, spending two or three hours a day interviewing Alexander or otherwise talking to his other guests, observing the general scene, and not aiming to join the wifelets' ranks. But I was altogether unaware of the paranoia at St Tropez where, in the absence of servants or other, non-wifelet, guests, the wifelets operate as a group of wives, cooking and generally ministering to Alexander and fighting among themselves for his favour. Unlike a Moslem polygamous marriage where there is a pecking order of seniority among the wives, each knowing her place, there are huge tensions. Even worse, therefore, when a group of individualistic women whose whole programming is to monogamy are placed in the same position: they are not going to find a happy way of sharing one man. As I am to discover, it is an intensely claustrophobic situation with three women cooped up with Alexander, and despite Alexander's reputation – or somewhat self-made myth –of sexual excesses, an atmosphere of pent up sexual frustration prevails. Alexander naturally sets the agenda for the day. He follows his usually rigid routine of rising to watch the satellite news about 8 am and then spends several hours after breakfast working at his computer on further instalments of his diaries. He paints during the afternoons, but by the time I arrive at the end of August his painting is virtually finished. He has, in the past six weeks, completed eight new heads to be mounted on the two staircases at Longleat, several being of recent wifelets, two of his recently departed Longleat housekeeper couple, Cuthbert and Eileen, and one vividly recognisable self-portrait which he did out on the terrace using a small hand mirror. Guests are free to do what they wish, provided they do not interrupt his work. The only snag is that anyone who wants to get away from the villa will either have to go to the beach, a rocky enclave, a short walk down the cliffs, or else borrow Alexander's car and drive to St Tropez. The latter is something that has to be organized in advance, depending on Alexander's own schedule of activities. As there is nowhere within walking distance – even the supermarket is a drive away – meals are all taken at the villa and prepared by the wifelets and any other women staying at the villa. Alexander, of course, never lifts a finger in the kitchen apart from when he decides on an inspiration that he will cook. I naturally expect to muck in with the others on the galley rota. I was unconcerned that the two women present at the villa would be Linda and Catherine. I had met Linda twice at Longleat and had thought her pleasant enough. She had told me that she had at one time taken hard drugs but that she no longer took anything other than marijuana. I had no idea of her mental state at this time. But I had not yet been told of certain behaviour patterns that she had exhibited on other occasions at Longleat.

The car is now climbing a steep winding road above the sea. 'It's also rather disturbing,' Alexander says as I turn to look at the dazzling view of the Med to my right, 'but I've discovered that a viper has shed its skin in the living room over by my writing desk.' 'Is that some sort of symbolism, do you think?' I ask, jocularly. 'Perhaps so,' he replies, serious and still unhappy. 'But one also has to wonder that if the viper has left its skin there, the viper may not be very far away.' 'Oh dear,' I say, also not relishing the idea of stepping on a snake. I look out at the beautiful heath and brush land that lie on either side of the winding road as we climb high into the rocky hills to the East of St Tropez. Olive trees lean precariously from outcrops of red earth, the Mediterranean stretches, brilliant and inviting, below us, a lapis sea, merging with the cloudless horizon. It is sad to think that such a paradise could harbour poisonous vipers or their human equivalent. It is also disappointing that women would exhibit their lowest natures in a possessive struggle over a man. Often, however, when more than one wifelet is present, there is a sense of repressed hatred. I also know that wifelets have their cliques and that there are those to whose cottages some will go but from which others will keep away. Invariably those who meet on the Longleat Estate gossip about other wifelets. New wifelets are an obvious target for calumny. Alexander clearly wants to avoid bringing deadly rivals into contact with each other especially when other company is expected, as at Longleat Sunday lunch. I am to discover that whatever goes on in private between himself and wifelets or between the wifelets, Alexander is embarrassed if his other friends are to witness any scenes. At St Tropez, however, it seems that several visitors, including myself, are to have firsthand experience of life in the vipelets' nest. But as we drive through the blindingly hot August afternoon I have no idea what kind of a psychodrama lies ahead of me.

Alexander's car winds up the twisting road and turns off through a gate into a shrub-lined drive and parking area. A residential village of rectangular red brick villas built in the early 1960s snuggles into terraces on the rocky hillside, the houses nestling in well-established gardens crammed with bougainvillea and oleander. Alexander bought his three-bedroom villa here when it was being built in 1964. It was part of what he called at the time his 'newfound independence.' He no longer has it, but for forty years he used it every summer for two months, from mid-July to mid-September. The rest of the time it was available for use by the family, but he complained to me that he had told his children that he would sell it if they did not use it more and indeed this is what has since occurred. On this occasion Ceawlin and Anna had both been there during the two middle weeks of August, but Lenka had not joined them. As we arrive, the early-evening air is luscious with the scent of gardenias, oleanders and jasmine. There is a distant sound of waves on rocks. One should have been arriving with the knowledge that a well-chilled glass of champagne would be waiting on the terrace and a scrumptious meal promised for the later evening. I am not, however, expecting anything of the kind as I know that there will not be any staff and, in addition, warring women await me. Besides, Alexander hates champagne and has warned me not to bring any with me as a gift. 'I like Bourgogne,' he told me when I asked his preference for a gift. As at Longleat and Notting Hill, he serves his St Tropez guests three kinds of boxed Provence wine: red, white and pink. However, it turns out that there were some bottles of digestif and other alcoholic drinks in the living-room cupboard.

Alexander carries my bag down some stone steps to the villa, entering through a door marked 'Viscount Weymouth' just like the door to his private apartments at Longleat. This does not refer to Alexander's heir Ceawlin, who has had the right to use the Weymouth title since Alexander himself became the Seventh Marquess of Bath on the death of his father in 1992. As at Longleat, Alexander simply has simply not got round to changing the name on the doorbell. 'They still call me "Weymouth" down at the local shop,' he says. 'No one seems to know me as Lord Bath.' Alexander was Lord Weymouth when he bought the villa in 1964 and it may be hard for the French locals to understand the passing on of English titles. After all, France has been a republic since the revolution in which so many aristocrats lost their heads under the guillotine's blade; and while aristocrats and titles still exist, no one considers them to be of great importance, except for the smallish clique of the holders themselves. In any case, it is not chic to use one's title. One may be a *duc* or a *marquis* but still only use the normal family name, perhaps with a *de* in front of it to signify aristocracy. As for knowing how to use a foreign title, Lord Bath could very likely be referred to as 'Monsieur Lord Bath' or, as in the case of his earlier title, 'Monsieur Lord Weymouth.' The French residents of Alexander's village also find it hard to adjust to the motley crew of women who fly in from mid-July to mid-September while Alexander is in residence. For one thing some of the women have no idea of how to behave with the formally courteous French bourgoisie who habitually greet even total strangers with 'Bonjour' or 'Bonsoir'. I am told that before I arrived there had been an ugly scene on the Residence Camerat's private beach over one of the sun mattresses which the French residents of the villas usually leave down there for their own use. 'The residents leave their mattresses down there overnight,' Catherine explains to me 'and I was using one of them one day when the woman whose it was came down to the beach. She asked for it back, and as I didn't understand what she was saying, she began to pull at it. Linda just flew at her screaming and calling her names in English. Eventually the woman called Linda a whore in English.' Linda had also been at work on her rivals up at the villa. There are three bedrooms, all downstairs: one, larger than the others, is Alexander's. This one contains a big bed in the middle of the room with shelves and tables surrounding it. Usually, wifelets will share this bed with Alexander either singly or together. Catherine is keen to make it clear that she is not a wifelet, more a friend who did have a cuddle with Alexander once, but it went no further. She has her own room at the villa and says that she has no intention of sharing Alexander's bed. Her nephew, Joe, is sleeping on the laundry-room floor on one of the grubby mattresses that are kept in a pile for use when the number of guests exceeds the supply of bedrooms. Two or three weeks earlier, I had telephoned Alexander to ask if I could visit the villa in order to see this part of his lifestyle and to do some further interviews. He had suggested that I could stay a few days from August 24 as a room would become free following Margarita's departure. Linda would be sharing his bed. He asked me to confirm all the arrangements with Viv, his Longleat secretary as she was in charge of scheduling the coming and going of the women by plane. She had been instructed to book flights for some wifelets: Alexander was buying Linda's and Margarita's tickets; while Catherine, who was not sexually involved with Alexander, was paying for herself and for Joe, who was quite happy, it was thought, sleeping on the laundry-room floor. Viv had told me that Margarita was leaving for Nice Airport on the 1.30 pm boat on August 24, whereupon, she said, rather like a hotel receptionist, a room would become free at 12.00 pm. She did not tell me the exact nature of the other guests' sleeping arrangements. It was Alexander who told me when I confirmed with him on the phone from Paris: 'Linda will be sleeping in my bed.' As he drove me from the port he told apologetically me that I would have to 'share a wardrobe with her'.

I told him that this would not be a problem, but, as I later discover, there is plenty of space in the wardrobe in Alexander's room. Linda simply wanted a claim on the bedroom I am to use and which she repeatedly and aggressively states is hers. Unaware of her agenda, I had no objections to sharing a wardrobe for a few days as on the two previous occasions when I had met Linda at Longleat weekends, I had found her civil enough. She had even been to my flat at Montagu Square for tea and to ask my advice on her professional and private projects, having told me quite a lot about herself and given me some insights into her relationship with Alexander. She had expressed her wish to be a promoter of events and I had suggested that she ask Alexander if she could put on a charity function at Longleat. Apparently, she had done so and he had agreed so she was now involved in trying to organize it. She was a hefty girl who wore black leather, fishnet and chains but she was demure in her manner and spoke so softly from almost closed lips that Alexander told me he could never hear what she said. Evidently this did not bother him, but I am to discover Linda's soft speech and demure aspect is a mask. She has another loud-voiced manner which involves constant shouting and abusiveness, much more reflected by her S&M clothes. Linda is also a liar. Nothing she says can be relied upon, as she makes up slanders about us all, including Alexander. Much of what had gone on the preceding three days before my arrival is related to me later by Margarita, who had left the day before my arrival. Margarita is a striking Scandinavian divorcee, tall with long blonde hair and a good figure. She is a painter who lives in London, where she shows her work and she has also held exhibitions in Los Angeles. She tells me she had met Alexander shortly before Christmas 1999 after her agent told Alexander about her work which is, like Alexander's, Expressionist in style. 'Alexander invited us both down to have lunch with him at Longleat, and so we went' Margarita says. 'I hadn't really heard of him before because I don't read the gossip columns but my agent said he was a colourful character. When I saw how nice he was I thought he would be wonderful to open my exhibition that I was organizing in a few months. I had no idea that anything else was going to happen. But later, after I'd met him a few times, I went down to Longleat for another lunch and we went up on the roof afterwards. It was so sunny and bright but it was incredibly cold. I was so cold that he gave me a big hug and it was so funny.' She laughs happily at the memory before continuing. 'We were both a bit pissed after lunch and then in the little roof garden, when he hugged me, Alexander slipped on the ice and he went flat on his back, and I fell on top of him and we were rolling around on the ice. It was very funny and we were laughing so much that we had to continue in bed.' Margarita is genuinely fond of Alexander. 'He is so warm and so affectionate and so kind,' she says. 'I never considered myself a wifelet, more a soul-mate and kindred spirit.' She is, after all, a fellow artist whose brilliantly-coloured paintings have something in common with some of Alexander's early work and certainly in his excellent use of vivid primary colours. Her work, she says, is post-Expressionist while Alexander's is expressionist, so there is a stylistic link. There have been a few artists in Alexander's life over the years, starting with the debutante Davina Merry. Alexander loves to meet intelligent accomplished women, but they have not been in the majority among his sexual conquests. In this respect, Margarita is one who stands out as being in a completely different category from many of the other wifelets. As to her surprise to be considered such a thing as a wifelet, Margarita adds: 'I went down one weekend and Sadie was there and Alexander introduced me by saying "We have a new member of the family."' She has not much cared for this inclusion in wifelet ranks. Once a woman friend becomes a wifelet, it seems it is open season for the longer-standing wifelets who evidently see all newcomers as a threat to their own tenure. They know only too well that the fringe benefits of being Alexander's current wifelet include going to London parties on his arm, having their pictures in the gossip pages and being written about in the newspaper diaries, then spending weekends at Longleat. Queening it at the wife's end of the dining table and sleeping in his bed will soon pass if newer wifelets elbow them from centre stage. A threat to all these perks and ambitions is evidently presented by any new women who come on the scene, whether purely as friends or as bed-mates.

Margarita, however, does not wish to be considered as a wifelet. She wrote to a newspaper which had published inaccuracies about her visit to St Tropez. 'I told them "If you want to write anything about me, why don't you ring me up?"' she says. Alexander, she adds, 'was quite pushy at describing me as a wifelet. But quite frankly, I was a little bit gob-smacked. One of Alexander's business associates said: "He's looking for respectability, Margarita, and you give it to him."' This may sound presumptuous, but, in fact, Margarita is able to invite the Danish Ambassador to open her exhibitions of paintings in London. 'Initially I was invited by Alexander to go down in the car with him to St Tropez and to stay for the whole summer,' Margarita continues. 'This was difficult because of all the things I have to do in London. One of the things I do is take architectural photographs, and I had a date for some work. So initially I said I would go down in the car to stay for a bit, but then the dates for the photography were changed and I couldn't go with him.

'I was also concerned about the small environment, not having rose-coloured spectacles about these women. Anyway, St Tropez was no big deal for me. My ex-husband and I had a villa there, and I had another friend who had invited me down. Then I had a phone call from Alexander's office in Longleat saying they had bought me a ticket. He really wanted me to come down.' Margarita agreed to go down for three and a half days in August, which was all her work commitments would allow. The arrangements seemed simple and agreeable enough. 'I learned that Catherine and Linda were both flying in on the same afternoon, August 20,' she says, 'and that Alexander would meet us at Nice Airport after he had dropped Anna there for her flight to Paris. We were all scheduled to get together at the cafeteria at Nice Airport and have lunch. How jolly!' She laughs merrily at the irony. 'Catherine was already there an hour before me. But Linda missed her flight and we had to wait for her to come in on the next one. Eventually she arrived, acting like a diva, in a big hat and looking very self-important. We were very kind to her, but there was an evil atmosphere.' Margarita later tells me about some of the events which had occurred during her three-night stay at the St Tropez villa. 'I was horrified at the way Linda behaved,' she says. 'She attacked me, and she attacked Catherine. She didn't say anything in front of Alexander but when I was on my own she would come up to me and say vile, insulting things. She also said in an ugly way that she didn't want to make love with me in Alexander's bed. I was shocked. I said, "I haven't come here for that. I'm not going to be involved in threesomes. I've come here to be with Alexander."' Margarita shared Alexander's bed during her three-day stay while Linda slept in the second bedroom which Alexander now offered to me. Catherine had the third room. After Margarita's departure, Linda was the only wifelet at the villa. She then began sharing Alexander's bed as he expected her to do but used the second bedroom as a refuge because, as she says: 'I need somewhere to get away from Old Snorey.' However, she had a particular reason for wanting Alexander to regard her as a special girlfriend, and she treated any woman on the scene as a potential rival. Until I arrived on Friday evening, Catherine was the lone target.

After Margarita's departure on the afternoon of August 24, Catherine later tells me, Linda concentrated her attacks on Catherine; and, as Alexander had outlined to me in the car, she began to undermine the relationship between Catherine and her nephew Joe. She apparently surpassed herself at lunch on the previous day when Tina Jorgenson, an old friend of Alexander's and an executive with the UN Association in London, was there with her husband, David Micklethwait, a barrister. As the lunch Linda began complaining that it was a scandal Joe had no computer. She made it seem as if the child was deprived and as if Catherine was spending money on herself while letting her nephew do without things. After the Micklethwaits and the other guests had left there was open warfare between Catherine and Linda, and this was the state of affairs which existed when a tense and upset Alexander picked me up at the port at St Tropez.

As soon as I enter the villa Catherine appears, smiling rather nervously, offering tea but clearly worn down by the verbal attacks which she then immediately proceeds to describe to me. From Alexander's description, I have no certainty who had started the affray. It is only later, after I hear Margarita and Catherine's stories in detail and experienced Linda's behaviour at first hand, that I realize that there is no doubt as to who was the instigator.

About twenty minutes after my arrival Linda arrives from the beach, wet black hair trailing down her back, wearing a large expensive hat under which her dark eyes glitter with hostility as she greets me in prima-donna fashion. I am puzzled by this as I had no reasons to suspect, after the kindness and sympathy I had shown her, that she would have any animosity towards me.

Joe follows her into the house. He seems to be unwilling to speak to Catherine and is glowering at her. I wonder what could have been said to him by Linda to create this atmosphere. I admire Linda's hat, which I recognize as coming from a very expensive bespoke hatter in St Honoré, and chat to her briefly. I ask her how she is enjoying the villa and the beach. 'Oh,' she says airily 'I've been working very hard on this big event I'm organizing at Longleat.' This is the charity event I had suggested she do if Alexander agreed. Later she tells me that Alexander agreed to the event provided she found all the funding and did all the organization herself. He did not wish to be involved, only informed of what was going on at various stages. Right now, Linda is making an exaggerated show of being the big executive producer.

'Oh, good,' I say enthusiastically. 'I'm looking forward to hearing all about that.' She smiles, showing her teeth. 'Oh, yes,' Linda says self importantly. 'I'm expecting a fax from London. Has it come?' she calls out loudly and bossily. 'Alexander, has there been a fax for me?' Alexander is on the terrace and does not reply, probably because he did not hear her. Linda goes over to the fax machine, which stands on the shelves running along the wall over the wine boxes, while I return to the terrace. I put Linda's tense manner down to the recent brawling with Catherine. Then I join Alexander at the rustic table under a vine-covered loggia and give him a CD of some of my songs. 'Nesta's given me a CD of her singing,' Alexander calls out joyfully to Catherine, who is in the kitchen making tea. Linda, by now changed into a halter-neck black leather bra with a fishnet inset, is seated opposite me on Alexander's left, and is watching us with jealous eyes as we chat. The atmosphere seems tense, but I still cannot believe that she would feel that I am any kind of a threat to her relationship with Alexander. After all, I am a friend and his biographer, not a wifelet. Surely that, or even my songs, do not trespass on her preserve?

I do not, however, appreciate the degree of paranoia operating in the villa.

These hints and glances are merely the opening chords of a sort of *danse macabre*. More is to come. I already know that the wifelets take turns to cook for Alexander, and Linda is quick to tell me that she cannot cook so her role is to clean up. I am quite willing to cook everyone a meal when my turn comes. Tonight's dinner is being prepared by Catherine, who has already assured me she does not need my help: so I go to the rocky beach for a swim. When I return the dinner is ready. It turns out to be a stew of chicken with what Catherine describes as anything else she found lying around. As I don't eat meat I ask if I can cook something for myself. Alexander comes out to the kitchen to find me some frozen fish, which I then cook with some onions, olives and tomatoes as garnish. The only other vegetables appear to be frozen peas and Alexander tells me that he has to use up all of the frozen vegetables before he goes back to Longleat in three weeks, which is why there are no fresh ones, despite the fact that we were in Provence where fruit and vegetables of all kinds grow in abundance.

At this point Catherine asks me if I would like to hear Joe singing. It seems that he has quite a good singing voice and can sing a number of popular songs, but when Catherine asks him to sing for me, he becomes too shy. To get him going again I suggest that everyone sing a song in turn. 'Okay,' he says, 'but you go first.' I oblige with a French song, which I had composed, and Joe then asks for an English one, so I duly sing one from my album. After this, it is Alexander's turn. He is lying in the hammock and from the shadowed corner of the veranda, his voice floats out into the humid evening air singing one of his own songs. It is then Catherine's turn and she sings an Irish folk song, but when it comes to Linda there is silence. This is odd as she has on other occasions been telling everyone of her ambitions to become a recording artist. We are able eventually to get her to sing a few halting bars of some unidentifiable song. 'I don't go in for all this spontaneous stuff,' she says irritably. 'Anyway, you don't need to be able to sing anymore to make a record. They can do all sorts of things to enhance your voice.'

I collect my dinner from the kitchen and put it out on the veranda. I go to get myself a glass of red wine from Alexander's row of boxes 'That looks nice,' I hear Linda saying in a nasty way. 'Whose is it? Nesta's?' I return to find her standing over my plate. I later find out that she polices the fridge, preventing the other guests from using any of the contents and hiding selected items such as avocados for herself. Catherine later tells me that Linda harangued her continually about various items of food, accusing her of taking them. Groceries are paid for by Alexander, but Catherine tells me that Linda, as the only wifelet currently resident, had charge of the cash for the shopping at the local supermarket a short drive away in the village of Ramatuelle. Joe now sings for us with some evident pride and then demands that I sing again. This time I sing a sad Welsh folksong, and then it is his turn once more. Our voices ring out over the darkened village. The scent of flowers drifts on the sea breeze over the terrace. The waves are still audible behind the constant sound of the crickets. Stars glint between the vines on the loggia roof. The mess of paint and other grunge on the terrace floor is obscured by the soft lighting. There seems to be a much more relaxed atmosphere than when I arrived and I genuinely hope that I have helped to defuse the tension. As I eat my dinner, Catherine sits in the hammock with Alexander, and it is swinging gently from side to side in the shadowed corner of the veranda. Joe is talking about songs with me, and there is no sound from Linda, who has left the terrace.

Sadly this harmony is not to last more than an hour. At 11 pm promptly Alexander gets up from the hammock declaring that 'it's Love Box time'. By this he means he is going to watch television. One of his necessities at the villa is a satellite dish and a TV in the living room, which is now referring to as his 'Love Box'. He has also sent out for a portable TV to go in his bedroom. It was intended that Catherine bring it with her, and it seems that Alexander made a histrionic scene at the airport when Catherine told him that she had not brought the set out with her as originally arranged. It had arrived later by air-freight. Alexander goes in to the living room to recline full-length on an old mattress to watch a film. Joe goes with him and imitates him by lying full-length on the sofa. They are like a pair of eastern potentates on their divans. 'You look all hot and bothered and flustered after being in that hammock,' says Linda meaningfully to Catherine. Catherine shrugs off her remarks but, despite evident bad vibes, she soon decides that she will go with Linda in Alexander's car to a disco at the nearby campsite. Although invited by Catherine, I choose not to go with them because by this time Linda has already given me a taste of things to come by launching a completely unprovoked verbal attack on me after following me downstairs to my bedroom. The main gist of the attack is that I am after Alexander and that my room is in fact her bedroom and furthermore that if I touch any of the things she has left there she will have me hounded out of France by her high-up political contacts. Clearly this is irrational, and I can only laugh at her threats, but it is unpleasant even to have to ignore the attack. I am not going to be incited to brawl, and I decide to limit my dealings with Linda to minimal civilities. But, as others have discovered before me, this will prove difficult.

I go for a peaceful walk around the oleander-scented village and down to the beach where the waves are crashing against the rocks with a soothing rhythm. The waning moon has not yet risen, and the stars glitter intensely in the black sky. As I walk back I am greeted in a friendly way by some of the local French teenagers who are gathering to take a picnic to the beach, and I return their greetings. As I walk on up the cobbled path, I can hear them murmuring. I assume that they know that I am staying at Alexander's villa and naturally think that I am one of his evidently notorious team of mistresses. As I am told later, Alexander's setup is a source of gossip to the other villa-owners and one of which they did not approve. Frenchmen may be famous for having mistresses, but they do it rather more discreetly.

When I return, Alexander has already gone to his room and I can hear rhythmic snores from within as I pass by his door to enter my own. I go to bed and read for a while, then, although it is still early for me, put out the light. However, it is now past 1 am, and Linda and Catherine are still out. I wonder whether they will come in relatively soon or stay out until dawn. I also wonder if they will be noisy, and I do not have long to wait for the answer.

At about 2 am I am awakened by clumping footsteps and loud voices, easily identified as Linda's and Catherine's, in the living room upstairs. Soon very loud pop music begins playing on MTV. I lie awake, wondering when it will stop. Alexander's deafness evidently prevents him from being disturbed: I can hear the rhythmic snores continuing, uninterrupted, from the next-door bedroom. Eventually, the music stops, and loud voices and a clattering of high-heeled shoes on the flag-stoned hallway warn me of Catherine and Linda's arrival in the bedroom area. Alexander continues to snore, but my bedroom door opens a crack and Linda peers in at me then storms off, shouting threats.

'I'll kill her,' she yells, bemoaning the fact that she has nowhere to sleep.

I am puzzled. She is supposed to be Alexander's bed-mate, but evidently she does not wish to join him. Catherine tells me later that Linda had shared her bed for the night. Certainly, this is the impression I receive from the voices, door slamming and general clatter. I am kept awake a long time after this subsided by a voice groaning over and over again: 'Oh, God. Oh help me, God. Oh, God...' It is a disturbing sound from someone who seems to be in torment, but I realize this might also be due to an excess of alcohol. Catherine tells me later that Linda has been desperate to find some marijuana and has kept on going up to young men whom they see on the beach after leaving the disco at the camp site, trying, as she says, to 'score' but without success.

Eventually, I fall asleep. I awaken very early and decide to get up. Suddenly the door of my bedroom bursts open and Linda rushes into the room, yelling personal insults at me. I tell her firmly to stop and to leave the bedroom. She continues shouting for a few moments before going out and banging the door furiously. Alexander, of course, is well out of earshot, being up in the living room working on his memoirs with his hearing aids off and with the English satellite TV on rather loud. I decide to go to the beach, so take a bath and get ready, further interrupted by Linda who barges in and sits on the bed hurling insults at me. I say nothing in reply. Before heading out, I greet Alexander who is at his computer in the corner where the viper shed its skin. The TV is tuned deafeningly to the news channel. I give him a good morning kiss on the cheek. He looks up at me in his usual smiling friendly way, bright eyes beaming out of a suntanned face, apparently unaware of any fresh tremors in his establishment. I tell him briefly that Linda had burst in on me bawling insults to which I was not going to reply.

'Good,' he says approvingly, but I can see that he is upset by this turn of events. I then ask him if we can do an interview before lunch, and he seems very pleased and agrees at once. Alexander adores being interviewed. Originally, I had meant to stay four days recording an interview each day, but I now decide that I will postpone some of the interviewing until my next trip to Longleat and do what I can to conclude my business at the villa quickly so that I can leave the unpleasant atmosphere there. I do not want to go into the kitchen to make breakfast so I pick some grapes from the abundant supply hanging from the vine-covered loggia and go down to the sea. From the beach, I use my mobile to call the four-star hotel where I stayed in Nice on the Friday night and arrange to return there. Before our interview begins I tell Alexander that I have changed my plans and now intend to leave on Sunday morning. He looks surprised and a little put out. I quietly explain my reasons. He seems crestfallen and later both I and Catherine, separately, hear him telling Linda off about her behaviour. Clearly Alexander realizes that it will reflect somewhat on himself if a guest who is there for professional reasons is driven away by a wifelet's bad behaviour. I later learn that Linda's behaviour is neither new to Linda nor to the villa during Alexander's visits there with wifelets. Catherine has learned from Gilbert, the village *gardien* or caretaker, of violent goings-on in previous summers. Screaming and brawling among the wifelets, often punctuated by shouting from Alexander, overheard by occupants of other villas is common. Catherine speaks to Gilbert of sending for the police because she has been so unnerved by Linda's behaviour, and she fears physical violence.

'It's nothing to have the police called to Alexander's villa,' Gilbert replies. He then speaks of a blonde woman who during the previous summer had suddenly acquired huge bruises and scratches on her arms, and after the police had been called late one night, she had been taken into St Tropez to a hotel.

I knew none of this before that Saturday lunchtime when I am scheduled to interview Alexander. When I arrive for our rendezvous, he says that he would like to give me the interview while lying comfortably in his hammock. I sit close by with my recording machine, while Linda watches like a jailer. She seems to be taking on the role of a dominatrix, trying to order Alexander around. She interjects a number of untrue allegations about me, which both Alexander and I ignore. Alexander looks embarrassed but relaxed again as soon as we begin to talk about his life. We have not got very far before Linda is intruding again, warning Alexander to beware of letting me tape the interview. Her next several interruptions are to announce that she and Joe want to have lunch, Catherine being in bed with a serious headache. On each occasion Alexander mildly tells Linda to have her lunch and that we will have ours later. Finally we adjourn to the luncheon table to find nothing waiting. Linda then goes into the kitchen and begins frying eggs, which she serves for herself and Alexander with some slices of avocado, ignoring me. Great piles of stale-looking food are brought out of the fridge. These consist largely of already cut and drying pieces of baguettes and some ancient-looking pieces of local sausage, which Alexander greets enthusiastically and eats with gusto. Catherine later tells me that these sausages have been left out overnight a few days earlier and then put back in the fridge. They have, however an indestructible air. Alexander also evidently has a cast iron stomach. Recalling what his old pal Sir Ian Rankin told me about Alexander's store cupboard being crammed with cans of fish from the UK, I ask if he has any tuna. He leads me to a large store cupboard which contains enough tins of sardines, mackerel, vegetables and pink salmon to feed an army. I select a can of pink salmon and in the absence of any salad materials, chop an onion with it. There seem to be no fresh vegetables in the fridge. All the fruit which had been there has mysteriously disappeared and I later learn from Catherine that Linda has hidden it. Alexander has already said that he is happy to lend me the car that afternoon to visit the supermarket, but Linda now announces her intention of taking the car to the shop that afternoon. As I am definitely leaving next morning, I decide I will wait to eat until that evening's dinner party, or if worse comes to worse, for a late lunch in Nice the following day. During this extremely messy lunch, I have been conversing pleasantly with Alexander rather than interviewing him. My tape recorder lies on the bench near the hammock well out of range of our voices. Suddenly Linda, who appears to have no aptitude for polite conversation, interrupts us loudly, warning Alexander to be careful of what he said as my tape recorder is probably still recording him. I say nothing, but Alexander and I look at each other.

'That's enough,' he says firmly, seeing how exasperated I am, 'Nesta doesn't need this.'

According to Catherine, Alexander does not intervene at all when the wifelets quarrel. Deeply upset by what she is going through with Linda, she has tried to get him to intervene on her behalf, but he refuses. 'He's colluding in these attacks,' she says. 'He lets it go on as if he's enjoying it. By doing nothing to stop it, he's encouraging these Rottweilers to attack the others.'

It seems more likely that Alexander has been used all his life to warring women, and he finds it better to let bitch eat bitch, unless it affects him directly. As he tells me, he cannot believe anything they tell him about each other, so he cannot act as an arbiter since it is impossible to discover who caused the ruckus in the first place. Now he has some evidence during our interview and the lunch that there has been one-sided provocation. He puts a stop to it because in this case it is an attack on someone who is not one of the wifelet clan. After Alexander's intervention, Linda falls silent. She takes out her and Alexander's lunch plates and the ancient bread and sausages, which go back in the fridge, and makes off quickly with the car keys. I take more grapes from the vine and go to the beach where I am soon in pleasant and jocular conversation with the local French as we collectively dodge the huge waves that come crashing onto the sunbathing area. Later Catherine appears and begins filling my ears with more of Linda's misdoings, and the locals become more distant, evidently registering my connection with Alexander's uncivil women.

From Soirée to Psychodrama

By the time I return from the beach Alexander has decided that Linda and Catherine have quietened down enough to go with us to the dinner. Alexander wears a long cotton caftan with no underwear, for the night is very hot and humid. We drive for about an hour to reach his friend's house. The party is held in the garden in air that is at first sensually scented by oleanders and soon is sizzling with mouth-watering scents from a delicious hot buffet. Most of the guests are mature people, and almost all are French. Later Alexander pronounces the party 'too French'. As a recent arrival in France, I thought that this is one of its charms. The food too is excellent. Although there are plenty of men there, as part of family groups, our table, oddly enough, fills up with women. Alexander sits at the head. It is just like Saturday dinner at Longleat. I spend some time talking to a French woman who is sat next to me. Alexander also speaks quite a lot of French. It is interesting to note, however, that none of these middle-class guests seem in the least bit impressed by the fact that Alexander is a marquess – the equivalent of a French *marquis*. There is none of the fawning and adulation that happen at the art-gallery parties he attends in London. He is simply a foreign friend of the hostess, more valued, as is usual in France, for being an artist than an aristocrat. One woman guest at our table is avidly keen to know where she could view Alexander's paintings. She seems quite puzzled by the idea that the only site is Longleat where his life's work is represented by his murals.

155

Catherine speaks no French and is silent except when speaking to me or Alexander. Linda sits next to Alexander in a wifely pose, with her black hair drawn back in a rather oily chignon, looking matronly and self-important in a striking long yellow dress, which she said she had got in the Lebanon which she claims she often visits. Ignoring the rest of us, she speaks to Alexander the whole while in English. The French woman wants to know if Linda is Alexander's wife. I explain that she is one of a number of mistresses, and that Alexander makes his mistresses very public. I translate wifelet as '*fammelette*' or a '*femmette*'. This lady finds it difficult to understand why Alexander would make such a fuss about having mistresses when everyone in France is used to the fact that many powerful married men have mistresses. No mention of the mistresses is ever made in the French press due to strong privacy laws so that when it was revealed after his death that Francois Mitterand had a mistress of twenty years standing and a daughter by her, there was surprise but no scandal. Mistresses have always been accepted, and sometimes an 'official mistress' such as Diane de Poitiers, mistress of Henry II of France, and the Duchess de Pompadour and later Madame Dubarry, serial official mistresses of Louis XV have been celebrated as important and powerful personalities in the lives of French kings. Nothing has changed except that there are no longer any French kings. There is dancing after dinner, and Alexander appears very relaxed. Much too soon, however, Alexander says we should be going home. In the car back to the villa Linda sits in front again and speaks aggressively to Catherine and to me each time we start to converse with Alexander from the back seat. She uses a governess manner and tells us angrily several times to shut up. 'That's enough,' Alexander says firmly, and Linda quietens.

She then acts in a solicitous manner with Alexander, ignoring us, and in a mock sweet voice, offers to drive if Alexander has had too much wine. There had been a seemingly endless supply of wine at the dinner, but Alexander drives us home impeccably.

I place some furniture in front of the bedroom door before getting into bed.

At noon the next day I am to be driven to the port by Alexander. Catherine follows me to the beach where I go for a morning swim and begs me to agree that she can come along. I do not have the heart to refuse since she is obviously terrified of being left alone within range of Linda; and of course both of us wish to avoid having Linda along for the ride. As we are returning to the villa from the beach, Linda arrives, shouting.

'Hurry up!' she yells like an irate hockey captain, 'Alexander is waiting.' With her furious face and loud yells, waving her arms and stumbling over the pebbles, she appears comical. I begin laughing at her. The real reason for her fury is that she herself has demanded the use of the car for the whole day and will have to wait until Alexander returns from the port before she can take it. Back at the house, Alexander takes my bags out of the front door and starts up the long flight of stone steps leading from the villa to the car park. Catherine urges me to hurry out the back way to avoid Linda, but as we follow Alexander to the car I also learn that Catherine is hoping that she will be able to use the journey to the port and back to warn Alexander about various aspects of Linda's behaviour which occurred when Alexander's back was turned.

'But I want to give Nesta another interview in the car,' Alexander says irritably as Catherine climbs into the car. 'Oh, Nesta invited me to come along,' says Catherine, not quite accurately. He says no more, and Catherine hops into the back seat. We drive off in silence. I have said nothing further to Alexander about Linda's extraordinary behaviour. My premature departure is enough of a comment, and he is clearly not happy about this. I try to put him at his ease by talking to him in a general way about his life in St Tropez over several decades of summers. This is not so much an interview – for which he clearly does not want an audience – as a background picture that emerges as we chat. I realize, for instance, that Alexander seldom goes out while he is staying at the villa. In fact he has never done so. He imports wifelets to stay and other guests for lunches and in between, works solidly at his projects: his memoirs and his painting. The wifelets clean up and cook but he will not be persuaded to take them out to local restaurants, partly because he keeps a tight hold on the purse strings. No wonder that a degree of cabin fever develops among the women trapped in this relatively small house with only the beach accessible on foot. And no wonder they are raring to get the car and to go off to St Tropez for a bit of night life because Alexander watches his 'Love Box' from eleven pm until he falls asleep. Any sensual goings-on develop when the current wifelet creeps into bed beside him.

I ask Alexander about the St Tropez scene. He bought the villa when the resort was becoming highly fashionable, but it seems that Alexander has never been one of St Tropez's beautiful people. Even in the resort's 1960s heyday, when Brigitte Bardot and Gunter Sachs had their big romance and the restaurants and streets were crammed with film folks and the glamorous followers of the jet-set couple, and when he himself was still the handsome and eligible heir to Longleat who could have been partying and pulling the girls, he stayed up in the hills. Aged seventeen in his virginal youth, Alexander had taken a trip to the South of France with another young man with the express purpose of finding a woman to lay. The mission failed, and there has been no sequel. Alexander's women are all his own imports; and he has never cruised the fashionable nightspots looking for fresh talent, never even had so much as a one night stand with a suntanned tourist. Despite years of tittle-tattle in the tabloid diaries about his glamorous lifestyle, the handsome but deeply shy and unconfident, workaholic Alexander always spends his summers ensconced at his villa hard at work on the panels for his murals at Longleat. He has remained in this reclusive routine for four decades with only his wifelets to cook and clean up for him, to satisfy his sexual needs and his even stronger need to be the centre of female attention.

Naturally, when several women are closeted together and competing for the attention of one man, there will be some sparring. Until he installed satellite television, the wifelets were his only entertainment; but, one must ask, does some of the entertainment verge on the Roman sport of watching gladiators fight each other to the death? Catherine, who has been a non-sexual camp follower for several years, has had ample opportunity to watch Alexander and his weekend wifelet scene at Longleat. This is her first visit to St Tropez and the first time she has been made the victim of such extraordinary beastliness. Her very pained experience over a ten-day period at the villa has given rise to a theory not very complimentary to Alexander. During my thirty-six hours at the villa, Catherine privately repeats to me many times that she thought Alexander was deliberately using the more vicious wifelets to victimize the others: an extreme view, perhaps, based on Catherine's own experience at Ramatuelle.

Could there be some reason beyond the competitive behaviour of the women themselves why Alexander's ménage so often breaks down into violence? Catherine declares that she believes Alexander is actually encouraging these attacks, that he is deliberately setting up the more normal women to be attacked by the Rottweiler element among the wifelets: that, in fact, he hates women and the whole extraordinary circus is deliberately set up to humiliate them. This suggests a psychopathic element in Alexander's makeup. The answer may be much less vile than this. Davina Merry, who was close to Alexander emotionally for three years and who still knows him and likes him, tells me that while Alexander had upset her, he was never cruel. However, Davina did not experience anything like the wifelet scene, nor would she have dreamed of subjecting herself to anything of the sort. In the meantime other wifelets have spoken of Alexander's kindness and gentleness. If there is cruelty lurking somewhere in his character, no wifelet is subjected to direct cruelty from Alexander himself, and, in fact, Alexander is often the victim of violence from the wifelets, who verbally or physically assault him. Some months after my visit to Ramatuelle, and, once more interviewing Alexander at Longleat, I ask him about this. He says that these violent antagonisms are something that happens quite often. 'I never seek them out.' he explains. 'And in that I never seek it, it's always a disappointment if it happens.' We speak of patterns that repeat themselves in relationships, and Alexander becomes rather quiet and sad. I ask him if he thinks his pattern is to foster combat among his women. 'Well, I don't see this as anything aimed at,' he says rather painfully, 'and I don't see it as necessarily happening every time.' Then he bucks up a bit. 'The relationships I regard as therapeutically good for me,' he continues, 'are the ones where there isn't this combat. Just pleasant.' As an example of such therapeutic relationships he mentions Mariella, who is coming to dinner at Longleat that evening. We speak lightly about the idea of psychological labyrinths. Alexander has a number of intricate mazes at Longleat, though none have a Minotaur or other monster at their heart. However, Alexander has recently acquired an impressive bronze statue of the legendary Cretan Minotaur. This statue is now in the garden where it has been positioned emerging from the bushes so that it threatens the stone sculpture of the two virgins. 'Is this a representation of the naughty, predatory Alexander?' I ask him.

'Well,' he chuckles, 'somebody approached me with a photograph of what she'd done and said, "Would it fit in your garden?" I felt it did.' Does this fit with the dark psychological element about which Alexander and I had joked at St Tropez? The labyrinthine rocks at the beach make the water very dark, and Alexander joked that people had to be on their guard when swimming because of all the psychological monsters which might be lurking in these shadowed underwater grottoes where the sunlight seemed not to penetrate. Indeed, when the sun is behind clouds, the water is black in the deep crevasses between the rocks, and swimming there is a daunting experience.

Due to his copious reading of popular psychology books in his twenties, Alexander is very aware of psychological depths and unconscious forces. We discuss the possibilities that the wifelets who start to behave violently are responding to something in Alexander's own psychological makeup and the possibility that Alexander is the trigger. Alexander is a man who is not at peace with himself emotionally. All his life he has had to deal with strife in his close relationships. Men – from his father and his brothers, to his mother's or his wifelets' boyfriends – have been a source of conflict. Alexander is undoubtedly volatile, and it seems also that he tries to suppress an element of violence in his own makeup, a violence that his father evidently perceived and decided to channel by sending his four-year-old son to a gym for tuition in the art of boxing. Alexander has only briefly revealed a violent side to his nature, such as the time a few years ago when he dotted a complete stranger whom he mistakenly took for someone who had previously offered him gratuitous insults. Alexander has told me of how he restrained himself from hitting his father during one of their huge rows despite the fact that he says Henry was shouting at him: 'Go on then, hit me. Hit me.'

Alexander acts out his father's part, his voice rising histrionically, his body leaning forward, chin jutting as if inviting a punch. 'I just kissed him,' he tells me, 'and walked out of the room.' This is not so with women, however. Alexander has been known to hit out at a woman. 'My father was known to hit women,' he also tells me. Evidently there is suppressed violence in Alexander, and his constantly remembered anger against his father is recognition of the fact that they shared the same problem of an anger which could become physical violence. Alexander's efforts to control his violent side are largely successful perhaps for the reason that from his boyhood boxing days onwards, he has learned powerful self-discipline. Michael Croucher believes

160

that much of Alexander's behaviour in relation to other people is very much that of an oriental martial-arts practitioner. Martial arts are about the strategic channelling of violent impulses. Sometimes this violence is channelled in such a way that the opponent expresses it. Or the martial artist responds passively to the attack, as in Judo where the opponent first translates impulse into action with an attack and the black-belt fighter merely steps aside and allows the attacker to lose his balance and fall over himself.

'He allows the attack,' Croucher says of Alexander. Allowing the attacks of wifelets on other wifelets may also come under this heading. While wifelet victimizes wifelet, it is deflecting the attacks from himself. However, there have been many occasions when Alexander has himself become the victim of an attack. Alexander evidently believes – hence his response of 'Good' when I tell him initially that I am not responding to Linda's attack on me – in the policy of passively receiving an attack. However, some of this could also come under the heading of timidity because, as I discovered, once one adopts a tough stance with her, Linda is silenced. Alexander has also succeeded in quietening the women by exploding at them and threatening them with a rapid return home. Perhaps he realized that passivity has its limitations at times. In the face of a determined and persistent aggressor it can become a wearying drain of energy. However, he did not pursue his threat on that occasion and had relapsed into his passive pose because he was either unaware of what was going on or chose to ignore the fact that Linda's attacks on Catherine continued behind Alexander's back after I had gone. Men can deal with male aggression more directly either by fighting or by acceptance. Like many men, Alexander is evidently intimidated by angry women: but with Alexander, this intimidation goes further. There is a visible fear of causing their displeasure. Familiarity with this kind of situation goes back to the tough governess, Miss Vigers, and her wars with the equally firm Nanny Marks. He would have had ample evidence of women's vileness to each other in those days and would also have known the unpleasant side of becoming the target of their anger.

As we drive along the winding road down the hills to St Tropez port it is evident to me that Alexander is more than nervous and really quite frightened. It seems that while Catherine and I were at the beach, he had an unpleasant scene with Linda. Not for the first time since I announced my premature return to Nice has he told her of his anger that someone who is writing about him was leaving before completing the interviews, and all due to her behaviour. Now, however, Alexander is worried about time – not about getting me to the port in time to catch the *navette*, because we are in plenty of time for the boat, but because Linda had demanded the use of the car for the whole of that Sunday for a visit of her own to St Tropez. Learning that Alexander would be driving me to the port before lunch, she has had to balance the displeasure of not getting the car for her own use during the morning with the relief of my departure. Alexander is himself inclined to be autocratic and to insist upon having his own way. It is possible that Linda was simply mirroring Alexander's character. Linda was silenced by a taste of her own treatment. What she wanted was that her 'victim' would try to fight with her, but when she was simply told in a governess voice to stop her behaviour, she wilted. Could it be that Alexander's fear of authoritative women is also being reflected by Linda? Alexander is clearly intimidated by loud-voiced angry women, but in turn is bossy and cross with the gentler ones. Several times during the journey to the port, Catherine quietly tries to interject remarks about Linda's behaviour, but Alexander imperiously squashes them. He will have none of it.

'No,' he snaps. 'I don't want to hear anything about it.' It is understandable that he would prefer to remain outside these 'women's squabbles' since he would then have to spend all his time trying to sort out inter-wifelet conflicts instead of getting on with his work. 'You can't trust anything any of them say to you about the others,' he also told me on the journey up to the villa from the port on the Friday. 'And if you say anything back, they twist that and go and tell it to the others.' He clearly does not trust Catherine any more than Linda and claims that he does not know who is to blame for the quarrelling between them. Poor Alexander! The whole point of having wifelets is supposed to enhance pleasure. His dream is one in which they all get on with each other.

'Alexander, this is not realistic,' I had told him on a visit to Longleat. 'Women do not function like that. They all want to have exclusive rights, and if you force them to coexist with each other, all you will get is a nest of vipers – or in this case vipelets.' Since my remark was meant to be humorous, Alexander had laughed. He likes to believe that he can defy human nature. He is trying to prove a sociological point and provide a blueprint for a new society.

He reckons without the dark side of the female psyche. The dark side is rooted in the instinctive nature: and in this case, the instinct is to attract an exclusive provider and to fight off all the competition. Linda is evidently right on cue for instinctive behaviour. Despite the fact that she has no love for Alexander, or even a sexual attraction for him, she has decided on him as her provider and is fighting like a jungle beast to fight off any rivals. 'You're after my boyfriend,' she repeatedly told me. She said other vulgar things about what I wanted to do to her boyfriend, and I began to wonder who this boyfriend could be. After a few moments of puzzlement, I realized she was referring to Alexander, the man she does not want to sleep with and about whom she speaks abusively behind his back.

The question must be asked, however: are the wifelets who behave like bickering governesses when with Alexander simply acting out the script which Alexander absorbed as a child when Nanny Marks and Miss Vigers fought their guerrilla war in his nursery? Linda was rather deliberately trying to act out the dominatrix governess in her treatment of Alexander and the rest of us. But she might have done better to have adopted the more gentle firmness of the nanny, for it seemed that Alexander's evident enjoyment at seeing someone who was making his life difficult taken down a peg harks back to the pleasure he took in those childhood wars when the benevolent Nanny Marks scored a point over the nagging Miss Vigers. If Linda's decision to act the governess was an attempt to gain power over Alexander, it seemed that she was really becoming a victim of her own role-playing. Unconscious forces were at work and during the period in which one could observe the pantomime of Linda's behaviour, it seemed that an element of panic and desperation was creeping into her manner as she was progressively losing control over her own conscious actions while something more powerful was pulling the strings. This problem of wifelet violence arises over and over again. But are those wifelets in control of their own reactions? Linda, for instance, may not have been able to understand her own behaviour. I concluded at one point that her mental state was a combination of her own boredom, frustration and desperation. However, she was expressing her inner disorder with increasing violence. Was she always like this? I wondered. I had only previously seen a civilized guest at two Longleat weekends. But she had been at the villa for over a week. This was a much longer spell of time to be subjected to Alexander's routine and the restrictions of living there.

There was also the fact that she was there largely as a career move and not out of affection for Alexander. The organization of the big event at Longleat was evidently crucial. She was also keen to get in amongst the beautiful people at St Tropez and further her cause there. This simply was not happening since she was trapped at the villa a good fifteen miles from the fun. Hence the psychological game she was playing with Alexander and it seems losing too, since Alexander had more experience at it than she did. I accidentally saw another side of Linda on that visit. On the night after the party, the second of the two nights that I stayed in the villa, I had been disturbed by a noise. I was on the alert since her irrational threats and exhibitions of violent rage and animosity might make her dangerous. I lay there in the dark, feeling apprehensive and then, unable to go back to sleep, decided to investigate. I crept out of my room and silently walked the length of the flag-stoned passage in my bare feet. I saw Linda, in a cotton nightie, standing in a bluish beam of moonlight. This fell directly onto her face which wore an expression of extreme – and I would say neurotic – unhappiness. As she saw me coming she slid sideways and went upstairs, vanishing like a ghost. I was disturbed by what I had seen: the tortured face of a woman who evidently could not rest easily with the daytime persona which she was expressing. Nor, evidently, could she rest at night.

It was also clear, however, that Alexander is nervous about her reaction if he were to be late back with the car. When I say that I have to get some cash before boarding the *navette*, the delay involved clearly worries him. We stop slightly short of the port, in a street with a bank. 'Please be quick,' he says, looking pink-faced and anxious.

'You don't mind if I don't take you all the way into the port?' he asks me when I return. He is if anything even pinker and seems agitated. Of course, I realize that Catherine has been talking to him about Linda's behaviour while I was at the bank. But that is not all. He says he wants to rush back. I know why. Linda is waiting and ready to fling her full governess act at an Alexander who has clearly been in terror of his childhood domestic regime and has not relinquished the response. 'Of course not,' I reply. My luggage is light and on wheels, and the walk to the dock will only take three or four minutes. In the car it might have been an extra one and a half minutes for Alexander to drive in, unload me and turn around. It seems that the only explanation for his reluctance to do this is his fear of Linda's wrath. Judging from the reports I received from Catherine after I had left, it seems that I was not mistaken. She tells me that Linda's behaviour became more and more impossible during the rest of her stay.

Aftershocks

I stayed some days in Nice, but after my return to Paris about a week after my departure from the Residence Camerat, I began receiving phone calls from Catherine. She had returned to London and wanted to tell me everything that had happened at the villa since my departure. According to Catherine, Linda once more directed her venom at Catherine. At a lunch with some of Alexander's friends at the villa, Linda was directed by Alexander to sit next to Catherine. 'Aha,' Linda said, 'I'm sitting next to my victim.'

Catherine was not Linda's only victim by then. Evidently hope of bringing off the big event at Longleat had crashed. There was nothing left to lose; an increasingly desperate-seeming Linda, locked up at the villa while a St Tropez full of potentially glamorous contacts lay a frustrating twenty-minute drive away, began to insult Alexander in front of his friends. 'These were old, old friends of Alexander's,' Catherine says, 'very sweet, older people. She called him "an old faggot" several times during the lunch. She told him: "You're a faggot. Your friends are faggots. You hate women. You denigrate women. You're a nasty man,"' Catherine continued. 'Alexander said to her: "Look, I don't want any more of this. I want you out of my bed, out of my room, out of my house and out of my life. I don't want you near me."'

But he did not send her home and later, Catherine says, Linda's bad behaviour grew worse. No other guests were due until Sadie arrived the following week, but that would be after Linda and Catherine had returned to London. This was an essential strategy for Alexander since Linda and Sadie were not on speaking terms. However, Linda had evidently begun to direct her extraordinary rage at Alexander. 'She was drinking more and more,' Catherine reveals, 'anything she could get her hands on: rum, whisky, brandy, all

Alexander's stock. And the more she drank, the worse she became. She started screaming at Alexander: "You bastard this and that." She was using his phone to make international calls during the night, and one night she was on the phone all night to Saudi Arabia and Lebanon.' Catherine continues her outpouring of Linda's misdemeanours. 'Then one night,' she goes on, 'when Alexander had gone to sleep about half past ten, she went downstairs to his bedroom and came up again to the living room with his trousers. She went through his pockets and helped herself to money from his wallet. I said: "You can't do that Linda." And she said: 'Yes, I can. That bastard! We're like caged lions here. That bastard! He won't spend money on us. I want to get out of here. Anyway, he owes me, the bastard. He owes me more. He gave me a sexual disease. I can't get to him. But I'm going to sue him, and I'm going to go to the German press." I said: "You're going to go to the German press? Why the German press?" She said: 'Well, then everybody else will pick up on it. They're very good. They expose things. And I'll get my lawyer, Ali, who is a lawyer to the Saudi Royal Family, to sue him.'"

'But what would she sue him about?' I ask Catherine, astonished. 'She says that he gave her a sexual disease,' Catherine replies, 'that he's ruined her fertility, that he wanted a baby with her, but he has cast her aside by saying "I want you out of my life, I want you out of here, I want you out of my bed, I don't want to see you." When Linda and I were in the car when he drove us to Nice Airport, he said to her: "*You* gave *me* a disease." And she said: "Oh no, you said you got it from Catherine." I said: "Excuse me, I've never slept with Alexander. I've never actually had a disease in my life. How dare you!" He argued with her about that. He said: "I never said that. I said I could have got it from any woman,"' Catherine continued, 'but she's a liar. Apparently she got something, Chlamydia or something like that, and he got it from her.'

'So that night, she went downstairs and brought the trousers upstairs and took the car keys and money. Then Alexander came upstairs. He woke up when he heard the noise. He said to her: "Have you got my keys?" "No I haven't," she said. She hid them under a cushion, and he said: "Catherine, if you go, you're a confederate in this."

'When Alexander went back downstairs, Linda went through the wallet. There was a letter in it from a doctor. She read it out loud. It said something on the lines of "I am happy to tell you that you are not HIV positive." 'Then she took the car keys and said she was going into St Tropez to look for some fun. She said she would take Joe with her, and of course he was desperate to go, and I couldn't stop him, short of tying him up, so I knew I would have to go as well. I couldn't leave a twelve-year-old boy to go off with her at that time of night knowing the sort of things she would do. I'd seen her going up to young men who evidently didn't even take drugs to ask for marijuana, trying to score, so I knew what would be going on. She was becoming more and more crazy.

'She was desperately trying to pick up rich contacts and she was obsessive when she knew that I'd met the captain of a very big expensive yacht which had been chartered by some very rich Russians. She kept demanding his phone number from me, but I pretended I'd lost it. The next day she was down to the port in a tight miniskirt and high heels, loads of makeup, trying to find the captain on the yacht. She kept saying: "It's important I meet these people. It's for my business."' It was becoming clear to Catherine that Linda made it her business to try to meet rich men who would then invite her on all-expenses-paid 'business trips'.

'So, that night we went out to St Tropez to a club,' Catherine continues, 'and when we came back it was five am and Alexander came upstairs. He had been waiting for us. He was upset. He said: "Where have you been? I was worried about my car." Linda just started screaming abuse at him. "You bastard!" she kept screaming, "You bastard, you gave me a sexual disease."' But whereas Linda could have been put on the next plane from Nice to London, evidently Alexander did not pack her off immediately. There were some days to go before Catherine and Joe also left, driven in the car with Linda to Nice Airport by Alexander himself. It had been a hellish few days at the villa, but for Catherine, especially. Since my departure on the Sunday, Catherine had been constantly hounded by Linda, who followed her around the villa and up and down to the beach, making verbal attacks so that Catherine never felt able to relax. Catherine had confided in the Residence Camarat's *gardien*, who told her some of the inside gossip about Alexander's summer visits.

'The *gardien* opened the garden of an unoccupied villa owned by a Swiss Banker so that I could go in there and have some tranquillity and Linda wouldn't know where I had gone,' she says. 'She couldn't find me when I was in that garden. She had no idea where I was. I was able to get some peace and quiet.' Catherine had earlier confided her fears to one of the two hostesses of the party to which we had all gone with Alexander. The woman told her that she could go there if things got too difficult. Catherine's problem was that she had bought fixed-date air tickets for herself and Joe and could not afford to pay for them both to stay at an hotel for the remaining week of what she said was 'supposed to be a holiday'. This may be a reason why other women guests have been unwilling to fly the nest when vipelet animosity became too violent for comfort.

Why would anyone want to put up with this kind of attack? Normally, anyone would do what I did and get out as soon as transport could be arranged. But why does Alexander put up with it? Although he had told Linda he wanted her out of his life, she was back again a few months later, screaming and yelling around the apartments at Longleat, shouting abuse down the telephone to the couple who were looking after Alexander, demanding that she be picked up at the station. Alexander's staff told me that they were upset by it and that they thought Alexander was too, since he had not been himself at all since his return from St Tropez the previous summer. They added that he had had few guests at Longleat all winter, other than Linda.

There may be more than one reason why the female infighting occurs around him and why he tolerates it. Firstly, the fact that women fight over him is evidence to a man who has a history of rejection by women at a sensitive period in his early manhood that he is desired. To the emotionally and sexually insecure man that Alexander became as he outgrew his confident and successful schooldays, the spectacle of women literally fighting over him would be immensely reassuring. Of course, for a man as deeply lonely as Alexander, the simple fact of an abundant supply of such competing companions would be preferable to the cold solitude of the man who in the depths of his soul fears and mistrusts his fellow humans to the point of – in his own admission – 'paranoia'. Alexander understands that many of these women have complex motives in befriending him. Although Alexander has an abundance of charm, he is not the virile hunk of his earlier days; and, as earlier chapters have shown, he was not attracting women in such droves even when he was young and single. Alexander has always believed in Longleat as a magnet for women. From debutantes and exotic beauties to other kinds of women, they have fallen for the glamour and the assumed wealth of an Elizabethan mansion, a marquess's title and a place in the tabloids. Charming, warm, hospitable, very rich and sufficiently famous, Alexander is a target and as such he realistically accepts and tolerates the rush of women of a certain type. As one of the loneliest people imaginable, he also accepts, gratefully even, the fact that he can attract a variety of women who will keep him company at weekends in his lonely den at Longleat; during the week in his bohemian penthouse at Notting Hill Gate and in his summer villa for two months of the year. Despite their company, Alexander works steadily, stoically, at his projects from the hours of 9 am to dinner, which is always served punctually at 8.pm. Only after dinner does he permit himself to stray into the erotic zone. Far from being the licentious free lover of his tabloid fame, forever pouncing, he is something of the clockwork seducer: he slots sex into his schedule somewhere between 10 and 11 pm. And then falls asleep.

For the rest of the time he is hard at work or watching his favourite TV shows. Effectively, he lives as if he were entirely alone, even when he has company. As at Longleat, Alexander works all day at the villa, never even going down to the beach for a swim. The wifelets are there to amuse him during mealtimes and for that night slot when he allows himself some erotic fulfilment before falling asleep. In describing himself as a recluse, Alexander is inaccurate. He adores his solitude, needs it in order to be able to do his work. But that solitude must be punctuated at regular intervals by fun and games with the women who follow in his train as if he were the Pied Piper of Hamlin.

No wonder so many of them, unable to amuse themselves with books or the beach and perhaps expecting a glamorous series of parties with the beautiful people of St Tropez, become fractious with boredom. What keeps them keen? Not his financial wealth, for he exhibits and shares little of that. Nor does he dispense money freely, even for the housekeeping. When Catherine and Linda came back from the Ramatuelle *supermarché* with a bottle of wine, which they had paid for out of Alexander's grocery allowance, he upbraided them furiously for spending his money on a single bottle of wine. 'We bought this bottle of wine,' Catherine says. 'It was only five euros.' That is above the plonk price in France where 3.5 euros will buy a quite good *vin du pays*. Meanwhile Alexander's bulk-bought cardboard boxes of very young Provence wine come in at under £1.50 a litre. 'We opened the wine in the kitchen,' Catherine continues, 'then Linda said: "I'm going to offer him this glass of wine. It's the least we can do." I said: "Oh, don't!" But she insisted, and then Alexander said: "How bloody dare you. I can't touch it. Catherine, I gave you that money to buy food. I can't trust you again with my money. You bought wine." 'Of course she knew that was going to rile him,' Catherine reflects. 'I told him: "She suggested it." He said: "I don't care. I gave you my money to buy food." She did it deliberately. She bought the wine and then offered him a glass of it on purpose to get him worked up.' Alexander watches his pennies, but he is never stingy with his wine, such as it is. There is plenty of wine on tap at the villa, and guests are told to help themselves. The wine is a side issue, however, perhaps evidence of a certain disappointment that entertainment *chez* Alexander is not quite on the level of the imagined lifestyle of a marquess in a stately home. What do these flocking females expect of Alexander? The great lover? The keys to Longleat? A backer for their career? Marriage into the aristocracy? Some of these women might imagine that by hanging around Alexander they will also move in exalted circles, meet other aristocrats and perhaps other eligible men who will snap them up and marry them. This is a forlorn hope, for wifelets tend to meet hardly anyone other than wifelets. No wifelet has ever made a socially distinguished marriage, certainly not a wealthy one. Few indeed have married at all, post-Alexander. Even the hope that hanging around Alexander will bring them connections to the magic world of show business to which many of them aspire, is one which would surely be dismissed after a few weekends at Longleat or a few trips to London parties on his arm. As for getting him to invest in a business venture, Alexander is too shrewd. He has been down that route before and now eschews it. Blackmail too is a poor business with Alexander as the subject. Some, he told me, have tried. But he has an easy solution. There is nothing, which is not known already, that a wifelet could threaten to expose. Alexander is as cool as the breeze about his private life. He lets it all hang out. He actively pushes his own mythology as the great stud, or as some wag aptly tagged him, the 'Loins of Longleat'. 'All these pictures of naked wifelets up trees,' Michael Croucher points out, 'the whole picture is in his albums at the house, left out for everyone to read.' They are there precisely to advertise Alexander's naughty goings on. There is even one rather ghastly snap of Alexander on the terrace at the St Tropez villa, in his robes, fellating a laughing Sadie, her knees wide apart, in front of other guests.

There is apparently nothing left to hide, except, of course, the disappointing truth that Alexander's sex life is nowhere near as prodigal as the advertising suggests: so much for the infamous Polygyny as a form of sexual and emotional fulfilment. Perhaps we will find more to excite interest in the inside story of his one and only legitimate marriage to Anna Abigail Gyarmathy, the Hungarian immigrant to France who picked Alexander up in a Paris picture house in 1959 and who, four decades ago became the Marchioness of Bath.

Chapter Six
'I'm A Happily Married Man'

Alexander laughs roguishly: 'I'm a happily married man,' he says, and the blue eyes swirl in their sockets. I had asked him whether he had ever considered marrying one of his wifelets. The answer is tongue-in-cheek and, knowing that he only married in order to legitimize an heir, I challenge him to explain himself. 'I regard it as happily married,' he says, laughing still more. 'Contentedly married, shall we call it? I don't foresee any change in that status,' he adds more soberly. Divorce is not on the cards. 'I think you could say that I have enough freedom not to have to worry about that problem,' he concludes. Divide and rule: the wife and the wifelets, each knowing her place. So Alexander has securely established himself among the few who have their cake and eat it. No wonder he is the object of envy for many a man in the street. They may think multiple marriages outside the law is one rule for the aristocrats and another for Mr Average. However, Alexander's Casanova-style self-rule does not cost him a penny. He decided to lead a polygynous life long before he became legally married. The man in the council house could do it too; if he could find the wife and the women who would put up with it. Of course, the stately home helps a lot; but is Alexander's married life all roses? How, and where, did it all begin?

Phase One: A Long Engagement!

Select an early volume from the many photograph albums that form a horizontal stack under a side table in Alexander's private drawing room, and you will find huge arrays of snaps dating from his youth. Some date from the 1950s and his years in Paris. Among them are several shots of a young woman clearly of strong personality, her poses, aggressive and arrogant. She has short brown hair a prominent nose and is by no means beautiful or chic. She clearly lacks the polish or the conventional beauty which she was to portray in the photographs taken a few years later. In fact, there is little in physical appearance to link the two sets of images: they could be pictures of two different women.

This is Anna Gayermarthy, the Hungarian whom Alexander met in 1959 during his second period as an art student in Paris. He tells me they met in a cinema one afternoon while she was still a schoolgirl, in her final year at a local *lycée*. It seems that Anna was being bothered by the man sitting next to her and moved to sit beside Alexander. When she left, Alexander says, 'I followed her and plucked up the courage to ask her to have a coffee with me.' The girl said yes. Alexander adds, with a shy laugh, that this may seem like pretty fast stuff for the 1950s, but this was Paris, the world of painting, the very alternative Left Bank and all that. It was not long before Anna moved in with him. Alexander said that this was the first time he had lived with someone but not the first time he had wanted to. 'I'd wanted to before,' he says indignantly Alexander had never spent more than a night or two with a woman before this and he found the experience of living *à la cocoon* and having total sex rather than the debutante 'only-so far-and-no-further' experience very pleasurable. Since he has told me he does not believe he has ever initiated a virgin, evidently Anna, despite her youth, was far from inexperienced.

This was also the first time he said that he felt free of the overwhelming sense that Longleat was still around him, even in Paris. Meeting Anna and living with her opened up new prospects. He says that he had felt unable to bring anyone home to his apartments in Longleat to live with him, but to meet someone in Paris and live with her there made it possible to bring a girlfriend back to Longleat to share his quarters. The only problem with Anna, he says, was that 'right from the start Anna was undermining me. Things were being said which undermined my confidence as an artist.' She was initially supportive and then soon very critical of his painting, for instance. This was at a time when Alexander had lost most of his self-confidence. He had far from fully emerged from the period of reclusiveness and intense introspection which followed his

Oxford graduation. He was desperate to prove himself as an artist; and that proof was, he felt, far from forthcoming from among his family. His second period in Paris was simply a continuation of the isolation into which he had retired after failing to prove himself at Oxford.

His friends refer to his disappearance after Oxford. Some of this was due to sheer depression arising from the shame of having lost the battle to prove himself in his father's eyes. He had wished to emerge, if not as an intellectual giant, at least as the possessor of a good degree which would have convinced his father that Alexander Thynne could be more than just a gentleman farmer and caretaker of a grand inheritance. It would also have proved him right: something he desperately needed to strengthen him in the disagreements with Henry over Longleat's finances which had, since his legal takeover of the estate, grown increasingly confrontational and stormy. It is the normal practice of the great estate to hand over for tax reasons the inheritance to the heir well before the death of the title holder. Alexander took over the Longleat inheritance in 1956 immediately after coming down from Oxford. Now he wanted to use his new power to curb some of his father's activities; but he had failed to win the authority that a good degree would have given him to win these arguments. He was now furiously intent on proving himself, not only as an artist but as an independent human being who could make choices separately from that Longleat identity. The power struggle which still characterizes Alexander's relationship with Anna began immediately. 'It was right towards the end of my time in Paris that I started my affair with Anna,' he says. 'I can't really talk straight on this, but she battered my self-confidence in many ways: but I lived through it and I was impressing her that, although she was being so battering and so aggressive, I was still unmoved and going calmly on.' Anna's onslaught was some kind of strengthening experience because Alexander seems to have been pushed forward by it rather than thrown back. 'She was surprised that she couldn't sink me with the fierceness that she produced,' he recalls. 'I think I was displaying the psychological muscles that these earlier years of pain had produced.' It was the success of surviving Anna's battering and undermining which enabled Alexander to continue with the relationship. He was winning at last in his fight for psychological survival against his detractors. 'The fact that I could endure someone who had set out to undermine me and was discovering that she couldn't, enabled me to continue with the relationship,' he explains. Perhaps his relationship with Anna was a continuation of his fight with Henry, a struggle for supremacy which was giving him more confidence, since it was with someone with whom he had a sexual relationship as well as a psychological battle to become himself.

Alexander's ultimate reaction to the challenge of the battle which Anna waged to undermine him was through his creativity. 'I started doing the murals at Longleat,' he explains. 'I was sitting in that drawing room downstairs, and the panels had been prepared so that a muralist could do them, and I got the feeling that I should be the muralist and that this should be my first major work. I looked upon it as a possibility, as a potential for display, that here I could demonstrate my true worth as an artist.' So Anna acted as a goad to prod Alexander into the first major expression of his work: one that was also, since it flawed the classical grandeur of the Renaissance palace, a statement of defiance against Henry and everything he represented. Indeed, his artist's life in Paris, living with Anna, who was hardly the consort whom his parents would have chosen to become the wife of a marquess, was also an expression of his rage against Henry and his wish to defy him in every way. There was also the sexual and emotional satisfaction of their attraction, which in the beginning at least, was greater than the forces driving them apart. There was, additionally, the fact that these two also felt that they were together against the world. 'We were two of a kind,' he says. 'We were two rebels, and two rebels is a very important point. You just don't think your parents are doing the right things for you. You have a free hand to think what you should be creating for yourselves. We were empathizing and sympathizing. Empathizing with the position of the other and seeing that we were aware of the problems of life. It was comfortable,' he adds, 'because it was shifting from my home environment and there were others in Paris at the time who were onto the same thing.' Anna was not from a Longleat background, however. Her mother, according to Tina Jorgenson, who knew both Anna and Alexander in the 1960s, was a poet and a journalist. The story was that Anna's parents were Hungarians who had come to live in France and had divorced. Her mother had also gone to the US. Their migration predated, and was nothing to do with, the Hungarian rising of 1956, and they were not refugees. More recently, Anna has allowed Wikipedia, the internet encyclopaedia, to write that she is a Hungarian aristocrat and a refugee. Alexander tells me that he has never been able to discover the truth. 'I never knew if what I was being told was the reality. I have been told things...' he says, leaving the sentence unfinished, his eyebrows rising. He describes Anna as 'a fantasist. I never know whether I am being told the truth about anything.' He does not think he has ever had the true story. Alexander himself is a little unsteady on some of the background to his eventual marriage. This did not take place until ten years after their first meeting in the Left Bank cinema. But he seems to have spent several years on and off in close companionship with Anna. After they lived in Paris together, the pair went off to South America in an old Jaguar. They travelled around, arguing and tussling. They also travelled in Scandinavia. Eventually they separated but did not part completely; and Alexander returned to England and Longleat while Anna went back to Paris.

In 1964, five years after the affair began, Alexander claims that 'I bought the villa near St Tropez in order to woo Anna.' But he has also confides in me that 'I would not marry Anna because she was too difficult.' In the meantime Anna married someone else: Gilbert Pinaud, a French film director some fifteen years her senior. While she was with Alexander, she appears to have had no particular profession, but on her return to Paris she determined to become an actress. After her marriage to Pinaud, her career in the films took off. Her clothes also came off, and her whole style underwent a revolution. From being the short-haired brunette with chutzpah and the aggressive profile, she became a voluptuous Bardot-style starlet with abundant blonde tresses, a delicately turned-up nose, and hugely made-up eyes. This was something akin to the transformation which occurred when the young brunette Jane Fonda, although already a beauty, was transformed after her marriage to French film director Roger Vadim into Barbarella, the plastic, space-age imitation of Brigitte Bardot, Vadim's ex- wife who had also undergone the transformation from brunette to blonde.

True to the style of Bardot and Fonda's 'Vadimization', Anna's transformation was very Barbarella. The studio photographs of that phase recorded in press cuttings, which now adorn the family album, show that Anna's profile had undergone a change: her nose now turned up at the end and was a more delicate structure than in the earlier photos, her eyelashes were long and curly

1960s false ones, her curling bleached hair now touched her only too visible nipples. She had also been taught how to pose. The effect was sensational. And this must have excited Alexander since he has told me that the blonde, busty model of womanhood is his ideal. Initially, at least, Anna's roles appeared to be nude and very sensual, and the films were described as soft porn. She starred in a film about lesbian love, and others which were all very 'Piccadilly Jacey': the blue cinema of that day. However, there were also some French TV slots in plays by Chekhov and other serious works, but only after her marriage to Alexander. She began visiting Longleat, and her appearance there evoked admiration among Alexander's Oxford pals. She was truly gorgeous, curvaceous, luminous, evidently exciting the pals. 'Anna wore long black boots,' recalls Laurence Kelly who saw her there – thigh boots being very chic in 1960s.

At St Tropez, Sir Ian Rankin was stunned to find 'Anna draped stark naked across a rock. She had the most gorgeous shape.' He thinks that Alexander did the best possible thing in marrying Anna. That was to come later. In the meantime there were more of the early wifelets and there was the 'anti-marriage'. Anna, however, although married to Gilbert Pinaud, came to Longleat. An actress and a 1960s beauty, she inspired the admiration of Shirley Conran, a frequent visitor to the glamorous house parties of those far off Halcyon days. 'I was quite entranced by Anna,' Shirley Conran recalls. 'She was absolutely beautiful, but she was so delicate. She could only eat certain things and could not drink wine. I saw her take a sip of red wine and immediately her face and neck turned a most hideous purple colour. There was this beautiful, fragile creature who was allergic to everything and she was taking homeopathic remedies, even in those days, well ahead of her time. It was quite interesting to see men falling in love with her.' She thinks that Alexander was genuinely in love with Anna. 'They were both very beautiful.' Conran, like many of her generation, remains in love with the 1960s and the glamour of that decade – Alexander too, although he says that 'for the 1960s, I was an oldie.' Then in his thirties, he never seems to have grown out of the 1960s. There he is, today, still in his hippie gear, velvet caftans, shoulder-length hair. Anna, however, has moved with the times. Once the glamorous starlet, everything a 1960s fan would adore; later the tough journalist, the novelist, autobiographer, she is now once more the bobbed brunette, gazing apologetically from the photo frames, modestly trouser-suited, chin down, demure. Not a nipple in sight. 'Demure?' Alexander burst out laughing at the very idea. 'You'll call her demure once too often. You might see another side.'

'You should be writing a book about me,' Anna told me huffily on the phone. But that sentence leaves so much unsaid.

Phase Two: The Marriage

There is an American joke that Hungarians are the people who come into the swing door after you and come out ahead of you. Anna followed Alexander into the revolving door of his relationships and came out of it ahead of all the other debutantes and putative models who had got in there before her and who had eyed Alexander as an eligible bachelor with a view to becoming his marchioness. 'I was thirty-seven,' Alexander says, 'and I thought it was time I produced an heir.' He looked around among his girlfriends. 'There was one particular girlfriend,' he wrote in his book about his philosophies, 'Anna, who had been coming to stay with me occasionally, or travel abroad with me, since the time I'd been at art school in Paris, back in 1959. In the 1960s,' he adds, 'she had married someone else, although her visits to Longleat had continued over the period.' Now, she was contemplating a divorce.

How casual he makes it sound, just like a business deal. No intimations of the passion and the intense emotional exchange which had bound these people to each other from 1959 to 1961 and continued to link them in relationship, however distant and rare, throughout the 1960s. Did Anna always want to marry Alexander? Did he consider marrying her at an earlier stage? If he says Anna was too difficult, why did he eventually decide that she was the one to become the official broodmare for the heir to the Seventh Marquess of Bath? Surely Anna would have found Alexander too difficult. Many of those close to him say that he is. And why had he met no one else in those ten years who would have been a possible mother for his legitimate heir? Alexander's gallery of wifelets for the next few years after 1961, when he returned to England and, as he puts it, 'rejoined society', shows a relatively sparse number of wifelet portraits. Considering that this was the 1960s when people were reputedly copulating like rabbits, it seems odd that he could not have sampled enough women from which to select a marchioness. Perhaps Anna was still in his head and evidently still, from time to time, married to Gilbert Pinaud or not, in his bed.

Old wives say the first ten years of marriage are the worst, and after ten years of an affair, interspersed with a few others, Alexander decided that Anna was the one. Of course, she was also the one with whom he had regained his self-confidence. She was the one he had, in fact, defeated in battle. She had prodded him into deliverance of his art, and he had begun his work in earnest. She accepted his other women. She could be a suitable wife. Anna, it seems agreed, but this was no conventional, aristocratic marriage. There was a deal. 'My lawyers told me that an agreement of the sort that I wanted had absolutely no foundation in law, Alexander reveals, 'so in the end it was a verbal agreement, mostly concerning property rights.'

Among other things Anna accepted that she would fund her own lifestyle without financial help from Alexander and that she would accept the polygyny system. She accepted that she would be the official wife who would breed a legitimate male heir to the title and the estate. This also gave her a title: the Marchioness of Bath. 'She agreed to the situation,' Alexander says. 'She said that it suited her better than a conventional marriage. She wanted to go on living in Paris and pursuing her career.' However, Tina Jorgensen, who knew Anna at this time, believes that Anna did not marry Alexander for love. The deal, Jorgensen tells me quite emphatically over a lunch at the Tate Gallery, was a means to an end for Anna too. She would receive from the marriage social status, the use of Longleat as a second home, a fairly imposing title and constant publicity in the tabloids which helped to move her career a step or two up from nude film roles to serious theatre. Before the marriage could take place, however, there was an important condition. Anna, still married to Gilbert Pinaud, had to become pregnant by Alexander. Of course, becoming pregnant was not an insurmountable problem. The question could only be, by whom?

'Was she still sleeping with her husband?' I ask Alexander.

'Well, yes.' he replies defensively. 'She wasn't going to divorce until she was pregnant.' Anna had no intention of divorcing her husband unless Alexander was committed to marrying her. Alexander had no intention of marrying Anna unless she could prove that she could give him a child. But if she was still sleeping with her husband, how did Alexander know that his firstborn child, his daughter, Lenka, was his own? 'Well, I take it from her that it's the case,' he says. And, indeed, women usually know. But has Alexander had a paternity test to make sure?

'No,' he says. 'But we're talking about Lenka, of course.' His tone of voice implies the lesser importance of this female firstborn. Lenka can never be the heir because she is female. Alexander does not know for sure that Lenka is his daughter. 'If you mean, could I bet Longleat on it? No,' he says, laughing slightly. Lenka's paternity is not important since she is not the heir, but Alexander's lifestyle would hardly inspire a woman to be faithful. Can he then be sure that either of his children, including the son and heir, Ceawlin – born five years after Lenka – is his own?

He blushes crimson. 'Of course,' he says, 'one goes through the questions, but I'm not going to start worrying about it, so don't push me to worry. Of course, I would be most upset if I ever discovered that either of them aren't my child, but I'm not going to start worrying.' For distraction from this difficult topic, he turns to speak to the dog. 'Woof, woof.'

Phase Three: A Thoroughly Modern Mirage

After the marriage, the tabloids adored the Bath bride. Beautiful, nude and near-nude publicity pictures from her movies were plastered across their pages. A lovely, photogenic actress married to an aristocrat: she could do no wrong. The interviews and the accolades proliferated. During her pregnancies and after the children were born, Anna continued to live in Paris. Her babies, who remained at Longleat, were cared for by nannies; and she visited Longleat, according to her arrangement with Alexander, for about one week per month. She still lives in Paris. Alexander has never visited her Paris home. Her present abode is an apartment in a grime-stained 1970s block in the 13th Arrondissement, on the edge of the more fashionable 5th Arrondissement. It has a central garden, visible from the street. On one side it's close to the touristic Rue Mouffetard, a street rich with *poissonerries, fromageries*, vintners, also packed with inexpensive little restaurants, shops selling oriental scarves and jewellery and Greek kebab houses, and on the other to a rather drab collection of 1960s and 1970s apartment blocks.

The area is a bit rundown. Not chic. Her street has a scattering of little shops, a *boulangerie*, a restaurant. Around the corner is a drab-looking clothing boutique. Her phone is listed in the name of a man. She still visits Longleat about one week a month. Alexander does not know which week that will be until quite short notice. 'She often arrives a bit sooner than expected,' he says. 'It's very annoying. I can't say "well you can't come that weekend." I have to alter my plans.' Is this because he wants to avoid any blowups as a result of Anna meeting a wifelet? This is a possibility. Anna has met wifelets occasionally, but 'she is usually seeking to undermine them,' Alexander adds with a smile.

He would prefer it if Anna's visits were guest-free because he does not know how she will react to his women friends. On the telephone from Longleat, Anna tells me that she will not give me an interview. 'But,' she says with a challenging note in her voice, 'why don't you come down to Longleat one weekend when I am there?' I suggest this to Alexander, but he does not feel he could allow it. He seems terrified at what might occur. Indeed, he may laugh and joke about it, but Anna clearly frightens him terribly. Yet it seems Alexander is the one who made the rules at the outset. So it seems curious that he is so afraid of his wife. Anna had overtly agreed to accept the wifelet scenario at the outset of the marriage deal. When the marriage was negotiated, Alexander said, she intimated that she might join in the wifelet games: in other words, share her marriage bed with one or more of the mistresses. In practice, she avoids them, and they are intimidated by her formidable reputation as a virago. They would also prefer not to be around when she visits. Anna would, of course, not wish to be introduced to wifelets. She can publicly ignore their existence. She has even, fairly recently, gone a step further and denounced the wifelets as 'a fabrication by journalists'; but that was in an item in a diary column which, according to Alexander, may not have been quite accurate. Indeed, under the circumstances, after more than forty years of press coverage, it would be difficult to deny the existence of the wifelets. Interpreting this curious proposition, Alexander feels that Anna may have changed her position on her long-distance, part-time marital status and would prefer to be a fulltime wife. 'Certainly, when we were first married she was saying this idea suited her,' he says. 'Whether she alters that theme in her answers to others now, I'm not sure what to make of that.' However, he also tells me that that Anna may have agreed to the terms about polygyny while hoping that the deal would change in time. 'Anna would have preferred a more conventional marriage,' he says

Indeed, this is borne out by an anecdote told by Christine, a wifelet of the 1970s, who met Anna at the Ramatuelle villa. It seems that, having read items about this rather gorgeous oriental wifelet in the press and seen her photographs, Anna arrived unscheduled at the villa. She rather imperiously dispatched a docile Alexander to the village to buy *patisserie* and then sat down with Christine and told her that her affair with Alexander was likely to cause a divorce. One wonders why the wifelet did not call Anna's bluff, save to say that by the end of her visit at the villa she was rather weary of Alexander. 'I only really got to know Alexander when I went to stay in St Tropez with him,' Christine tells me. 'He's very conservative underneath that hippie stuff. He was very inclined to talk down to people. He would point at someone and ask them questions as if to say "Hey you down there. Tell me your views on life." It was as if all the 1960s hippie stuff was just a camouflage and that underneath it all he looked down on people. He wagged his finger at them when he was talking. I didn't like that at all. The final thing on that visit that really turned me off was his selfishness. When we were leaving to go back to London, he stopped the car in the village and went into the shop to buy himself something and a lolly for his daughter. He came back with something for each of them. He never even asked me what he could get for me. After that, I didn't want to tell him that I didn't want to see him anymore. I went on seeing him, but whenever I was with him in London or at Longleat or wherever, I did everything I could to humiliate him. I would insult him at a dinner party in front of all his friends. He didn't know what was going on.'

Did Anna play the divorce card again with later wifelets, and did she try to play it with Alexander? If she did, it evidently did not work. The wifelets kept on being featured in the newspapers and tripping down to St Tropez to the villa for their summer visits. Anna's attempts to head off the humiliating experience of being the poor wife, spurned sexually in favour of mistresses, did not work in the case of Christine – nor would it have worked with any others. Alexander, after all, controlled the game. Anna could fight back by threatening a divorce with all its financial implications for an adulterer. The fact that she had verbally agreed to accept wifelets would not be of much help to Alexander when faced with the legalities of the wife's position in an English court. However, Anna evidently had more to gain from staying married than from divorcing. In the first blush of her youthful beauty and success before the cameras, in her triumph at becoming the Marchioness of Bath, Anna may have overlooked the distressing side of being constantly upstaged in the British press by a succession of fresh faces at her husband's side. No doubt the ensuing years of being portrayed as the long-suffering wife of a highly public Casanova have taken their toll on her self-respect. She may be Lady Bath at public gatherings, but privately, and in terms of tabloid gossip, she is one face in the crowd: the wife of a man who publicly parades his mistresses, often at the same parties at which she presides as his wife. What a constant experience of rejection! Yet she prefers not to divorce, despite the fact that divorce might bring her financial benefits, perhaps because nowadays she is getting more financially out of staying married. That does not diminish the ignominy of being the public woman at the side of the man who makes it clear to the world that he has more enticing things to do at bedtime than accompany his legal partner to the marriage bed. This is a real humiliation for any woman, not only for one whose sexuality was overtly flaunted in her 1960s films. There is an element of cruelty in this continual upstaging, even by a man long past his prime, of a woman whose beauty and fertility have peaked. Not that many of the wifelets can compete for looks with Anna in her days of glory. There are times, however, when Alexander seems to be trying to have his revenge. But against whom? Against Anna, for the ways in which she so brutally tried to dismember his fragile self-confidence during their early years together? Or against some archetype deeply buried in his unconscious memories of that elusive phantom of female seductiveness, Daphne? He once told me that his father's treatment of him during his teens, beating him and denigrating him, was 'punishing the son in order to punish the mother'. But it seems that in his treatment of Anna, Alexander is punishing the wife in order to punish the mother. By subjecting his wife to the constant public display of his infidelity, he is punishing his mother Daphne for her very public displays of her extra-marital affairs. In doing that, he is getting his own back on his mother for the fact that he was made a scapegoat by Henry for the destruction of Henry's and Daphne's marriage. 'My children think I have treated Anna very badly,' Alexander tells me. Some of this must have come from Anna herself, but Lenka and Ceawlin are also embarrassed at Alexander's parade of wifelets. They too would have preferred a conventional marriage for their parents. So much for the fairy tale of Mummies and Daddies walking into the sunset together, free of illicit sexual passions, united in ideal love for each other and their families. Is it ever so except in dreams, or perhaps in photographs? The family snaps on Alexander's sideboard showing him and Anna, a brunette once more ("gentlemen prefer blondes but marry brunettes") but looking lovely, cooing over their newborn babies, seem the very image of a perfect union. The looks which the couple give each other in these pictures are of deep and close love. The pony-tailed Alexander bending tenderly over his babies is the dream father: handsome, caring and virile. Alexander and Anna seem the ideal couple. Other snaps show them walking together outside the stately pile with the two children toddling beside them. So much for polygyny – this was the image of successful monogamy. Or was it just for the cameras?

Anna's decision to accept Alexander's proposal for an extraordinary marriage has haunted her throughout the thirty or so years of this polygynous compromise. What may have seemed a victory over all Alexander's other mistresses, when, in 1969, she married one of Europe's grander titles and became the Marchioness of Bath, has turned into a forty-year struggle with the humiliating reality of her husband's sexual publicity. No wonder she has continued to live abroad where she can lead her own life and avoid constant blushes at tabloid accounts of Alexander's affairs. Her life in Paris has changed considerably from those crazy days when the *beau monde* moved from party to party, where her fantasist nature could play games with other people's realities. She is no longer an actress, having given it up during the 1970s in favour of journalism. She has also published some books: two novels and an autobiographical account of her war reportage from Vietnam, all in French. Once Shirley Conran was riding in a Paris taxi and discovered that the driver was reading Anna's Vietnam War memoirs. 'He was,' she says, 'enthralled. He said it was really terribly good.' Anna no longer has to support herself entirely unaided, however. She is now a director of Longleat Enterprises and receives a director's salary; but her role with regard to the estate remains limited to certain domestic issues. 'She takes enormous interest as to whether the carpets are kept clean and that sort of thing,' he remarks to me, as if to put her down. 'She's not involved in the running of the estate. She doesn't have any role there. That's delegated. I wouldn't want Anna having anything to do with that. I wouldn't want her coming between me and the manager.' Anna seems to have a proprietorial feeling for Longleat. Her son has said that she feels as if the house owns her. Alexander continues rather disparagingly, 'She wants the staff to feel she is "Boss Lady" sort of thing, although, except for cleaning matters, she wouldn't be telling them what to do.'

In effect, Anna is a terror for the bottom line. She evidently tells Alexander what to do and what not to do. When I ask Alexander if Anna questioned him about his sex life, he smartly retorts: 'She's more likely to ask me about what I've been spending.' Alexander does not like dealing with record-keeping and accounting, only going so far as filling out his cheque stubs. 'I don't want to know about checking the accounts,' he tells me. 'I leave all that to Anna.' Since Alexander does not give presents to his wifelets or take them to restaurants, there is no danger of a drama about cheques to Asprey's or extra cash drawn on his London visits to pay for candlelight dinners. Pub lunches at *The Windsor Castle* do not stretch the budget much. Even so, Anna tells Alexander off sharply if he seems to have loosened up on the purse strings.

Anna's visits to Longleat are reputedly a torture for everyone there because of her keen eye for detail, her obsessively critical nature, her temper and the abrasive tongue with which she lashes Alexander and his housekeepers. No one has an easy time when she is around. 'Anna is a very ferocious lady,' Alexander says. 'I think a fair section of the staff is quite frightened when she comes.' Indeed, her reputation with Alexander's personal housekeeping staff is that of a scold. They report that she attacks them furiously, to such an extent that it would be quite difficult for them to contemplate staying on at Longleat if she were permanently resident. As it is, there are also some wifelets who behave in a similar fashion. It is as though Alexander's hidden anger infects some of his women and they act it out. One of the extraordinary stories about Anna concerns the wine brought by weekend guests as gifts. Friends have noted that this wine disappears before the bottles can be opened. The friend of Alexander's who claims that a housekeeper had shown her a cupboard in the kitchen crammed full of assorted bottles of wine brought by guests also tells me that some of them had been opened but were still on the shelves. She was told by the housekeepers that Lady Bath would not allow even the oxidized contents of long-opened bottles to be thrown away or even used for cooking. Parsimony indeed!

One of the problems which Alexander describes is that Anna nags. It upsets and agitates him to the point where he must do something to stop it. The answer is that he hits her. 'Nag, nag, nag goes on,' he says, 'and if you happen to be driving along in the car it becomes too dangerous. It could cause an accident.' He starts to shout in re-enactment of one such scene. He jabs his finger in a ferocious demonstration of relived fury. 'I say,' he shouts '"Are you going to stop? No? All right! Are you going to stop? Are you going to stop? If you don't stop right now, I'll stop the car and I'll slap you." She doesn't, so I stop the car and *bang, bang, bang* I slap her. Then I start the car again and if she starts to nag, I say, "If you don't stop now at once, I'll slap you again."' Alexander is yelling, wild-eyed, puce of face, and the whole scene is repeated. '"It's got to stop,"' he shouts. '"It's got to stop. Stop that at once. I'll slap you again." She doesn't stop so, *bang, bang, bang*. I slap her face quite hard several times.' Anna, it seems, takes it quietly. She does not fight back physically, but she often does not give up, and the violent scene has to be repeated several times on a journey. One day there was an accident with Anna in the passenger seat. In June 2007, Alexander accidentally struck a pedestrian on a zebra crossing while driving his gold-and-black BMW in Central London. According to a report in the *Daily Mail*, the pedestrian was lying in the road bleeding from a head wound. He was taken to hospital, and Alexander was taken away by the police for a breath test. Asked about the crash by a reporter, he replied: 'It was a very frightening experience.' On hearing that the pedestrian was not as seriously injured as first thought, he said: 'That is a very great relief to me.'

In or out of a car, it is not only Anna whom Alexander slaps. 'I have also slapped certain wifelets,' he says. 'Only some. It's not a great pleasure in my life.' There is a whole other side to the relationship. Anna, who has always been a health fanatic, shows wifely concern for Alexander. She feeds him vitamins, leaving pills for the staff to put beside his plate at breakfast. 'They're probably drugs to keep me tranquilized,' Alexander says, laughing.

He usually does not invite other guests when Anna comes for her monthly stay, since Lenka and Ceawlin sometimes come and the family can be together. The children are less likely to visit on other weekends as they dislike having to meet the wifelets. The Longleat sleeping arrangements are not intimate, however. Anna has her own suite of rooms in the house and sleeps there while Alexander sleeps, as always, in the penthouse. Anna had not been to the Notting Hill apartment for years until one day, a few years ago when a train cancellation forced her to take refuge there for a night. Apparently she was horrified by the filthy and chaotic condition of the place and reported this to the Longleat housekeepers.

Alexander admits that he and Anna still sleep together in his double bed at the villa in Ramatuelle. 'When we're down in France there's one bedroom that is shared,' he tells me. 'There are three bedrooms, and often two are occupied if the children come, but in any case I'm not moving out of my bedroom and that is where she would expect to be.' There is a distinct absence of pillow talk. 'I go to sleep rather quick,' Alexander laughs. In the morning Alexander gets up first, early rising as ever, to go to his desk and the satellite news so there's no talk then either. At Longleat, he says, 'Anna gets up late and stays downstairs for breakfast. She tells me that in Paris she gets up early to work.' He says this disbelievingly, as if he suspects that she does no such thing. It is also part of Alexander's attitude that there are important virtues in early rising. Getting up early and getting on with the day is not the normal artists' life, but Alexander's disciplines are very much those of his experience in the Life Guards and at Eton. So the couple who do not talk in bed or at breakfast talk at lunch and dinner. 'There are other times when we talk,' he observes, 'and yes, we talk at lunch.' At Longleat it is the same. Because of the separate sleeping arrangements, with Alexander in the penthouse and Anna downstairs in her suite, the couple don't meet until lunch. This is usually a meal prepared by the housekeeper and served on a trolley in the downstairs drawing room. The conversation is often difficult.

'Anna is very secretive,' Alexander reveals. 'We don't talk about her career. I certainly did when it was acting, and what the reviews were. But now it's journalism, I suppose I don't know exactly what she's been writing about.

'I don't probably get all the answers I might want,' he adds rather disconsolately. 'It was always very difficult to get factual information. People like this have got their lives, and so they give you a story and change it when necessary. Also, perhaps, they feel it's none of your business.' Some people lie by omission, allowing one to string together a story of one's own from the few things one is told. 'Yes there was a lot of that going on too,' he says 'but she's got more cautious now, because my having worried and worried away, fretting and fretting about well, what is the story? And having finally got out of her some semblance of the truth, I think she's much more cautious.'

Right from the start of the relationship Alexander realized he was not getting the truth from Anna about her background or her life. He does not know if she was simply trying to hide a background that she considered might not come up to scratch for an aristocrat. 'I think it was partly the mentality of a fantasist,' he admits, 'and partly that she was also not satisfied, herself, with the factual details. There was a lot of what I was told that wasn't the same next time.'

Needless to say, there were no wifelets at the villa during Anna's annual two-week summer stay. This was a family holiday interlude timed according to Anna's whim; and around it were arranged the visits of the squads of wifelets and other women friends who were flown in and out of St Tropez for short stays, their visits coordinated by Viv, Alexander's Longleat-based secretary. In contrast to when wifelets were in residence, Alexander cooked every night when the family were there. 'My speciality is big meaty stews,' he says, 'but I also do paellas, things you throw everything into. At Longleat too, I'm quite happy to cook, but I'm not so sure that other people like my cooking. I don't think I cook so well that other people want to go on eating my cooking for long. After a few nights there woul be a general cry of "Oh, can't we go out, Dad?"'

Alexander clearly enjoys these family occasions, but they are rare. Lenka, forty with a career in television production and a baby; and Ceawlin, now in his mid-thirties, developing a career as a banker and currently living in Russia, are both leading their own lives. Ceawlin has gone on record saying he hopes he can make a lot of money to fund a Longleat less intruded-upon by the public. This seems the idealism of youth. His vision of Longleat, private and non-commercial, is unrealistic unless he can bring billions to the cause.

Alexander's declared object in life is that Longleat should survive. His belief at one time was that the place would become a giant public concern with the family camping out in an apartment there. However, the success of Longleat as a commercial enterprise and the changed aims of Labour governments over the years have made that notion redundant. In accordance with the need to evade large-scale death duties, the estate has now been transferred to Ceawlin. So the present Viscount Weymouth has been made aware of the practical realities, the funding, the sheer magnitude of the cash flow required to maintain such a place. He now knows that it is a business and that his father is not only Chief Executive but also, and more importantly, Head of Public Relations, the star of the show. Ceawlin is said to have remarked that when he takes over, things will be very different. This is the boy that Alexander sent to the local comprehensive school and who, in his teens, when he became Viscount Weymouth and began to receive an income from the estate, decided, after taking advice from lawyers, to check himself into Bedales, a mixed progressive public school. He was thrown out for smoking pot, a drug which his father is in favour of legalizing. Ceawlin has also told certain members of his father's staff that when he takes over, and this may be quite some time in the future, he will evict the wifelets from their cottages. This tells the story of his feelings about his father and his mother's marriage. His attitude, a throwback to the old days of the very private aristocratic estate, entirely financially self-sufficient, is also conservative in terms of marriage. The children of that rebellious generation who threw out conventions during the 1960s are often conservative, traditionalist and staid. The only way to rebel against a rebel is to embrace the status quo, but Ceawlin is doing so in a world where, as his father seems to understand, commerce responds to promotion. Alexander is the king of marketing techniques. Ceawlin, with his desire for the conventional aristocratic life may find himself stranded, lacking the promotional skills with which to draw in the customers. However, Ceawlin seems to have a slightly wild side to his persona. Some of the colourful genes of his parents may be expressing themselves at times. Being expelled from school is a good start. In July 2001, a warrant was issued for Ceawlin's arrest for failing to turn up at Horseferry Road Magistrates Court to face charges. The magistrate said that he could not have bail if found, so it looked like jail for the viscount, who had been breathalysed while driving a Maserati and had already been excused one hearing on the grounds of absence on business. No doubt he will wish to assert his own personality on Longleat when he eventually takes control as the Eighth Marquess. Will he remove

189

Alexander's murals? Alexander hopes that he will not. The murals are Alexander's life's work. Ceawlin also wants a conventional married life. A tragic accident in India, where the hotel he was staying in was blown up by terrorists, deprived him of the girlfriend whom he said he had hoped to marry. Her death may be something he still has not accepted. In this he reveals himself to be as sensitive as his father but less reactive. The relationship between father and son is something which Alexander says he has sorted out. When Ceawlin was a child, Alexander once had to slap him for disobedience, but it only happened once. He has not, he said, slapped his children: unlike his father. He feels the father-son relationship is far better that the one he had with Henry. If both children seem closer to their mother, it is because they cannot accept their father's lifestyle. Even as Alexander admits to resenting the fact that his father chose divorce because he wanted a new bride, he cannot avoid realizing, as he first realized in childhood, that happy families are not easily forged when husband and wife lead separate lives. 'Happy families are not something I've had experience of,' he says wistfully.

Chapter Seven
Paranoia

Seeds of Psychodrama

Alexander talks a lot about his paranoia: so much so that one has to wonder why he wants to draw attention to something that most people would consider to be a manifestation of insanity. Evidently Alexander's paranoia, like everything else about his personality, is under strict control. It remains the object of Alexander's interest and the subject of much of his artistic output. Indeed, it was at one time a big feature of his life. He eventually created a mural entitled *Paranoia*. His paranoia is evidently not of the clinical variety. His use of the term seems to be an exaggeration of a state of mind which in his case seems to be the result of genuine persecution, although, the word persecution is too strong. 'Severe criticism' would be a more accurate description of what Alexander was experiencing. It became full blown when Alexander came down from Oxford, tail between his legs, having failed to get the kind of degree which would have made Henry, his father, see that Alexander was, indeed, an intellectual cut above the average farming Thynne.

Several of his Oxford contemporaries mentioned the year in which Alexander apparently disappeared from social life and became a recluse down at Longleat. This period also coincided with the handover of the Longleat Estate to Alexander for tax reasons and with him receiving some money of his own as well as his own apartment in Longleat House. It was a time of change, of shifting balances and of sudden furious conflict with Henry. 'The estate was handed over to me to avoid death duties in the event of my father dying suddenly,' he tells me before adding: 'Well, then all the estate was mine, but I was still letting him go on making decisions in the forestry, even though it wasn't his.' The legal handover of the estate to Alexander meant that he was now able to examine the books and learn about the way his father had been running things. In actuality, Henry was still heavily involved in the estate, and it was the fact that Alexander now wanted to take financial decisions with which Henry disagreed that brought about a crisis. There were furious rows. 'My father consulted some lawyers who found out that the will of the First Marquess did not include the contents of the house,' Alexander says. 'So my father found out that he could do whatever he liked with the contents of Longleat House. He was selling valuable books from the library to allow him to finance whatever he wanted to do and he had also been secretly and illegally selling valuable pictures and putting up copies instead. My father had always been saying Longleat was everything. "We must do our best for Longleat. The survival of Longleat comes first." Now, here he was, once he found out he could do what he wanted, he was just selling things and stripping the estate of its heritage to finance whatever he wanted.' Alexander's voice expresses disgust.

Henry had remarried by this time, and soon there was to be a daughter, Silvy, from that second marriage. From this point on until Henry's death in 1992 there would be fights about what Henry was doing with money from the sale of Longleat treasures. It was as if his father was trying to rob Alexander of his heritage by the backdoor. Some of these arguments account for the state of extreme anger in which Alexander says he found himself and which was the background to a paranoia which had been developing since he was a schoolboy. 'We used to be very angry with each other,' Alexander says, 'but then it was a matter of why is he angry about me? Does it have a factual basis? Are our visions distorted? I suppose I was thinking: "his is distorted, mine is clear thinking."'

The first betrayal of what had been the son's adulation of his soldier father occurred, he remembers, when he was just a baby. Henry held out his cigarette and asked little Alexander to hold out his hand. He touched his son's hand with the burning end of the cigarette and laughed at the pain he caused. That breach of trust had gone into Alexander's memory but had not meant too much. Then came the second incident. While Alexander was at Ludgrove he tried to implement Henry's teachings of fascism and strong leadership by having one of his schoolmates disciplined by being shut into a chest of drawers. 'My father had been saying that Hitler was giving the right message,' he says. 'I was listening, absorbing his teaching. I was captain of the school, and I went back there and ran a little fascist dictatorship. There were cases when there were two people who had disobeyed the monitors and also someone who had been bullying someone so we gave him a dose of his own medicine by shutting him in a drawer. He'd done exactly the same to someone else.' When Henry was informed of this by the school, he agreed with the Headmaster that Alexander should be disciplined for this event. That was the first major disillusionment for a boy who was trying to follow his father's line. It was the first crack in the wall of his admiration for Henry. The beating over the dog-washing incident, which came several years later, brought the wall tumbling down. Alexander gave up respecting his father's authority. From then on it was war.

Before this, Alexander says, 'I was trying to be everything my father would have wanted a son to be.' He does not understand why he allowed his father to beat him as a child for washing his dog in the kitchen. 'It could nowadays be a case one complained to the police about,' he says bitterly, 'but not then. It was ridiculous. I hadn't been there. I'd been away for a week, working in the woods where he'd sent me; and the other children had been there, getting on his nerves apparently, as he explained to me later. But there was no need to beat me for washing my dog, making water on the linoleum floor which had to be mopped up, as he was saying, by the housekeeper.' His voice is full of anger, indignation and incredulity. 'The humiliation was unnecessary,' he goes on. 'The fact that I submitted to it is humiliating because I was bigger than him. He couldn't possibly have done it if I'd resisted.' The humiliation still wounds. It was the turning point in father-son relations. Indeed, the problem was why did Alexander feel that his father was angry with him? It seems that the root of the paranoia was that beneath the surface of the rights and wrongs of every argument about the estate, Alexander sensed another motive for his father's attitude. It seemed to him that his father had it in for him: that his father resented the handing over the estate to his virile young son and that he was manoeuvring stealthily to cheat Alexander out of his legal right to inherit the lot. The problem of overtly manifested anger began to alienate son from father when Alexander was quite young. By 1945, Henry had also had some three years in which to brood about his wife's love affairs, which were continuing. Did he come to the conclusion that Daphne had been unfaithful to him long before the mad days of the war? Did she actually tell him as much?

Alexander says that Daphne had implied that she had had affairs before Henry went off to the war but that Henry had accepted them. If, however, there was any doubt that his son and heir might not be his own child, would he have taken it so calmly? Alexander does not physically resemble his father at all closely, apart from being tall – as, indeed, was Daphne. Nor does he resemble his younger brother Christopher. The latter resembles Henry quite closely. Like Henry, he is tall and thin with an angularity of face, head and body that Alexander did not have, even in his slender youth. Christopher's facial structure is also very similar to that of Henry's. But the most prominent feature is the long thin nose, which could indeed be called the 'Thynne nose'.

This nose appears on most of the Thynne descendants, including the young nephew of Alexander, who is also named Alexander and who is the love child of Christopher by a mistress who lived in Tangier. Also Silvy, Henry's daughter by his second wife, having a similar nose, more closely resembles Henry than Alexander does. She has the same lean frame and similar facial structure to Henry. Alexander, however, seems to be built quite differently: not lean, and although slim enough in his youth, never thin in the way Henry and Christopher are thin and angular. Alexander's facial structure certainly does not resemble that of his father, his brother or others on Henry's side of the family. I asked Alexander about this. He seemed not at all phased. 'I haven't heard it suggested before,' he replies. 'Sons don't resemble their fathers that much, but usually they do so sufficiently.' I suggest that a suspicion that his son was not of his own blood is a possible cause of Henry's irrational treatment of Alexander. 'I think it was because I was refusing to endorse his lines of policy and backing the opposition to him which irritated him enormously,' he maintains. This, however, was a later manifestation, which came when lawyers became embroiled in legal struggles over the estate and Henry's management of it. The irrational anger towards Alexander began earlier, while Alexander was still at Ludgrove, when Henry found out the extent of Daphne's infidelities. However, in the next moment, Alexander, referring to that earlier period, asserts that: 'I was trying to exemplify his attitude to life; and I was, in fact, exemplifying it very well, but he couldn't see that.'

This attitude of trying to emulate Henry was at its height while Alexander was a schoolboy, but there were shadows of it even during his period in the army. Alexander's full-scale rebellion came long after the beating. It came after Oxford and after the handover of the estate. It was then that Alexander discovered much of his father's secret activities with regard to the Longleat Estate, and any remaining shreds of respect for Henry vanished. The disillusionment with his parental teaching was complete. By then it was evident that something very important had occurred which had not only turned Henry against his eldest son but had at the same time caused him to favour his second son, Christopher, in everything. The result was that Alexander's view of the world was turned upside down. Instead of being the exemplifier of his father's attitude to the world, he became its chief challenger. He challenged it in head-on confrontation but also by acting out his rejection of it in his bohemian lifestyle and his political stance. The more he challenged, however, the more he found himself in collision with his whole family and ultimately his class and his entire social cohort. Here, in the disintegration of his relationships with his family and his rejection by them, we find the birth of Alexander's rebellion against his cut-glass world. Here, also, are the origins of what he calls his 'paranoia'.

Turning Experience into Art

One of the murals outside the dining-room door in the downstairs quarters at Longleat is entitled *Mental Disorder*. These murals were all done in the 1960s after Alexander's return from Paris and his travels in South America and Western Europe with Anna. However, the source of much of the material, recollected in anger, is that period of his late teens and early twenties when his great disillusionment and rebellion set in. The first mural painted is *The Ages of Man*. This is a series of panels representing the stages of life, starting with birth and passing through various phases to maturity and to death. It is well-planned with a harmonious pinkish colour scheme. The ceiling is adorned with a vivid sunflower-like sun which represents an existence outside physical life.

Alexander describes this quite often to tour groups who pass through his drawing room while he is in there alone or with guests: 'We have, innocence, disillusionment, maturity, toil, success, decay and, on the ceiling, an eternity panel where I've inset a symbol from all these other panels. In the other panels, there are three small insets in each of them and they talk the same language as dreams. If you describe one of these insets to a psychiatrist, treating it in the same way as the contents of a dream, you would find that the pictures are talking about the problems of life and I'm sitting here in the middle of it and it all comes crowding in on me, and I go out and then come in again and then start all over again.' By the time he painted this mural and his others, Alexander had read considerable amounts of psychological literature. He says that he 'read paperbacks on the work of Freud, Jung, Adler, and more things like group psychotherapy, the Tavistock Clinic and what they were about.' Alexander was doing this to understand himself, to try to sort out what was happening to him, to find the answers to what he perceived as paranoia. The result of this was, he says, 'a double-edged sword. I understand others.' He laughs a jolly laugh. Alexander even interprets the dreams of many of his wifelets. 'They tell them to me,' he says, 'and I often understand much more about them than they think they are telling me. So I often go straight into the language that I was using at this time, and I'm seeing what is troubling them.' It's not that he's trying to tell their futures. He had a spell at that. Palmistry was, at one time, he says, a way of getting girls interested in him. He could start by holding their hands. He no longer believes in all that. He finds all forms of prediction a threat to his own powerful sense of materialistic determinism. He tells of how his father had his, the young Alexander's horoscope cast, and how the Indian astrologer predicted that he would become a diplomat. Enough said. Alexander, a Taurus, does not believe in astrology. He has striven, however, to understand much of his psychological depths without referring to anything beyond the normal timeframe; and he is still trying, he says, to understand himself. Up to the age of twenty-five, Alexander had been struggling with disillusionment and trying to make sense of it. Once finished with disillusionment he realized that he was terribly angry. He says that he was then preoccupied primarily with trying to find out why he was so angry.

The 1950s, he says, when he was in his twenties, were his 'Angry Young Man' period. 'Angry Young Men' were a notable feature of that decade, many of them writing books and plays: John Osborne's *Look Back in Anger* was typical of the genre. Alexander wrote a novel called *Angry Young Men*. He is relieved that it did not get published. There was another called *The Millions and the Mansions*, which he also binned. Anger may have been a prevailing psychological force of the period as the post-war younger generation examined the class system and rejected the illusion of upper-class superiority which had been accepted by earlier generations of all social classes. Alexander was from the aristocracy and had been brought up to believe in its mystique of hierarchical supremacy. His perception of the illusory nature of the mythology of his own class superiority was equally strong. Perhaps, above all, he realized that, despite his expectations as an aristocrat, he was unable to demonstrate that his membership of the ruling class gave him abilities to be superior and to become a leader and ruler of other men. 'Yes,' he says of the latter, 'intellectual disillusionment and leadership; disillusionment that things went so wrong sometimes in my army officer training. Yet I was aware of having had a higher opinion of my capabilities than the outcome suggests.' There is no doubt that his feelings were registering a mighty quake at all levels of his being; emotional, intellectual, personality issues were all being confronted. It was not only what he perceived as an upper-class society that had regrouped after the war and returned to 'business as usual'. It was that he, Alexander, was personally experiencing a huge revolt against the attitudes of his own class, especially the ones exemplified by his father's views. Even if his revolt was part of a general historic sea-change, he did not perceive it as such. For him, the revolt and its causes were intensely personal, hence the fact that he felt so personally victimized to the point of paranoia. However, the times in which he lived lent huge force to his personal crisis. 'Disobedience may be regarded as the greatest luxury of youth,' Jean Cocteau observed, writing at about the time Alexander was experiencing his internal revolution, 'and there is nothing worse than those times when young people are too free and consequently denied the opportunity to disobey.' Alexander experienced the extreme opportunity to disobey. He was brought up to believe absolutely in a rigid aristocratic elitism; but when he understood that this view was a fraud, that his father, his mother and everyone else in the cut-glass case were in fact no more special than the others, that they did not even follow the rules of their own social strictures and formulations, he had no alternative than to try to find another way. Of course, he had been personally betrayed, and the pain of this had been the trigger that had forced him to scrutinize the myth he had been educated to uphold. Had Henry shown Alexander that he valued the ways in which he was trying to emulate him, Alexander might have gone on to be a right-wing aristocrat of the old school. He might never have rebelled. As it was, much of Alexander's anger related to the way he had allowed himself to be fooled by the myth of aristocratic superiority and by the way in which he had tried to model himself on a man whom he now perceived to be unworthy of his admiration.

Henry's betrayals brought Alexander to the point of realizing that his hero was a hollow man. From this point onwards he began to question not only his father and his immediate society; but, because he seemed to be alone against them all in his views, he also questioned himself. The shock of this breakdown of his belief in an absolute view of society, which his father upheld, disturbed Alexander deeply and is still disturbing him. At the time of this breakdown of belief, he was suddenly stranded, with no foundations to his world. He wobbled. He questioned his mental state, questioned himself as to whether he was in fact in 'mental disorder,' a phrase which supplied the title for one of his later murals. Eventually he found reassurance in the fact that he could explain himself, but this took years and is still going on. The self-analysis went on throughout his second period in Paris. 'I was a loner,' he says of his time there, 'reading psychology, writing the novels which weren't up to standard and painting paintings without any place to put the paintings.' If this realisation was slow to come, it was because of the pain of rejection, of being wrong-footed, of being made to feel that he was out of step with 'English Society'. That was the main reason that he could not stay in England after Oxford. England, he observes, had won the war but the old system had remained virtually intact. England was ossified. However, French society of the time, certainly the artistic and cultural world of Paris, was busy forging new values. Alexander was swimming daily in this dynamic intellectual climate and doing so via his painting. He was gradually absorbing new elements, more egalitarian, more freethinking; and these elements harmonized with the views he had heard expressed by the liberal-thinking masters at Eton and their counterparts among the dons of Oxford. It was a thread in the labyrinth which might lead to a way out for Alexander personally. It is perhaps no coincidence that even today

Alexander goes on creating new mazes for the entertainment of Longleat's tourists. No wonder he accepted the statue of the Minotaur for his private garden. Alexander has found a workable way of being, but he is still looking for clues as to who he might become, who he really is under the seesaw imagery of randy roué and sad recluse, for the way out of the maze. By the time he began painting murals at Longleat in 1964, eight or nine years had passed since he had experienced that massive humiliation of being beaten by his father at the age of fifteen. It had taken all this time to turn his anguish into art. It was eight or nine years of introspection, self-analysis, a lonely quest for self-confidence and self-respect after self-perceived failure, rejection and humiliation. 'In 1964,' he says, 'which was the end of this period, I was playing around with psychological dream symbolism and making sense, so all those images are visions of what you get in dreams.' Then aged thirty-two, feeling some success under his belt because he had survived the psychological onslaught from Anna and the ongoing denigration by his family, his painting benefited enormously. Suddenly, he was painting rapidly, translating these dream images, these well understood psychological images and experiences into painted images: visionary themes at times so huge and so ambitious that only the walls of a great house could accommodate them. And he had that house.

After the near decade of feeling stymied, there was a rush of activity. This was no rich man's playtime, no desultory doodling to keep oneself amused. It was planned, coherent, driven work. According to Michael Croucher, Alexander created a colony of young artists on the estate, housed them, fed them and paid them to paint the swirling red and purple backdrop onto which his hardboard panels for the various murals would be fixed. It was the speed with which he accomplished it that staggered Croucher and made the whole effort seem like 'desecration'. Yes, Alexander had discovered his artistic muscles and, impassioned by the anger that still burned violently within the furnace of his recollected hurts, he rapidly covered the delicately traditional Chinese Eighteenth Century wallpaper of rooms and galleries in his half of the conventionally-furnished house with his removable boards bearing his expressionist, autobiographical statements.

His work is historically as well as personally relevant. It relates to the current times in which Alexander developed his revolt against the aristocratic conventions and the arthritic class structures of the pre-war world and of their dogged perpetuation into the post war period. It relates to the other attacks on that resurrected choreography of class relationships which drove Alexander out of that 1950s 'never had it so good' England to find a new self. It relates to the political and social changes that swept in during the 1960s as the floors of the old world finally gave way and collapsed in a cloud of dust, taking with it the tulle-frocked debutantes and their dancing partners. No wonder schoolchildren are writing theses about Alexander's painting. There is far more here in these huge murals than a Bluebeard's Gallery of wifelet heads could possibly express about human nature, human life on earth, about Alexander's carefully crafted philosophies. In the end, with titles like *Paranoia, Mental Disorder* and *Prey into Predator*, it is also a personal statement, and therein lies its vigour, its vitality and its arresting audacity, individuality and personality. But the paranoia and its causes had not burned out. If anything, they were more evident.

'A Traitor to My Class'

Returning from his foreign travels in 1961, Alexander once more installed himself at Longleat and attempted to rejoin society. So far there were no indications that he was 'socially unacceptable', which was a phrase he had used to describe his previous experience of being an undesirable in his sister's marital home and of having disapproval showered upon him from all around. It was the purchase of the Notting Hill maisonette, which became possible now that he had money of his own from the estate, which helped to bring Alexander back in from the cold. Now pony-tailed and glamorous and with his own place in a smart residential quarter, he once more became a figure on the London scene. While he began by having invitations to the cocktail and dinner parties of his old friends, the prevailing sense of being 'in the wrong', that paranoia of old, was a shadow haunting his newly found sense of self. 'Thinking people are thinking bad things about me,' Alexander says of this condition, 'and that they are incorrect and so I'm always defending myself against such assumptions being made.' Guilt, often nameless, is usually at the heart of feelings of being persecuted. There is no doubt that Alexander feels guilt for having exposed to his father his mother's behaviour with other men. He has a strong feeling that if he had not said what he said out of his ten-year-old curiosity and mischief, his parents could have stayed together, his father might not have turned against him and his life would have followed a more comfortable, more conventional course. His paranoia problem relates, he says, to 'not being the person my parents were saying I ought to be. I think it was their criticism that made me feel I've taken a wrong tack and that I've somehow gone wrong when, in point of fact, I don't think I've gone wrong. The fact of not being in step with everyone was a fact of my life and I can justify that, but I'm talking about it in the sense more that one feels persecuted by it. And that persecuted feeling does exist. I had the feeling I'd done very well at school, and there was my father not seeing it that way. Or not seeing that I'd actually been a wonderful heir for him, and instead was doubting me and saying, what a pity it isn't his younger brother who's the heir. Yet my brother had never done anything in school and so there was that sort of feeling of "What's going on in their minds? Are they all against me?" and there was lots of thinking "Well, how much of it is in my mind, and how much are they really ganging up and doing things against my interests?"' The real cause is hidden, but the criticisms and backroom activities of his family, of which Alexander often complains, are tangible results of that cause. However, it was not only these that were troubling Alexander when he returned from Paris. That return predated by several years the massive upheaval in social mores and class values which were to be the hallmark of the 1960s. Yet Alexander was already the bohemian, the scruffy artist, paint-spattered, revelling in being somewhat grubby and longhaired. He was more than thirty years old, and most of his old friends were living sedate married lives. He had to find new people with whom to cavort, and these tended to be the colourful elements: of assorted extractions and social origins, not just the women but also the men. He was not alone in his alternative stance on many of the new ideas which characterized the period: he had two male American friends who supported his arguments at dinner parties. The press were to play their part in the defining of Alexander as the 'alternative aristocrat'. Long before his Parisian incubation, the young Viscount Weymouth had been featured in the tabloid diaries and social columns. Gradually a mocking tone had developed. Now back from Paris, a pony-tailed artist rather than a proper chap, Alexander was widely described in a manner which often suggested both in text and in headlines, that he was 'loony'. He played up to them. He was, after all, enjoying the fact that every time he was mocked as an eccentric, he was promoting his own cause, which was to wage war on his father and his father's values. Over the years he has often been told directly and aggressively by other aristocrats that he is, in his own words, 'a traitor to your class'. He does not try to argue with his attackers. 'There are people who feel that I've not upheld the status of my class or whatever,' he says. 'But I'm not even thinking to defend myself to them. I don't try anymore.' He does not try to justify himself to them because, he says, 'they don't justify themselves to me.' Alexander believes that these people are mistaken in following the old ways. 'But I don't ram it down their throats,' he says. 'If these people don't adapt themselves to a changing world, it's their problem. I'm not trying to make their way of reacting to things a problem by the way that I talk. I'm just talking about the worlds that they believe in.'

However, the reaction of his peers has made Alexander feel even more isolated. He blames that too on the attitude of his family. He feels that it is an extension of his family attitude that certain contemporaries and aristocrats are critical of his way of life. He also thinks that the family attitude caused reactions against him in the smaller community close to Longleat. 'The family attitude against me was being talked about so much that I met people in the village who were thinking that way, who said nasty remarks to my children because of that attitude having got to them,' he remarks. 'And the press, you see, and those two,' he adds, meaning his father and older brother, 'were always with the press around them; and their little remarks spilled into the conversations, so the press were talking about me as this absurdity. I was being very badly represented by my family, and then the press was thinking that if even the family think badly of him, there must be something wrong.'

This part of the paranoia went on and on. It was strikingly visible as far back as the late 1960s when TV films were being made about Longleat and the family. His half-sister Silvy remembers one TV programme where Henry and the family were filmed having dinner. 'We were all at Job's Mill having dinner and Alexander wasn't there,' she recalls. 'I don't know why we hadn't invited him. Then the film showed him all alone on the roof of Longleat House, barefoot, playing his guitar. It was awfully sad really.' Alexander could not speak his mind at home without being mocked. 'I would have thought I was getting it all into perspective and therefore seeing how it was all coming about,' he says.

'But if I talked about psychology in my father's presence or even my brother's presence, it would have been "Oh, there he is pretending he knows something about psychology."' Alexander raises his voice to a hideous screech. 'Psychology! Psychology!' he screamed. 'That's how my father used to react if I said anything about psychology.'

His sense of isolation was overwhelming. At home, where he should have felt supported and among friends, he had the sense of being a pariah. No wonder he has had little faith in conventional family life, seeking instead his multiplicity of female relationships, but so many of these too have been difficult. It is as though the obstacle to good relationships is somewhere within Alexander. His anger is so deep-rooted and so strong that it erupts all around him. 'I'm aware that anger is a football that gets kicked around,' he remarks. This is why he has sought, through psychology especially, to understand himself. Like many an artist, he has been obliged to do this in the deep loneliness of his own mind and heart. The fact of his being an artist is also part of his isolation in a social order, indeed in a culture, where artists are misunderstood. Sadly, his lack of confidence has prevented him from mounting exhibitions of smaller works outside the walls of Longleat. Some of this is due to the way in which the media constantly mock his work. His lack of confidence is also part of that configuration of mental and emotional responses which he calls 'paranoia' and which goes back to the way in which his family criticized him and closed ranks against him. Once again, one must ask if their behaviour was not due to some unconscious perception that Alexander carries some great guilt within him. We do not know if that guilt is his alone or the one he shares with his mother for her wartime escapades, which destroyed her marriage. We only know that when there is a deeply-buried guilt, the person feels constantly as if they have done something wrong or are in the wrong and tend to attract the attack.

Fears Without Foundation

Alexander has experienced a fear of guilt at various times in his life. There was the constant fear during his army years that he was a homosexual. This was largely due to his experiences at both his schools but also due later to Henry's mocking of him as a man because he had chosen to be an artist instead of opting for some overtly macho role in life. Alexander seems to have erased that fear quite well, unless, of course, one interprets his display of being the great seducer of women as part of the myth he has created to mask the fear that he might also have enjoyed sex with other men.

However, one of the worst episodes of paranoia for Alexander was a psychodrama that developed when Lenka, his firstborn, was a baby. The child was repeatedly badly battered on her arms and legs. Alexander admitted that he was under suspicion. He says of the nanny that 'she left saying it was me that did it, not her. The paediatricians sent a psychiatrist out. She was seeing the psychiatrist, and the psychiatrist gave me a clean bill of health. They said that my tale was exactly like the documented baby battering. So I was clear with the hospital that Lenka went to.' There was no court case against the nanny, however. 'I could have taken a private lawsuit against her,' Alexander says, 'but no one was urging me to prove that she had done it. They were saying, "Yes, we know it's her", but they weren't going to say anything because, you know, they like to keep out of things. They weren't going to give evidence in court on my behalf if she sued. And so it was all a bit of a worry at the time. But there was no doubt at all in their mind or in mine. Here were other people saying what had happened to their babies.' The employee, who had very good references, went on to work for another family and was later found to have bruised another child at her employers' home. 'It was only bruising,' Alexander says of the second case, 'but in Lenka's case it was four broken bones.' Of the effect on Lenka, he says: 'She ordinarily was more pessimistic than a child is. Nobody knows really, but I think it's possible that she was given a more pessimistic view on life, more a feeling that people might come up and batter you, sort of thing.'

So physical violence had erupted around Alexander, and he was subjected to the fear that he would be accused of causing the harm. It was another cause for paranoia. Once again, however, he turned his suffering into artistic product. He wrote a novel based around these events, *The Carrycot*, which became his first published novel and was made into a feature film with Anna playing herself. Alexander's paranoia is not over. He still feels exposed to attack. On one occasion he did not know whether or not he could eat the sweet dessert served to his Sunday lunch party. His own dessert was supposed to be prepared with a sugar substitute. It turned out that this was not the case, but he had not been told when the food was brought in. He sent for the housekeeper, who confirmed that there was sugar in the dessert. Why wasn't he told? 'They're trying to poison me!' he exclaimed furiously. This accusation was levelled at Cuthbert and Irene, who had been his housekeepers for a number of years. Another problem he would complain about in relation to this couple was that they were trying to seduce his pet dog away from him. He referred to Toya when she could not be found, as being, 'with the enemy'. Toya was his loyal dog who sat devotedly with him in the penthouse day and night until she had to be put down because of illness in the spring of 2001. For a lonely man, the sleeping dog was a faithful companion. Sometimes she would disappear and this was because she had, according to Alexander been lured into his housekeepers' basement flat to keep company with their own dog. It was perhaps an exaggeration of the situation which Alexander perceived as disloyalty on the part of his staff to be seducing his dog away from him, but his reaction was on the level of paranoia. It may simply have been that this rather old dog felt warmer in the housekeepers' cosy basement flat than in Alexander's often chilly quarters.

Perhaps the nub of Alexander's problems lies with the press. He has constantly been portrayed as the eccentric, offbeat, loony marquess, the 'aristo' with the lose screw. Some of this is due to the whispering campaign of his father and brother. Some is simply due to the fact that the press love a colourful character, and if they can apply a label to an individual, they do so and it sticks. Since English culture finds it hard to accept artists, Alexander's artistic life would present a broad target for the writers who want to dramatize his extrovert image. Alexander appears in the guise of an entertainer. He is certainly more stable and correct than any pop star, yet, in contrast to many of the latter, who are often taken rather seriously, he has frequently been written about as if he were mentally aberrant or deficient. The fact that Alexander is a highly intelligent man, very often ahead of his time in terms of the views he has expressed, does not fit with the popular perception of the more entertaining showbiz side of his persona. Alexander has already been packaged some thirty to fifty years ago as a freak aristocrat, a rebel against the system; and that's how the media still like to portray him. Alexander longs to be taken seriously, yet he accepts, even enjoys, his portrayal as the extrovert womanizing artist and the publicity it attracts. However, his peers cannot forgive him for 'tarting' himself around in the tabloids and for that apparent betrayal of the elite class. One has to inquire as to whether Alexander's 'paranoia' is partially provoked by the press coverage of his various activities, going back to his teens and the consequent reaction to this by more sober conventional aristocrats. Give a man a label...

Was there a deliberate campaign to disparage him? Was it perpetrated by people in remote places who thought a rebellious aristocrat would be a threat to the system? Were his father and his brother deliberately trying to discredit him? Or was it simply that Alexander didn't fit into the British system? If Alexander ever made himself dangerous to the status quo, it might have been by his intervention into politics. Although clearly ahead of his time when he stood as a Wessex Regionalist in 1974, he was described as a 'loony' for doing so. 'There were things written by *The Times* and other papers which ridiculed me for proposing regional government,' he recalls. 'They wrote things like "He wants the world to be governed from the Sinai Peninsula."' As one of his Eton, Oxford and Guards friends remarked, it was not appropriate for an ex-member of the Life Guards to say they were against the continuation of the monarchy or even likely that they would do so. Nevertheless, Alexander is simply aware that the present direction of policies for the European Union will lead to the end of the British monarchy, as they will lead to an end to Great Britain as a national entity. He does not state that he is either for or against such a conclusion. He simply supports the policies that will bring about that end because he believes regional government will be better for the regions than national government. Is part of his anger directed against the smug superiority of his parents and their class? He said he is no longer angry with society; but a deep rage is still burning against his family. Yes, his 'paranoia' was brought on by his father turning against him, and this in turn cause his rebellion against his class. He has, however, exacerbated the reaction of his peers to him by rebelling so openly and so violently against the old aristocratic conventions which he felt had been purveyed to him as the real McCoy but which had turned out to be *faux* jewellery. Alexander has spotted the flaw in the system, which is that it depends on people's belief in it to persist. For him, at least, that belief has long since died. The myth has been stripped naked. Alexander has never intended to fight a political battle. He created universal arguments in the form of a philosophy in his essays, merely to support the views he had formed in order to work out his own anger. His philosophies and his arguments are simply a way of justifying his personal responses to the notion that he was persuaded to accept a fraud as a reality. Even if they seem to be applicable to the times in which he lived and the historic changes of the eras through which he has passed, his beliefs and his ideas of new social orders are, as he himself admits, entirely devised for himself, to solve his own dilemmas, provide himself with a workable philosophy of life to replace one which had collapsed. All of his questions, which could well be questions about the whole human condition, are basically questions about his own psychodrama. Like many an artist, Alexander has translated the personal into the universal and hit the problem right on the nose. One wonders if any of this would have happened if his mother had not given in quite so frequently to her erotic impulses.

Chapter Eight
The Inheritance

The Importance of Being a Marquess

Until 2000 marquesses had an automatic right, along with other landowning aristocrats, to sit in the House of Lords and decide which legislation already passed by the elected House of Commons would eventually reach the statute book. This odd anachronism in the oldest of the world's democracies was tolerated by successive governments. Lords' reform was often mooted but never carried out often for very practical reasons connected with the support the Lords gave to successive governments in power. The bulk of the hereditary peers have traditionally been Tories, but there have been many Labour hereditary peers. There was also the might of patronage. Life peers, created by Prime Ministers, and often Labour or Liberal in their patronage, held the balance in the House which might otherwise have been dominated by the – traditionally Conservative – hereditary peers. There was a time when Labour governments went in fear of the might of these Tory backwoodsmen. If controversial legislation were passed by the House of Commons, it still had to face its final reading in the House of Lords. It has long been expected that this would be dealt with by a nod and a wink, but only if the new law were relatively moderate and did not threaten the property rights of the aristocracy. Indeed, there were some occasions in the 1960s when Harold Wilson's government was brought up hard against the might of the Lords. When the chips were down, those peers who did not normally exercise their right to sit or to vote in the Lords would suddenly descend on the House and vote the legislation back to the Commons for amendments acceptable to the Lords.

The existence of the House of Lords as so constituted has been the reason for the slow pace of constitutional change over matters which have affected the entrenched wealth and power of the landed aristocracy. Leasehold Reform under the Thatcher and Major governments was one such matter; but there have also been other issues, and at times it seemed that the only voice of reason to be exercised in a matter of reform was that issuing from the House of Lords. There is no doubt that a Second Chamber constituted from hereditary peers and those created by government patronage has been a stabilizing force in some ways, although a block on real radical change in power, wealth and property ownership in Britain. The House of Lords was also a direct route to political power for individual aristocrats. Peers have become government ministers without having to be elected to the Commons. A hereditary peer could also become prime minister if he stood for election to the Commons. A hereditary peer may not, however, stand for election to the House of Commons without resigning his title, but from the 1960s it became possible to give up a hereditary title and stand for election to Parliament as a member of the Commons. The Act of Parliament which enabled this originated as a private Member's Bill proposed by Lord Stansgate, who after the passage of the bill became Anthony Wedgewood Benn, was elected to Parliament as a Labour member for a Bristol constituency and later became a cabinet minister in Harold Wilson's governments. Alexander's arrival in the House of Lords was just a little too late for him to make a mark. He inherited his title of the Marquess of Bath in 1992 on the death of his father, but he did not take his seat in the Lords immediately because, he says, 'I had a lot of family business to sort out.' By the time he did take his seat, two years later, there was little sand left in the hourglass for most for the hereditary peers. In the reforms passed by the Blair government, which was elected in 1997, only ninety-two hereditary peers retained their seats, out of 750 who had been in the habit of turning up from Monday to Friday and collecting their daily expenses, which, for cash-poor landowners, was a comfortable bit of assistance.

Alexander was not going to the House of Lords for the money, however. He was doing it because it provided him with a respectable platform. He was thrilled to have the possibility of entering Parliament at last and made four speeches there on the abolition of the hereditary peers, on the regional development agencies, the leisure industries and House of Lords reform. He was well qualified to speak on all of these subjects. Regretfully, he admits that 'I did not permit my name to go forward for election as one of the surviving hereditaries on the grounds that I was not prepared to put in the hours of attendance that would be expected for any life peer.'

Having tried his luck at standing for Parliament as an Independent Wessex Regionalist in 1974 and losing his deposit, he could, until the Lords Reform Bill was enacted, walk into the Second Chamber as a marquess and take his place among bishops, law lords and ex-prime ministers who had accepted peerages, plus numerous other life peers created by the governments of their day for services rendered. Of course, he was also taking his place among his fellow aristocrats, like a returned prodigal son, able to stand proudly among them, even if still not quite one of them, for the first time since his departure from Oxford in 1956. Alexander could thus legitimately fulfil his inclination to 'go where the power is'. Parliamentary politics offered him the authentic power for which he had long wished. His voice could now be heard with the authority of the House of Lords behind it and as a well-known figure he was invited to make speeches outside the House and TV appearances, including some on the Continent. Aware of this somewhat awesome heritage, he began to play his part very properly. For his appearances at the House of Lords, he abandoned his habitually colourful public dress and opted for convention, slipping into a pinstriped suit which, for his investiture and other ceremonial occasions, was then worn under the traditional ermine-trimmed robes of the Lords.

At last, Alexander was following in the footsteps of his ancestors. The death of his father had made possible this sudden curtsy to tradition in two ways. One was that Henry was dead and Alexander could relax his revolt somewhat. The other was that Henry's death simply opened the door to the full range of possibilities available to a marquess, one of which was to accept an automatic position of power in the realm. He was in his element: the aristocrat in his rightful place, helping to run the country and reform the machinery of government. Even in the liberal climate of modern Britain, a marquess is worthy of a certain amount of awe. The title, the wealth and the vast estate place such people on a level which automatically seems to win respect. They will still be called 'your lordship' when most others, whether they wish it or not, are called by their first names by bank and shop employees and total strangers. Alexander had long secretly wanted to prove that he was capable of becoming the aristocrat of his inheritance. 'I've never got away from the idea that I will be a better marquess than any of them and that was always there in my thoughts,' he reflects.

A patrician self-image under the bohemian kaftans? Was this a total capitulation to all the old traditions? Was the poacher about to become gamekeeper? He sat on the Liberal Democrat benches and, when the opportunity presented itself, he made points or speeches which promoted his progressive ideas on nursery education, regionalism, the arts and Lords reform. The House of Lords: what a platform! He was in his element, and he owed it all to the hereditary principle. Was he going straight at last, now that the cause of his rebellion, Henry, had been laid to rest? Was the 'traitor to his class' now coming back into the fold? 'I've never got away from the idea that I will be a better marquess than any of them,' he repeats proudly. 'That was there in my thoughts all along, and I've never actually departed from that. But what did depart is what I've got to do to be a better marquess.' He smiles gently before going on. 'That is to understand the regime you're working under and then to provide some of the things that people want.' In other words, to be a thoroughly modern marquess is to understand and respond to the commercial, political and social currents of the age. So the showmanship, the turning of Longleat into an entertainment for the masses, the business of being written about saucily, filmed frequently, going on chat shows, wearing extraordinary robes, attracting the multitudes to the estate, being different from the old stuffy style of aristocrat: that is what Alexander meant by departing from the old paternalistic, landed-gentry methods of being a better marquess. It's the clearest statement Alexander has made of where his real priorities lie. The rebellion against his family was a distraction. His heart really lies in the preservation, the permanence of his inheritance. This is the endgame to his double-sided act. 'Alex is a great actor,' his Oxford friend Sir James Spooner says. 'I remember when he was Viscount Weymouth, there was a time when he dressed in these ghastly robes and bare feet, and he used to turn up at one's parties with one or a couple of the wifelets, not often with Anna, I have to say, and then after he became the Marquess of Bath, I saw him somewhere and he had shoes on and a velvet jacket, although his hair was still down the back of his neck. Then I was in the House of Lords for a Christ Church reunion with a number of our contemporaries, and I was absolutely amazed when I saw, coming up the stairs, Alex in a double breasted grey pinstriped suit, which I hadn't seen him in for decades. So when he was in the House of Lords he was playing a part.' Although he has played the socialist, the political rebel, with his Wessex regionalism, he was genuinely in awe of the House of Lords. He was totally on edge one Monday morning when he was due to deliver a speech that afternoon. He was intending to take a wifelet, myself and another female guest back to London with him in his car. He had invited us to go with him to the House of Lords to hear his speech. Because he dared not be late for the 2 pm opening of business at which he was to deliver a speech on the reform of the Lords, he drove off even while we were searching the house for him, leaving us behind. He had not been able to find us just prior to departing and due to some mischance he had passed down in the lift while we were slogging up the spiral staircase to the penthouse. For Alexander, a seat in the Lords was a longed-for chance to rejoin the respectable world. This was an opportunity to put forward his views from the august position of a member of the Upper House of the British Parliament. Albeit unelected but able to claim his constitutional right as a peer of the realm, he could use the power of his aristocratic inheritance. He did so with great seriousness, taking the whole business in his stride. It was like coming in from the cold. For so long an outcast, treated satirically in the press, considered 'not one of us' by his own class, he had never sought re-entry to the world he had left behind him when he went down from Oxford, but he had wished for it. This was an opportunity to be taken seriously, to prove himself more than the intellectual mediocrity which his father believed was all any Thynne could become. The political world of important affairs of state, of elder statesmen, was also the world of intellectual acceptability: the world where people who had influence, people who were listened to by those who had power, were the ones who were admired and respected. Alexander had longed to be part of that world, but he had turned his back on it because it had failed him in his fight with Henry. He had therefore gone on the left-hand path to self-respect, but in doing so he had lost the automatic respect due his rank by birth. Through his speeches in the Lords, he had a fresh chance to show the other side, the philosopher, political thinker and the liberal patrician. Of course, whatever he had done, nothing short of his untimely death would prevent him from becoming the Seventh Marquess. It was his inherited right. Alexander was, as he told the two footmen, destined to become the Marquess of Bath. He was also going to inherit and control a 10,000-acre estate and a fine Renaissance palace, a further tourist attraction with vast paying potential, plus the Cheddar Gorge and Caves, all organized into a thriving business concern worth anything between £40 million and £175 million according to various estimates. However, even this inheritance may have seemed doubtful at times in the immediate years that followed his legal takeover of the estate from Henry. Alexander has told me that, despite his emotional uncertainties, he felt secure in who he was and what he was legally going to inherit. There is no doubt that this security was shaken by his father's activities. At other times Alexander expresses this uncertainty. Alexander had no idea why Henry would want to deprive him of all but the shell of his inheritance, but evidently something was afoot. 'I didn't know what he would do,' Alexander says, still reflecting unhappily on the anxieties of the past.

The Battle Over the Inheritance

The first problem was mismanagement. 'The trustees were telling me that they'd always restrained him,' Alexander says of the time in 1956 when he first took over the legal ownership of the estate from his father, 'but that now it was up to me to restrain him because he'd now handed over the estate to me and I'd got to stop his expenditure on the estate because the estate would be utterly broken in five years. So I was doing what the trustees had told me to do and what the lawyers were telling me to do, and he never forgave me for that.' A great deal which was untoward had gone on before Alexander's legal takeover of the estate. Alexander is too cautious to tell all, but he says enough about his father's activities to reveal how much he himself doubted Henry's honesty.

'My father was a crook,' he angrily tells me. 'It was found out that he was doing illegal things like selling pictures and putting copies up on the walls. When that was discovered he went to different lawyers, so that when two sets of lawyers were studying it, they found that the will of the First Marquess hadn't been included in the breaking of the entail and it was found that broadly speaking the chattels of the house were my father's. And then, though he had been selling off these things, he could still say, "OK, I'll sell that to pay for the things that I ought not to have done." So he'd been caught out in very bad behaviour, but there was a way out of it, and that led to him selling off all the books.' Alexander is still angry about the sales of books, which destroyed a valuable library. Some of these books were sold after Henry's death because he willed a certain amount of money to his other children, Christopher and Silvy, and for his second wife, Virginia. Alexander turns red and grinds his teeth when he talks about this. He won't talk about the figures but, in fact, about £1.5 million had to be raised to fulfil Henry's bequests.

'He had set them up from the sales of the books,' he says. 'He forced my hand. He was in the clear legally, and he left it so that I would have to sell, not all the books but enough books to give Christopher and Silvy and my stepmother vast amounts. Just to add on to that,' he goes on furiously, 'he was selling the paintings while he must have known that after his death when they found that they were missing they would make me pay for them. So in fact,' Alexander shouts, 'he'd found a way that by doing an illegal act he was making sure that I would be funding him.' However, it was not Henry's last act to rob Alexander of his expected full inheritance, which was the cause of years of gut-chewing anxiety. It was his constant undermining of the financial underpinning of Alexander's inheritance by other manoeuvres. How could he continue to do this when the estate now legally belonged to Alexander? Only by virtue of the fact that the transfer was purely a formality and the estate was in actuality being run by the father and his heir together. Alexander was in charge of the estate while Henry ran the tourist side and the park: hence the continuing acrimony over the financial side. Undoubtedly, Alexander had a clearer head when it came to reorganizing the management of the estate in order to make it a paying concern. His friend Sir James Spooner, who became an accountant, was asked to do some work for the estate after the legal handover. He is tactful in his comments, since, like most of Alexander's pals, he liked Henry very much, but he makes it clear that Alexander was the one who had a business head. 'Remember,' he says of Alexander, 'he's a split personality in many ways, because he's extremely shrewd and down-to-earth in business matters. I used to act for both him and his father while I was practicing as an accountant, and Henry was absolutely hopeless at detail, but Alex would go through invoices in immense detail, wanting everything to be very successful. He's very keen on detail, which I admire him for. I suspect the estate is in rather good shape, much better shape than when his father and his brother were running it, because Alex is very down-to-earth.'

Henry was commercially creative and inventive, however. Before 1956, he had sought various desperate ways of paying the huge bills for running Longleat, but there was also the ingenious idea of opening the place to the public. In 1947, Longleat became the first stately home in Britain to welcome paying tourists. This was Henry's response to the Labour Government's savage increase in death duties. The gimmick was soon copied by other stately homeowners, who also followed suit by installing swings and roundabouts in the grounds. Henry was also the originator of the famous Lions of Longleat. He brought in lions later, after Alexander had become the estate's legal owner, and he did so with the help of Jimmy Chipperfied of the well-known circus family. Again it was a first, and now the Safari Park is one of the finest private zoos in England. Henry may have been a poor manager of the estate's finances, but he had a showman's instinct for what the public would love; and Longleat and its famous lions became a big public attraction. Alexander, no less a showman but a much sounder businessman, has put the place onto a sound financial footing. 'Its in the black,' he says me. 'Getting Centerparks,' Sir James Spooner says, 'was an amazing coup.' Although one of Longleat's biggest controversies, allowing Centerparks to build and run one of their indoor leisure centres on the estate was indeed a big financial boost. This was entirely Alexander's doing. In dealing with Henry, Alexander had to fight, but he also had to deal with the deadliest weapon which Henry had to deploy: his charm. He said that Henry was 'always trying to persuade me to his point of view, using his charm to try to get me to do things. He would say, "Come on. We can work together on this."' Having an enormously stubborn nature, Alexander was not to be won over by charm. 'I was not going to be persuaded to do something that was against the interests of Longleat,' he says.

Alexander has the gift of imagination. He is, as his old pal James Spooner observes, a shrewd businessman. He is constantly thinking up ways of drawing more people to visit Longleat and more ways of getting them to spend money, on top of their entrance ticket, once they are there. There is an ice-cream parlour, a gift shop, a cafe, fun castles, boat rides on the lake and the Safari Park. He has also enjoyed creating mazes. A family can easily spend a day at Longleat and spend a packet while so doing: the entrance and other money from punters visiting Longleat every year is of vital importance to its survival.

One seldom sees the house without scaffolding somewhere along one of its vast walls, but many of the costs are less obvious. There is staff looking after the grounds, taking money for entrance to the estate, the house, the Safari Park. There is the feed and the vets' bills and other expenses of caring for the animals, the costs of running various other attractions. There are cleaners and coffee-shop staff, management, secretarial help and security guards. The outgoing is considerable. Part of the estate, but less directly connected with tourism, are such income-producers as the tenanted farms and the forestry: more the old style landowner activity, it is also needed to keep Longleat going. When all of the income from tourism was stopped while Foot and Mouth Disease kept Longleat in quarantine for most of the winter and spring between 2000 and 2001, Alexander was visibly very worried at the drain of expenses on the vast estate with vastly less income to sustain it. The profits from gate money for the Safari Park, Longleat House and other attractions were halved to £239,000 on sales of £6.1 million in 2000. Subsequently Christies were asked to auction treasures from the vast Longleat collection of paintings, manuscripts, furniture, silver, porcelain and books. The sale of these sleeping assets was intended to bring in £15 million to augment the estate's maintenance fund. In fact, the auction, in June 2002, raised £24 million. This became a cash-pool, producing income and also providing liquidity in case any other bad luck such as the Foot and Mouth epidemic strikes again to cripple the estate's cash flow. It provides a fund which will also pay for the maintenance of the vast buildings of Longleat House for many years to come.

Did Alexander feel remorse that he was actually following Henry's example in selling off Longleat's treasures? He says that he regretted having to sell beautiful antiques, but that most of the items sold came from members of the family who were not closely associated with Longleat House. They included manuscripts and books belonging to Beriah Botfield, a Victorian bibliophile and antiquarian whose collection arrived at the house during World War Two.

The Botfield collection sold for £12.4 million. Other works of art auctioned included Dutch old masters. However, unlike Henry's secret and illegal sales of paintings which were replaced by fakes, this sale was a widely publicized event, open and above board and sanctioned by the estate's lawyers. The selection of works for auction resulted in a great deal of rummaging around in the Longleat attics, which brought to light many forgotten treasures, most of which remain as part of the estate and which contribute to its overall value. The full extent of Longleat's value may still only be estimated, but a figure of £157 million for art, property and land is the most recent, according to *The Sunday Times* Rich List in 2009. The Rich List bases this valuation largely on the art treasures and books. Clearly these values can and do change yearly depending on the fluctuation in market values for paintings, silver, porcelain and other antiques. These valuables do not produce income save for that brought in by the cash-paying public who tour Longleat House and admire its contents. Otherwise there is forestry and agricultural tenancies and the Cheddar Gorge, a Longleat asset which is also the scene of tourist attractions. Without doubt the income from tourism is the life and soul of Longleat. Hence Alexander's considerable efforts in the press and on TV to keep up the level of interest in Longleat, which generates the vital flow of paying punters. Without Alexander as its chief executive and cheerleader, Longleat might find itself unable to pay its enormous bills. Alexander, in return, has the good fortune to be able to live in this splendid setting. He is not the owner of the great house so much as the tenant for life. He has an income of his own from investments, but his position is curiously halfway between that of the rich and powerful owner and that of the poor relation who lives in the great castle, which he does not own but who does, thanks to that error in the will of the First Marquess, own the rich haul of that castle's contents. Or does he? The whole estate has now been handed on to Alexander's heir, Ceawlin, but even he does not own all this. Such is the nature of legal protection of the great family estates, those who inherit titles and estates do so only as life tenants with limited powers. Hence Alexander is rather like the chairman of a public corporation. He cannot sell art treasures, land or property at will even though he – or rather Ceawlin – legally owns them. He can only do so with the agreement of his trustees. In terms of his personal spending, he is restricted to the income from his private investments.

Nevertheless, despite all these legal manoeuvrings, Alexander is a very rich man on paper. The degree to which a marquess has power to control the way the estate is run is largely a question of choice. One marquess might let things ride, another might watch every penny that comes and goes while looking for additional ways of augmenting the income. Alexander is very much the latter type; and while there is no power without responsibility, he wields the power and also accepts the responsibility as the estate's Chief Executive. There are always a few problems for Alexander as the Chief Executive of Longleat, but these are nothing compared with the problems he had to deal with before his father's death. For quite some time, it was a case of battling with his father and then, increasingly, with his brother Christopher, whom Henry had placed in charge of Longleat House. To the outside world it seemed as if Alexander was pottering with his painting and writing while his father and his brother were running things. In reality, Alexander was an eagle-eyed defender of the financial expenditures and profits. So there were the constant power struggles. The 'difficult days', as he calls them, were especially the 1980s, before Henry's death. 'That's where the sibling rivalry came in,' he says, 'in that my father was promoting Christopher as the second voice on the estate after himself. And in particular the PR lady was working with my father to promote Christopher. I was getting promotion through television documentaries and things, but the angle that was being taken by everyone was that I was the difficult black sheep.'

Finally, when Henry died and Alexander was clearly the sole owner and controller of his inheritance, he found that Christopher was becoming a problem. His relationship with his brother is now very cool. Lord Christopher Thynne and his wife, Lady Antonia, do not live on the estate any longer. The brothers do not speak. 'I think what went wrong with my relationship with Christopher were two things really,' Alexander says, looking back to the origins of the problems between them. 'One was that he married Antonia. If he'd married Lucy, the previous girlfriend, she would have been wonderful and that might have cemented us together. But with his marrying Antonia, and with my father promoting him to what really amounts to above me, that made it unattractive and I just had to get rid of him as soon as possible.' After Henry's death, Alexander spent two years at Longleat sorting out the administration of the estate, going into all the areas which had been controlled by his father and his brother, uncovering the details, setting things in order, putting his stamp on the business and his own staff in place. He waited those two years before taking up his seat in the House of Lords, because, he says, 'I needed to gain the feeling of control. I was in control in actuality, but I needed to feel that I was controlling.' However, Christopher was still where Henry had placed him, and something had to be done. 'I would have been an atrocious businessman if I had let Christopher go on in the job,' Alexander observes. 'It would have been the most silly decision of my life, and I would have regretted it all my life.' The day of getting rid of Christopher was very soon precipitated by Christopher himself. 'My reasons for not having Christopher there,' Alexander recalls, 'are first of all that he wasn't trained to be there. He wasn't trained in business management. He was there only because my father had got him doing my job, and I can do better. What Christopher was good at was being lord of the house. He wasn't as good as me, but he could work with my father and that was because I and my father couldn't do it. But to have my father try to plant that situation as a permanence was ridiculous from my father's point of view. Of course I wasn't going to let my younger brother be lord of the house. Of course I wasn't going to take that line. And Christopher simply wasn't good enough at anything else. He's pretty bad in some ways, but I don't want to start running him down. He would have been an impossible manager of the house if I had had to put any responsibility on him. I knew the break had to happen,' he continues, 'I told my father: "This is not going to work. It's not going to happen." He knew that. He just inflicted it upon me. Then there it was, within a week, three days after the funeral, I discovered that Christopher had arranged an interview with the *Independent*. I was in the drawing room with Anna. We were looking out of the window, and we saw that there were press arriving. I said: "What's going on? Why are the press here?"' 'Christopher described it as a thing about how he "runs Longleat House". In fact that was the article which appeared. So that was the thing that hit me. It's not good. It's got to happen now. I can't wait for another thing to happen. He's got to go; and if I hadn't done it, anybody on analysis of the business would have said of me: "He's not a business manager. He deserved the problems." Yes, it was absolutely necessary and I have not the slightest regret. It would have been the worse for both of us in the long run.'

Alexander did the deed very coolly. 'I was very, very cool,' he recalls. 'It was: "I've got to do it now." I think any idiot would have done the same thing. I can be a good businessman, and I had a bad businessman in control and foisted upon me, and it would have been hopeless. I've appointed the person who was my estate manager to become the general manager,' he continues. 'He's been trained in such business matters and I find our relationship excellent.' However, Henry seems to have had plenty to laugh about from beyond the grave. 'It wasn't that he wanted to hang on after death,' he growls. 'He wanted to hang on in this life by appointing Christopher to do what he wanted. He'd set up Christopher in this way, so when the end was coming he couldn't say: "Well now it's time to step down, Christopher." He couldn't. He'd got himself into a trap. I think he knew he was leaving chaos behind him. I think he knew that I would sack Christopher, but then he did find a way to see that Christopher got some of the treasures of Longleat from the sale of the books.'

What angers Alexander even more is that after all these treasures had been sold, Alexander had to pay all the tax on the sales as well. 'He was a crook, this man,' he rages. 'He was doing some very crooked things.' Some of Henry's complex dealings went on well before his death. Alexander does not state specifically what they are, but in his novel *Pillars of the Establishment* (more or less a *roman à clef*) he tells a story whose characters and events are cleverly based on real people and events. The question is: how much of this story is imaginary and how much true to real life? Alexander laughs a lot when talking about the way he created this book. He is coy about what is fact and what is fiction. He has melded characters from several sources. In his plot, he tells the reality but he disguises the actuality. One significant part of the story in relation to the manoeuvrings of Henry is the one where the character based on Henry creates a company called Buddlea, named after the fictional marquess's daughter from his fictional second marriage. Buddlea turns out to be a device for siphoning money from the estate into a separate corporation which is intended to cheat the heir of the estate, a character modelled on Alexander. Alexander will not come clean on this for legal reasons. Although Henry had to read the proofs of the novel before it could be published, there is a legal minefield involved in disclosing what really went on. 'It would not be fair to bring in Silvy,' Alexander says of one of the beneficiaries of Henry's will. 'You've got to look at other people.' When I mention a name, he laughs. 'Again I can't tell you,' he says. 'It's far too dangerous.' Indeed, the novel does not imply any problem with Silvy; but the fictitious company was being used by the fictitious marquess to channel funds away from the estate for other purposes. Alexander will not give an answer when asked about this. 'I'm not going to give you this material,' is all that he will say. 'My father was a rogue and I'll leave it at that.' Alexander foresees no problems with his own legal handover of his estate to his son Ceawlin, the present Viscount Weymouth, as it has already taken place. However, Ceawlin appears to favour running the estate on conservative lines. He has also declared himself ambitious to make a lot of money in his own right, which he would then like to use to fund Longleat. If one ignores the glamour of the title and its four centuries of history, one might consider Longleat to be a family corporation, and the Marquess as the chief executive officer and marketing director for life. There are strict laws governing the identity of the CEO (primogeniture) and others (the entail) that limit the CEO's powers to dispose of assets or reorganize the capital resources; but the remuneration package, as such, is also linked to inherited sources of money such as the trust fund which Alexander came into after he left Oxford. However, the legal framework is geared to protecting the rights of the inheritors, who are also the unpaid executives or workers who have a choice of whether they will bother to do any work at all or leave it to trustees and hired management.

Nevertheless, it is quite something to be born into a job with such splendid accommodation and ready-made respect and connections – and has there ever been a case of trustees of such an estate removing the hereditary CEO from office? Jobs for life exist in other sections of some countries, where employees of state-owned enterprises or government departments are virtually undismissable and where they are given 'tied' apartments for life at rents far below the market rate but hardly on such a grand scale as Longleat House and its parklands. The choice of whether to work at the job or simply take advantage of all the assets and enjoy life is clearly available to the inheritor of a family-owned enterprise such as Longleat Estate. Alexander, undoubtedly works very hard at his 'job' of being a marquess, but the position is unique and he can hardly be said to have worked his way to the top. Nevertheless, he prefers to be considered a meritocrat.

Meritocracy

Despite his deep concern for Longleat, the marquessate and his inheritance, Alexander is not a believer in inherited advantage. He is also against the conventional perceptions of class. 'Upper class?' he says. 'I think it's a passé word, passé conception. I don't even think of myself as upper-class. I hope, but I'm never quite sure, that I'm acceptable within the meritocracy.' It is true that he has earned his passage as a published author, a celebrated painter and a sort of media star, but has he actually earned his living at these skills? It is a moot point. It is also open to question whether he would have attracted any interest to it or earned anything at all from his work had he been born into an ordinary lower middle-class family with no connections. Going to Eton and Oxford, serving in the Life Guards, having an entrée into upper-class society is networking at the highest echelon. To postulate that he is a meritocrat after all this inherited advantage seems a mega-illusion.

In some ways, however, it may have been harder for Alexander automatically to succeed just because he was the son of a marquess at the metier he has chosen. He might have been better off as the son of another artist, since meritocracy seems to breed nepotism. The son or daughter of an actor, musician, painter or TV presenter is more likely to be accepted as an artist, actor, musician, painter or TV presenter. Or the children of a celebrity can succeed in their parent's profession or another sphere through social introductions. This is usually because the parents have the contacts. They can introduce their children in the right circle and put the pressure on a bit. Alexander thinks that nepotism is still better than people simply inheriting wealth. 'Oh, I can forgive the generation that said: "Here's my lovely daughter, see that she gets a good job,"' he says, 'I can forgive that, provided the system of them being wealthy enough to have that position is taken away.'

It is the inheritance of money which bothers him. So, in Alexander's world, everyone must succeed on their merits and not by inheriting wealth. This does not sit well with his rage that his father should have tried a little egalitarianism with regard to the inheritance at Longleat. Alexander is furious that his primogeniture, his right to inherit every last penny and every last clod of earth or lump of masonry, every painting, artefact or furnishing from the estate, was apparently tampered with by his father in order to provide for his other children and for the widow of his second marriage. This conflict between his views does not make a lot of sense. Alexander does not consider himself rich because he has tight limits on his cash income. In addition to that, he gets a petrol allowance and some other perks related to his role as the CEO and Front Man for Longleat Enterprises: and of course, he lives rent-free in the house and free of charges. Additionally, improvements to the property are not paid for out of Alexander's pocket. For instance, when the central heating system, including that for his private apartments, was upgraded in 2000 the estate naturally paid the bill. With most of his living expenses at Longleat taken care of by the estate, he still has to pay running costs for his other residences, the duplex at Notting Hill and the villa at Ramatuelle until he sold it. The impression that he is short of cash is based on the reality that he does, in fact, live on a relatively small private income. Again, this is from inherited capital assets. All said and done, he earns little from his art or his writing.

True, he does not have a stupendous life style. Alexander could live in his present fashion in a council flat; but Longleat House is no council flat, and it is clear that Alexander's wealth includes the grandeur and prestige of life in one of England's historic houses with all the hidden advantages of the power to have final word on the running of the estate. Not to mention the distribution of cottages. Owner or not, Alexander has inherited the use of a fabulous house packed with treasures and a prosperous estate with its own income-producing enterprises. Not to mention a title which carries with it influence and door-opening prestige. With all this inheritance behind him, it is hard to see how he can consider himself a meritocrat. Alexander believes that he has succeeded in becoming a celebrity in his own right. However, he has not, nor did he need to, succeed financially on his merits due to the fact that he has a hereditary investment income and an inherited business with a capital base of £157 million. Even without the mystique of the title, Alexander could be considered to be in the same position financially if he inherited only the property and the right to live there, plus his trust fund. But how would he have attracted the interest to himself that has enabled him to make his name? He says good things about his school, Eton: a very elite, very expensive, fee-paying school with a high scholastic standard. He says that it is also a school which encourages individualism. He admits that he enjoyed it very much, but despite this, he is against fee-paying schools. He wants everyone to go to state schools. He sent his two children to the local comprehensive. It was only when Ceawlin came into some money from his trust that he paid for himself to go into Bedales.

Alexander tends to have double-vision about all these matters. For instance, when he talked about his daughter Lenka going to Oxford, he was rather amused that an Oxford College would be accepting a comprehensive pupil at the same time as she happened to be a marquess's daughter. It's part of the doublethink in which he indulges. For instance, it's okay for him to inherit a title and live at Longleat, enjoying all the benefits of life in a stately home. It's also okay for him to inherit his title and enjoy the privileges that go with such a title. But he still wants inherited wealth highly taxed. This hardly squares with the fact that he has just gone through the legal handover of his estate and all its trappings to his son Ceawlin in order legitimately to avoid heavy taxation which would otherwise destroy the estate.

The unresolved conflict between his heritage and his desire to see social justice began in his teens. The elite schoolboy was the father of the egalitarian man. At Eton, Alexander said he thinks that 'there was the good person inside me, looking for what made the good world. I would like to think that I'm a good person. I was just finding difficulties in finding that route because of the people who'd been giving me ideas to follow before. I just knew they felt I was a good person,' he says of his housemasters and tutors, 'that they were in some senses the father I never had. They were encouraging me to think. Of course, when I'd started, I didn't stop.' But times were changing, and such was the extent of the liberal teaching that went on at Oxford that 'there were parents of my contemporaries saying that they didn't want their children to go there because they would learn all this socialist nonsense, sort of stuff.' He chuckles. 'You must remember that I was never militant on socialist theory,' he continues with regard to the views that stuck with him. 'I voted Labour in my time, but at the same time I'm a Wessex Regionalist, working for that and working out my position and could only be held responsible for that.' Alexander has never been inspired to give up his title and his wealth and go off and take his chances with the rest. He did not want to follow Anthony Wedgewood Benn, who had given up his peerage in order to stand for Parliament. (But then Wedgwood Benn was married to a very rich woman). Alexander does, however, expect his son to be a meritocrat: not that the present Viscount Weymouth will be expected to forgo his inheritance of Longleat or of the marquessate. He will inherit the title and the estate: unless the law changes to remove all chances of families passing on their assets to their children, as Alexander would wish it to, his boy will also inherit any cash and capital that goes with the title. 'I've sent him out to be a meritocrat,' he says. 'I think he feels a meritocrat and will show it. Not that I'm demanding it, but I think he's proud of it.'

Lady Lenka too is a meritocrat, earning her keep in television. She is not entitled to inherit the estate or any of its valuables; and it is unlikely, with his views on inherited wealth, that Alexander will find a way of giving her a bequest. She can visit Longleat for long or short stays, and Alexander might even make a cottage available to her, for which she would pay rent and the cost of repairs as do the wifelets. Her main advantage is that of being a marquess's daughter. Even heavy taxation of private wealth will fail to remove the privilege of birth and connections, or the glamour of a title.

Permanence

Alexander jokes about a group of people who believe that Longleat is built over the site of an ancient parking bay for a large flying saucer. This spaceship will only be needed again on Planet Earth's Judgment Day when the extraterrestrials decide to head for the stars. He conjures up an image of Longleat House rising vertically on the back of the escaping flying saucer. 'Oops,' he laughs, 'something strange is happening. We're getting rather high.' The house has stood for more than four hundred years and seems likely to manage a few more centuries, barring major earthquakes, a meteor strike or nuclear attack. Hungry for funds to keep its ancient masonry, roof and battlements in good order, it survives on a steady diet of cash provided by the people who come to spend the day on the estate and enjoy its weird mixture of entertainments. It is not surprising under the circumstances of living within such a strong material entity that one of Alexander's principle beliefs is in permanence. His view of the universe is also one of permanence. He does not accept the concept of eternity. His God is the universe. He believes there is one universe, which goes on, permanently.

Likewise, his own existence is a form of permanence. He transfers from one

225

body to the next after physical death but lives exactly the same kind of life without evolving in any way. Some of his theories of God and the universe are elaborated in his novel *The King is Dead*. It all seems a rather dreary repetition without any of the transcendence and evolution of reincarnation beliefs such as those of Buddhism or Hinduism, but the concept of permanence is part of Alexander's persona. For a man who has been through the traumas of his family experience, he remains remarkably resilient. If the weakness of all flesh troubles him, his considerable optimism carries him along. For Alexander, there is always the hope of new beginnings, of new wifelets, new excitements and the hope that, after all, there will still be the babies, and the happy-ever-after polygynous group of women, sharing and supporting each other as an extended family while the babies grow up in the big house under the eye of their great stag of a Dad. Whatever the outcome of his theories of male-female relationships, Alexander has already been proved farsighted about regionalism and the European Union. He has also found a unique way of perpetuating his own form of aristocracy, through populism and a rather zany individuality. He has put his precious Longleat onto a firm financial footing to face the future. His greatest hope is that his art will outlast him: his murals, above all, and his novels and other writings. He expects his online autobiography, an oeuvre of some seven million words to make his name for him as one of the first ever authors of an online autobiography. He believes then that he will have made his mark on history, as an individual rather than as a marquess. Even as a mere marquess, however, he will rest in legend as unique.